HALLIE RUBENHOLD

Hallie Rubenhold is an historian, a curator, broad-
caster and an authority on British eighteenth
century social history. In addition to being the
author of the acclaimed study of Georgian low-
life, *The Covent Garden Ladies*, she has written
two works of fiction: *Mistress of My Fate*, and
her forthcoming novel, *The French Lesson*.

HALLIE RUBENHOLD

The Scandalous Lady W

An Eighteenth-Century Tale of
Sex, Scandal and Divorce

VINTAGE

3

Vintage
20 Vauxhall Bridge Road,
London SW1V 2SA

Vintage is part of the Penguin Random House group of companies
whose addresses can be found at global.penguinrandomhouse.com

Copyright © Hallie Rubenhold 2008

Hallie Rubenhold has asserted her right to be identified as the author of
this Work in accordance with the Copyright, Designs and Patents Act 1988

This edition reissued in Vintage in 2015

First published in Vintage with the title *Lady Worsley's Whim* in 2009

First published in hardback by Chatto & Windus in 2008

www.vintage-books.co.uk

A CIP catalogue record for this book is
available from the British Library

ISBN 9781784701932

Penguin Random House is committed to a sustainable future for
our business, our readers and our planet. This book is made from
Forest Stewardship Council® certified paper.

Printed and bound in Great Britain by Clays Ltd, St Ives plc

For Frank

Contents

List of Illustrations

Plate Section I

Plate Section II

The author and publishers would like to thank the following people and institutions for the permission to reproduce their images:
The Earl and Countess of Harewood and the Trustees of the Harewood House Trust, 2, 3, 4, 5, 6; The Lewis Walpole Library, Yale University, 8, 11, 14, 18; The Trustees of the British Museum, 9, 12, 15, 16, 17; The National Portrait Gallery, London, 13, 19; The Ashmolean Museum, University of Oxford, 22; The Bridgeman Art Library/Private Collection, 18; The Guildhall Library, City of London, 24; Private Collection, 1, 26, 27.

Introduction

'What do you know about Sir Richard and Lady Worsley of Appuldurcombe?'
I asked my taxi driver as our car rolled along the undulating road to Newport.
I had just disembarked from the hovercraft at Ryde after gliding across the
Solent from Portsmouth. The Isle of Wight, lingering off the coast of the
English mainland has always held a reputation for its insularity and
secrets. I was eager to learn if the secrets of the two subjects who had
brought me there were retained in local memory. 'Oh the Worsleys,' said
my driver, rumpling his brow. 'There was some sort of trouble, wasn't there?
Some sort of scandal. Something bad', he responded. It was an answer I
received from almost everyone I quizzed on the island; hoteliers, parish
priests, publicans and long-time residents. 'The Worsleys?' one man questioned with a hint of a snarl. 'They were a bad family'. I was intrigued by
the use of the word 'bad'. No one seemed to know what precisely it was
that made the Worsleys 'bad' or what 'bad' events had reduced their once
imposing ancestral seat of Appuldurcombe to the ghostly shell that stands
today.

I had come to Newport hoping to discover the story that lay behind one
of the eighteenth century's most sensational legal suits: the trial of Maurice
George Bisset for criminal conversation with the wife of Sir Richard Worsley,
an MP and Privy Counsellor. In February 1782, the case and its lurid sexual
details made headline news. The country gossiped about it for months while
the newspapers hounded and lampooned its protagonists for the better part

of their lives. Yet remarkably, a story that was as familiar to the inhabitants of the late eighteenth century as the Monica Lewinsky scandal is to living memory has virtually disappeared. All that seemed to remain on the Isle of Wight was a vague sense that disgrace clung to the family's name.

I was certain that within the archives of the island's Record Office lay the answers to the many questions I had about the calamitous union of Sir Richard and Lady Seymour Dorothy Worsley. If I was to truly know the Worsleys and understand their legendary 'badness' I needed to read their own defences. I wished to hear what the Worsleys, now dead for nearly 200 years had to say and what explanations they might offer for their own failings. But as my days in the archive passed I realised that someone or perhaps even a number of people had beaten me to their correspondence.

The Georgians were astonishingly prolific people with pen and paper. As frequently as we send e-mails and make phone calls, they wrote letters. Literally tens of thousands of little notes and lengthy narratives might be penned in the course of an individual's lifetime. Messengers and servants were constantly dispatched to post the latest missive filled with tattle, politics and information on the day's events. Fortunately, the correspondence of a number of the era's more illustrious families and noteworthy literary figures has been preserved. The Lennox sisters, the Duchess of Devonshire and Horace Walpole all captured the minutiae of daily life and the complexities of human experience. However, for all the sheets of writing paper we have managed to salvage we have lost many more. While a good deal of correspondence was disposed of by the recipient or simply forgotten and left to rot, still more was systematically destroyed by priggish descendants. Entire collections were thrown into the fire in the hope that their secrets would burn away. Usually the first letters committed to the pyre belonged to people who went against the grain, who broke with tradition or flouted the norms, the very voices that we now really want to hear.

What I discovered was that two lifetimes of private letters from Sir Richard and Lady Worsley to a vast assortment of friends and family had been all but eliminated. I was certain that it was more deliberate than haphazard. Nevertheless what I found fascinating was that in spite of all attempts to blot it out, their reputation in some form persisted, especially on the Isle of Wight.

Undoubtedly, that which has fanned the dying embers of legend has not been what remains in writing about the Worsleys of Appuldurcombe, as much as what remains in paint. It was Joshua Reynold's iconic portrait of Lady Worsley that originally sent me on my quest. This image of a proud, strident woman in a blazing red riding habit with one firm hand set on her hip and the other gripping a riding crop excites as many gasps today as it did when Reynolds first exhibited it in 1780. It is a very public picture which frequently appears in print and at major exhibitions. When not travelling, it hangs quite prominently as one of the masterpieces at Harewood House. What I hadn't appreciated until recently was that the artist had also created a companion piece of her husband. He too is depicted in full length and dressed in the red regimental uniform of the South Hampshire Militia which he commanded. The portraits were intended to be thought of as a pair, but due to the history of its sitters, never hung together. In this case, art has mimicked the life of its subjects perfectly. Just as they had positioned themselves roughly 225 years ago, Lady Worsley stands under the public gaze, attracting attention for her brazenness as 'a scarlet woman', while her husband remains hidden from view, sequestered in a private family collection.

Until now, no one has ever attempted to reconstruct the sordid history of Sir Richard and Lady Worsley and the star-crossed marriage which exploded and re-formed their lives. As they were among the first to harness the power of newspapers and publications to wage war against one another, their legal dispute might rightly be identified as one of the first celebrity divorce cases. A vast amount of contemporary gossip, journalism, pamphlets, and lampoons exists to help tell their story, as well as meticulous transcriptions of the criminal conversation trial which catapulted them into infamy. I was also able to unearth hundreds of pages of painstakingly recorded witness depositions from their 'divorce' proceedings which open the private recesses of their tale even further. The richness of detail contained in the testimonies of servants, hotel staff, friends and family not only offers a blow-by-blow account of events but even captures the facial expressions, conversation and emotional responses of those caught up in the drama. This fascinating collection of documents allows for an unusually vivid insight into the crucial week of 19th November 1781. Together, these materials tell a captivating historical tale of love, wealth, sex, class and privilege, even without a large cache of personal correspondence.

I cannot pretend to have unravelled all of the mysteries of the Worsleys' dark and complex tale. There are many sides to this story and many angles from which to view it. Like an archaeologist piecing together an ancient mosaic I have laid out the fragments and it is for you to visualise the entire picture.

1

The Heir of Appuldurcombe

In the early morning hours of the 8th of October 1767, a small packet ship sailed out of the harbour at Calais and on to the white crested waves of the English Channel. In addition to a cargo of parcels and letters bound for Dover, the vessel was ferrying an introverted and slightly awkward sixteen-year-old by the name of Richard Worsley. The boy's inquisitive mind and his pocket watch kept him occupied throughout the rough sea passage. As the hulk rolled and dipped with the swells he lost himself in the ticking seconds. By his calculations he and his family endured a crossing of precisely 'three hours and five and thirty minutes'. He jotted a notation of this into the back of a journal alongside a table of measurements. In the course of their long journey from Naples to Dover the young man had charted with meticulous care the expanse of road they had travelled, converting the distances from the Italian and French standards into English mileage. They had, according to his reckoning, 'been exactly absent two years, five months and twenty days'.

It had been on account of his father, Sir Thomas Worsley's deteriorating health that the 6th baronet's entire household were uprooted for a curative sojourn amid the orange trees and crumbling ruins of the warm Mediterranean. Two years earlier, on the 23rd of April 1765 his wife, the polished hostess Lady Betty Worsley, his seven-year-old daughter Henrietta and his son, Richard assumed their seats inside a carriage which would trundle across the pitted roads of Europe towards southern Italy. The historian Edward Gibbon,

5

a friend of Sir Thomas's, had condemned the baronet's 'scheme' as 'a very bad one'. 'Naples', he warned, had 'no advantage but those of climate and situation; and in point of expense and education for his children is the very last place in Italy I should have advised'. However, contrary to Gibbon's fears, the journey which wound them through the valleys of France and over the Swiss Alps into Italy offered the Worsley children a scholastic diet far richer in experience than any provided by tutors in England.

In spite of his doubts, Gibbon recognised that Sir Thomas Worsley was an individual who valued knowledge, more so than many of his acquaintances. Although the historian marked him as 'a man of entertainment' he also admitted that he possessed 'sense' and an interest in antiquity. The library at Pylewell, his Hampshire estate held well-thumbed volumes of Cicero, Plato and Herodotus and bound illustrations of Roman temples and villas, many of which he and his wife had visited in the early years of their marriage. As a devoted traveller Sir Thomas believed that whilst such works offered a useful introduction to the classical world, a greater understanding of it could be gained from standing in the shadows of ancient monuments.

Before he and his family left for Italy, the baronet decided to remove his son from Winchester College, where after only a year's enrolment, Richard had been dubbed 'Dick Tardy' because 'he lagged so far behind'. As it was unusual for a gentleman to travel abroad with his wife, let alone with his children, a parent less concerned with his son's academic welfare would have left him in the hands of his tutors. However, Sir Thomas felt compelled to take command of his son's studies, to create his own programme of education and hire instructors that met his specific criteria. He was also determined to assume some of the burden of his heir's education by exposing Richard to the art and architecture that lay on their route to Naples. He placed his son between the buttresses of cathedrals, in colonnades and under rotundas. He plunged him into the jewel boxes of Europe; the gilt-embellished interiors of Catholicism, the private gallery walls aching with the heavy adornment of Michelangelo, Caravaggio, Titian and Raphael. He supervised him as he trod the paving stones of the freshly excavated Roman towns of Pompeii and Herculaneum and sent him up the side of the still gurgling Vesuvius so that he 'could walk upon the coolest part of the lava'. This wealth of spectacles was difficult for Sir Thomas's son to digest. Although the baronet encouraged him to keep a travel diary, Richard was unable to put anything into it beyond notations of his father and his tutor's discourses, indicating which paintings were 'executed in the highest taste' and enumerating 'the profusion of different marbles' used in the Palazzo Farnese. Perhaps an indication of the domineering character of his father, the young Richard Worsley seemed hesitant to hold opinions of his own or to express them, even in the privacy of a travel journal.

When Sir Thomas took his son's education in hand, there were many lessons which he intended to impart. The importance of duty, role and legacy were foremost among these. He taught his son that the world was a rational place, one that rotated around the principle of fixed truths. The baronet might have taken the watch from his pocket and opened its cover to the boy. The eighteenth-century mind often likened the workings of the era to a timepiece. Civilisation might operate on a smooth continuum only when each gear and cog ticked and turned as it should without question. Each object beneath the clock face had been designed for a purpose from which it would be unnatural to depart. Unlike the other notched circles that moved within, Richard Worsley would have been told that his function was exceptional, and that the other gears worked to ensure his existence. As the heir to his father's title and an estate that generated an income of over £2,000 per annum, Sir Thomas's son was a member of one of 630 families that made up the ranks of the aristocracy and gentry. What ensured his position of privilege over approximately 1.47 million other English families was the Worsleys' possession of land.*

Historically, only the ownership of property bought respect and influence. After the King and the royal family, those entitled to the greatest obeisance were the varying ranks of the aristocracy and gentry. Both Parliament and the judiciary served their interests. Neither politicians nor judges were much concerned with the travails of the average man or woman, and the recently fashionable concept of 'liberty' was a privilege savoured most by those whose estates sprawled the widest. The basic principles of this were explained to Richard Worsley as a young child. His tutors and father instructed him that the dark wood-panelled interiors of Pylewell, his home, and its 228 acres of field would one day pass into his care. But this estate would form only a small portion of his inheritance.

The family's principal seat, Appuldurcombe lay on the southern part of the Isle of Wight outside Ventnor, though it is unlikely that Sir Thomas

---

*Statistics come from Joseph Massie's 'Estimate of the social structure and income, 1759–1760', in Roy Porter's *English Society in the Eighteenth Century* (1990).

took his son beyond its gates on more than a few occasions. In the middle of 11,578 acres of 'rich soil and excellent pasturage', surrounded by beech trees and 'venerable oaks of uncommon magnitude' sat an incomplete baroque manor house, mournful and abandoned. At the start of the century his relation, Sir James Worsley, had planned to construct a spacious, modern home but diminishing funds eventually slowed building to a standstill. Neither Sir Thomas nor the 5th baronet had demonstrated much interest in resuming the project, but to Richard, Appuldurcombe held great possibilities. From its windows he might one day look across the hillocks and troughs of his parkland and survey those farms, villages, orchards and fields that secured the Worsleys' wealth and political influence on the island.

Between the two estates of Appuldurcombe and Pylewell generations of Worsleys since the reign of Henry VIII had passed their lives. Many of Richard Worsley's ancestors had slipped without remark through the fingers of history, while others, more noteworthy, had been captured on its pages. The stories of the Tudor courtier Sir James and the first baronet, Sir Richard, were recounted to him with pride. In their lifetimes, sumptuous banquets were spread across Appuldurcombe's tables, marriages were contracted with some of the most powerful families in England, and his relations were favoured with places at the courts of Henry VIII and Queen Elizabeth. It was the preservation of their name and the legacy of their deeds with which he would one day be charged.

Sir Thomas approached his parental duties with seriousness. While many of his contemporaries relegated the care of their children to servants and tutors, Sir Thomas enjoyed the company of his son and regularly had Richard at his side on journeys to London or Newport. Although this type of affective parenting was coming into fashion by mid-century, many found the baronet's constant influence on the boy worrying.

Since the early seventeenth century, the reputation of the Worsleys as a family who enjoyed access to the monarch's ear had diminished. Preferring a quiet local existence as gentry, they had retreated to their estates and bowed out of the prestigious circles of power. By the time of Richard's birth they were known simply as country squires; backward, uncouth and fierce supporters of the Tory party. Their prominence had long been forgotten. One anonymous scribe dismissed the family as 'never having been remarkable for producing either heroes or conjurors'; rather, they were a stock whose 'hereditary characteristics' had a history of 'association with vanity and folly'. With his boisterous and colourful behaviour, no one promoted this image of the Worsleys more than Sir Thomas.

The 6th baronet's aspirations were not lofty ones. Unlike many of his ancestors, he had no desire to hear his voice echo through the halls of Westminster. He did not wish to command a ship or assist in the governance of Britain's growing empire. His primary interests lay in Hampshire where he executed his occasional duties as Justice of the Peace for Lymington, listening to his tenants squabble over the ownership of a cow or the paternity of an illegitimate child. From 1759 his time was chiefly occupied in the command of the South Hampshire Militia, one of thirty-six battalions raised to protect Britain from the possibility of a French attack. These legions of what Horace Walpole called 'demi-soldiers' were considered 'a thing of jest' among the military establishment. Led by 'country gentlemen and men of property' who were 'imbued with a . . . looseness of conduct', the militias were never destined to wield their bayonets in any real combat; instead they existed as a type of home guard and were marched futilely from county town to barrack and back again for no discernible purpose.

As the Colonel of the South Hampshire Militia, Sir Thomas presided at these activities, both official and extracurricular. According to Edward Gibbon's account of his commanding officer, the 6th baronet cut a clownish figure. 'I know his faults and I can not help excusing them,' he wrote somewhat apologetically. The baronet may have been a man who valued the classical lessons of stoicism and self-control but his outward personality betrayed no hint of this. Sir Thomas's manner was distinctly 'unintellectual' and 'rustic'. He was a man 'fond of the table and of his bed', Gibbon wrote. 'Our conferences were marked by every stroke of the midnight and morning hours, and the same drum which invited him to rest often summoned me to the parade.' Unreliable and fanciful, the baronet was better known for his musings on 'sensible schemes he will never execute and schemes he will execute which are highly ridiculous' than engaging in the practicalities of life.

Undoubtedly this behaviour was due in part to his severe dependence on the bottle. When Gibbon first encountered him in 1759 Sir Thomas was already an incorrigible alcoholic and it was through 'his example' that 'the daily practice of hard and even excessive drinking' was encouraged among the officers of the battalion. A significant amount of time was spent in 'bucolic carousing' or the pursuit of drunken antics, like the incident when the inebriated Sir Thomas roused his friend, the equally intoxicated politician John Wilkes from his sleep and 'made him drink a bottle of claret in bed'. Although hard drinking among men of the landed classes was widely accepted as a normal part of masculine behaviour, Gibbon suggests that even by the liberal standards of the era, Sir Thomas's attachment to drink was immoderate. By 1762 he had begun to feel the effects of gout and possibly other alcohol-related disorders. In the hope that the therapeutic waters of Spa might cure him, he travelled to Belgium that summer. Upon his return, Gibbon commented that 'Spa has done him a great deal of good, for he looks another man', but the perceived improvement lasted only until the first glass was poured. '. . . We kept bumperizing till after Roll-calling,' Gibbon wrote 'Sir Thomas assuring us with every fresh bottle how infinitely soberer he has grown.'

While the baronet's drinking caused his relations and friends concern, his unpolished conduct and rural habits were a source of true humiliation. He felt no obligation to own a town residence in London, as was the practice among fashionable families. Eschewing the lavish suppers and card parties which would have established his name in the capital the baronet chose to live simply and when he had to visit town, he took a modest rented house. This error of judgement left a poor impression on his associates, who in an age of conspicuous consumption interpreted scantily furnished rooms and a sparsely laid table as the hallmarks of poverty or a coarse character. Gibbon was horrified by what he encountered at Sir Thomas's London residence. The house he described as 'a wretched one' and while there he was served 'a dinner suitable to it'. Having been offered so meagre a meal, the historian stayed to finish three pints before departing 'to sup with Captain Crookshanks', a proper host who provided him with 'an elegant supper' and a variety of wines. Embarrassed at having glimpsed such a striking example of the Worsleys' lack of cultivation Gibbon marvelled how his friend, 'a man of two thousand pounds a year', could make such 'a poor figure' in London.

Sir Thomas's insistence on maintaining a lifestyle of 'great oeconomy' did not suit the tastes of his wife, Lady Betty Worsley. As the daughter of the 5th Earl of Cork and Orrery, one of the eighteenth century's most celebrated literary patrons, Lady Betty had enjoyed a position at the centre of cultural activity in London, Dublin and at her father's estate in Somerset. The earl's drawing rooms had been warmed by the witty conversation of Alexander Pope, Jonathan Swift, Dr Johnson and his friend, the accomplished actor

David Garrick. What hopes Lady Betty may have had of continuing her father's tradition of arts patronage were quashed soon after marriage by the force of her husband's personality. While her name and connections facilitated an entrée into the most elite circles, the 'great contrast between the baronet and his wife' did not go unmentioned behind fluttering fans. In her attempts to sidestep social disgrace, Lady Betty's appearances in the capital became less frequent. She preferred to remain in Hampshire and reign as the mistress of Pylewell or to slip away to the continent where she and her husband passed several years of their marriage untouched by social obligation. It was only after Sir Thomas's death in 1768 that Lady Betty re-established herself in London. Taking a town house on Dover Street, she made her home a centre for lively musical parties and artistic gatherings.

Between Lady Betty's graciousness and Sir Thomas's boorish temperament, it appeared to some observers that the heir of Appuldurcombe had taken on more of the roughness of his father's character than the smooth gentility of his mother's. Like the baronet, Richard had a hungry intellect which thrived on classical history, philosophy and mathematical conundrums, but while his mind had been honed, his manners had been left untended. Lady Holland, who encountered the boy in Naples, thought him to be 'rather pert'; the product of parents whom she dismissed as 'mighty good but deadly dull'. Described as 'an honest, wild English buck' Sir Thomas's son had the smell of the country about him. Fresh faced and unaffected, Richard had enjoyed a rural boyhood, removed from the unhealthy air and corrupting morality of London. But although this upbringing represented the era's ideal childhood, it had left the young man unfinished, gauche and lacking in gentlemanly manners. This was a situation which his mother, his godfather, Sir William Oglander and his father's cousin, James Worsley, thought required an urgent remedy.

Since the 23rd of September 1768 responsibility for Richard Worsley's education had been placed in their hands. After a year of declining health, Sir Thomas's exhausted liver and kidneys finally failed him. It became common knowledge that the baronet had made himself 'a sacrifice at the shrine of Bacchus' at the relatively young age of forty. The door of the family tomb had hardly swung shut when preparations for his son's grand tour of Europe began. At the time of his father's death, the 7th baronet, who now proudly bore the title of Sir Richard Worsley, had been wearing the velvet cap and silk gown of a privileged 'gentleman commoner' at Corpus Christi

College in Oxford. His guardians would not have him waste his time or his mind in the collegiate environment for long. Like most gentlemen they recognised that Oxford and Cambridge offered little in the way of a useful education. In the eighteenth century few who began their studies at a university did so to obtain a degree. The colleges were home to an assortment of wealthy young men, idling their time away before inheriting their fathers' estates or marrying. It was widely acknowledged that drunkenness and gossip preoccupied the tutors while their students were left to engage 'in every disgraceful frolic of juvenile debauchery'. The guileless 7th baronet would never receive the refinement his character required in such an environment. For this it was necessary that he go abroad.

The traditional grand tour was designed to plug the deficiencies in a young man's education. A period which might span several months or several years was spent under the direction of a specially appointed tutor, or 'bear leader', who escorted his charge around the major sights and cities of Europe in pursuit of intellectual and personal improvement. The standard curriculum generally included immersion in the languages, art, architecture, geography and history of the countries visited, but also might involve instruction in additional subjects such as music, fencing and dance. As the study of classical and Renaissance art and architecture was the focal point of most tours, Italy was given precedence on the itinerary. A stay in Paris where a gawky young man might better his deportment and dress sense was also considered *de rigueur*, while a test of nerve in the form of an Alpine crossing by mule or sedan chair rounded the experience. At a time when the cost of travel was beyond the reach of those without a considerable fortune, the grand tour was a luxury reserved primarily for the elite male. Multiple visits to Europe for the purpose of study were a rarity and so the decision Sir Richard's guardians made to send him abroad for a second time in less than five years would not have been undertaken lightly. In return for this extravagant investment, the results would need to be demonstrable. Richard Worsley was to return to Pylewell with his rustic edges smoothed and his character shaped into that of a fully formed gentleman.

The man whom Sir William Oglander and James Worsley employed to implement the young baronet's metamorphosis was an individual well known to the Hampshire gentry. Since 1766, Edward Gibbon had been hosting the Swiss writer and scholar Jacques Georges Deyverdun under his roof at

Buriton. Gibbon's 'dear friend' had been hoping to find an income as 'the travelling governor of some wealthy pupil' when the historian recommended him to Sir Richard Worsley. As his student had already acquired a substantial knowledge of Italy, both modern and ancient, Deyverdun devised a course for Sir Richard which departed from the usual grand tour programme. On the 22nd of April 1769, the pair embarked on a fourteen-month exploration of the less traversed regions of Switzerland, France and northern Italy. They were also to spend several months in Paris and at least a full year in the scenic surrounds of Lausanne, the town of Deyverdun's birth. This bracing location beside Lake Geneva was an ideal spot for the improvement of the mind, body and soul. As Gibbon, who had lived in Lausanne several years earlier had found, Switzerland was devoutly Calvinist. Laws prohibiting gambling, and in some towns attendance at the theatre, made evenings in this region quieter than in other European countries, while Voltaire's decision to reside near Geneva brought serious scholars of philosophy to its shores.

Under Deyverdun's guidance, Sir Richard applied his intellect to a critical investigation of the 'French and Latin classics'. Where previously the baronet's education had focused on achieving a grasp of the Italian language, he had come to Lausanne to improve his French and possibly to learn German. His tutor was fluent in both languages but as Deyverdun 'never acquired the just pronunciation and familiar use of the English tongue' it is likely that they conversed almost exclusively in French and Latin.

Months were spent scrutinising and discussing the works of great historians, orators and poets. Yet, remarkably, Sir Richard's travel journal demonstrates very little intellectual growth. Its rambling pages read like a roll call of inanimate objects and sights between Paris and Turin. Void of objectivity or analysis and with barely a note to document human interaction on any level, Sir Richard's method of regarding the world around him was perfectly scientific, stoic and absolutist. Only the factual was recorded; the distance they rode between villages, the length and width of fortress walls, the age and height of a cathedral. On the rare occasion that he gives an opinion it comes in the form of a pronouncement. He provides no elaboration and no explanation of his conclusions. Towns, roads, inns and churches are rated as either 'miserable' or 'of the greatest merit', 'execrable' or 'the finest example', and whether he referred to a work of art as being 'fine' or 'excellent', what made it so was never discussed or even questioned. Sir Richard's universe was one of blacks and whites and by engaging in the ordering and ranking of it he demonstrated his eagerness to assess his own place within its grand scheme. At the same time his adherence to accepted perceptions limited what he was able to see. In spite of his learnedness his diaries reveal a persistent fear of independent thought.

Attaining an understanding of one's role in society formed the very essence of the grand tour's purpose. Its broad syllabus was designed to introduce an elite young gentleman to his inherent privileges and responsibilities. Intellectual polishing played a large role in this, but learning was not confined exclusively to an investigation of antiquity. The tourists were also expected to gain an insight into the workings of contemporary Europe, from its politics to its agriculture. A knowledge of its people and cultural habits, its topography and technology could only add to a gentleman's effectiveness as a law maker when he returned to his own country. Likewise, it was held that an inspection of the practices of Catholic Europe might serve to bolster his natural Protestant biases and patriotism. The acquisition of the precepts of taste, where it applied to art, was also considered instrumental to well-rounded education. Wealthy men were society's patrons; their inclinations dictated the tone of paintings and architecture and it was their duty to impart their exalted wisdom to the plebeians. The grand tour provided a baptism in the waters of eighteenth-century manhood. From this formative experience the tourist was to emerge with good deportment, confidence, and a command of etiquette useful in a variety of scenarios, from how to address a monarch to how one might undress a lady of pleasure. As it was considered preferable for a boy to learn nature's lessons from the degenerate women of France and Italy than from his father's household servants, sex also featured on the grand tour's agenda. Upon his return home, the sly smiles of a young man's guardians would belie a shared acknowledgement of that which had come to pass in a foreign bedchamber.

Although he possessed a familiarity with the sights and customs of Europe, until his second continental excursion Sir Richard had not yet experienced all that a grand tour had to offer. The gap in his knowledge was only filled upon his arrival in Paris, a capital believed to be 'a theatre of more vice than any city in the world', where it was impossible to escape the noise, filth, prostitutes and beggars, even in the more fashionable quarters.

The lodgings which had been arranged for the baronet lay on the rue Saint-Honoré, in one of Paris's better areas. From his windows on the first floor at the hôtel des Quatre Nations he enjoyed a clear view into the glowing rooms of the opposite building. After observing for some time its female occupants open and close the shutters or carelessly leave the drapery askew, he was able to conclude that the residence 'was a *bordel deternie*, or a *positive* brothel'. Naturally curious, the young man became compulsively drawn to his window. His stares were soon discovered by his powdered and rouged neighbours, who began 'paying him not only their respects by ogles and signals, but verbal communication'. Over the course of several days the baronet's will was sufficiently eroded for 'their charms . . . to conquer his virtue'. One evening he determined that he would cross the road and pay them a visit. However, before he departed, the hotel's proprietress asked to speak with him. She had heard of the baronet's plans from his manservant and had grown anxious. Where brothels were concerned, the establishment across the road did not bear a good reputation, she warned, and 'gave him such cautions as induced him to forgo the expected pleasures he had promised himself'. It was a fortunate escape, 'for that night a man was murdered in the house'. The following morning his body 'was found after the ladies and their bravoes had decamped'. Sir Richard had observed it from his window. It was a sight which bled deeply into his consciousness. The prostrate customer lay stretched out on a drenched bed, 'naked and . . . stript of all he had been possessed of'. The baronet could not shake the belief that the corpse might have been his own. The experience made him 'very cautious how . . . he viewed females' and persuaded him in part that the sexual act was best enjoyed when observed from afar. Beyond everything he had learned on his grand tour, it was this lesson which would shape the events of his life.

Sir Richard's homecoming in the early spring of 1772 had been greatly anticipated by his relations and friends, who were eager to see how his experiences had changed him. Indeed there were alterations, as Gibbon remarked, but surprisingly 'little improvement'. The young man knew that his guardians had expectations and was determined not to disappoint. The new master of Pylewell hid his youthful lack of confidence behind a grandiose façade. He believed that his studies had made him a sage at the considerable age of twenty-one. 'Sir Richard Worsley . . . has grown a philosopher,' Gibbon proclaimed archly. While 'Lord Petersfield displeases everybody by the affectation of consequence; the young baronet disgusts no less by the affectation of wisdom'. This attitude was not what either Sir William or

James Worsley had had in mind for their ward and they were quick to chasten him, pointing out 'that such behaviour, even were it reasonable, does not suit this country'. But behind the puffed-up projection of himself was a son, wrought with insecurities and desperate to demonstrate that he was not the inebriated, bumbling image of his father. Instead, the 7th baronet embraced an entirely different persona. Gibbon was astonished. 'He speaks in short sentences, quotes Montaigne, seldom smiles, never laughs, drinks only water' and, most importantly, 'professes to command his passions'. To this list was added one further detail. Ready to assume all the responsibilities of adult-hood, Sir Richard made it known that 'he intends to marry in five months' time'.

2

A Girl Called Seymour

In an era that valued attractiveness above all other feminine attributes, no one ever raved about Seymour Dorothy Fleming's beauty. No poet ever sang the praises of her prettiness, no gossipy matron ever remarked on her fine figure and in the many printed paragraphs which appeared during her life, at no point did any writer mention her comely features. Although she was not plain, her blue, almond-shaped eyes and mousy hair were considered distinctly ordinary. She had inherited her small stature and later her predisposition to plumpness from her mother, Jane Colman. From her father, Sir John Fleming, she had inherited an enormous fortune.

She had arrived in the Fleming nursery on the 5th of October 1757, the fourth child to be born in as many years. Her father, a career soldier who had served as a lieutenant in the Royal Regiment of English Fusiliers, had at the considerable age of fifty-one only recently married her mother. The son of a minor Irish landowner in County Sligo, Fleming had followed his uncle Colonel James Fleming into the army. By his late forties, a lifelong devotion to his family regiment had still failed to provide him with the means necessary for attracting a socially acceptable wife: his loyalty to his uncle had only yielded him a single bequest of £350. Had it not been for the unusual benevolence of his commanding officer and 'best of friends', Lieutenant-General William Hargrave, John Fleming might have ended his days as a bachelor. Circumventing the wishes of his family, Hargrave, His Majesty's Governor of Gibraltar, willed his entire estate to Lieutenant Fleming. In

1751, this comprised 95 acres of land and a dilapidated manor house in Brompton on the outskirts of London, as well as smaller holdings throughout Middlesex, including a new, spacious town house on Grosvenor Street. Fleming's windfall prompted an immediate quest for a spouse and in 1753 he married Jane Colman, granddaughter of the Duke of Somerset.

The war-weathered Lieutenant Fleming and his twenty-one-year-old bride soon settled down into a routine of domesticity and urgent breeding at their Grosvenor Street home. As men in the mid-eighteenth century could not expect to live much beyond their fifth decade, John Fleming applied himself vigilantly to the production of an heir. His young, fertile wife remained in an almost constant state of pregnancy. Her childbearing began with the delivery of Jane Margaret in 1755 and ended with the birth of the last of five children she carried to full term, Margaret Mary in 1762. The much wished for male heir, Hargrave William, arrived in 1756, followed closely by Catherine Elizabeth and then Seymour Dorothy in 1757. Seymour, the surname of the Dukes of Somerset, was an odd choice of Christian name for a girl, although the practice of bestowing a mother's maiden name or a family name of importance on a boy was common enough. There was something prophetic in this decision, as an unorthodox name came to shape an even more unusual girl.

Shortly before her sixth birthday in 1763, Seymour lost both her brother and her father within a month of one another. Whether the two deaths were related is unknown. The family monument which the newly entitled Sir John Fleming, baronet had erected in Westminster Abbey to himself and Lieutenant-General Hargrave records the dates of their demise, but not its causes. Tragically, within six years, two further names would be engraved into the marble: those of her ten-year-old sister Catherine and of her youngest sibling Margaret. Although such an extreme loss was a misfortune, it was by no means exceptional while diphtheria, scarlet fever, whooping cough and tuberculosis ran unchecked through the urban population. It is estimated that between 50 and 60 per cent of the capital's boys and girls died before their tenth birthday. Those who survived, such as Seymour and her eldest sister Jane, frequently reaped more than the benefits of a strong immune system.

As the Brompton estate had lost its male heir in October 1763, Sir John Fleming amended his will in the final weeks of his life so that the majority of his holdings, valued at approximately £52,000, might be divided evenly between his daughters. In theory, the four girls would have each enjoyed a substantial £13,000, an amount large enough to calm the anxieties of their widowed mother. At a time when a quantifiable worth could be placed on the head of every woman of genteel birth, the Fleming girls had been blessed with exceptionally bright prospects. Their futures, like that of any eighteenth-century woman, resided upon their ability to marry within or above their class, a feat which would have been impossible without the prospect of a sufficient marriage portion. By mid-century the daughter of a landowner might feel unease if her family could not entail more than £1,000 on her. The amount of £5,000 was the smallest sum considered worthy of mention in the *Gentleman's Magazine*, whereas £20,000 was regarded as an extremely generous settlement for Anne Pitt, the daughter of Baron Camelford, a minor aristocrat. As the sole beneficiaries of Sir John Fleming's wealth, the baronet's two little girls might one day be able to enter the most powerful and wealthy circles in Britain.

Unencumbered by concerns for her daughters' welfare, Lady Fleming now in her early thirties entered the enviable state of wealthy widowhood. Described as 'wonderfully agreeable', 'animated', and possessing 'charming, easy' and 'polite' manners, she knew how best to represent herself among society's eligible gentlemen. Where financial considerations and family obligations had played a role in the selection of her first husband, personal preference alone would dictate her choice of a second. This was to be Edwin Lascelles, a widower who was only slightly younger than the man whom she had lost. Lascelles, the long-reigning MP for Yorkshire was a man of bold political and personal ambitions who, according to George Selwyn, could 'divert' his friends 'beyond imagination' with his hearty conversation. He was also staggeringly rich.

Born in Barbados to a family who had accumulated their wealth through the trade of sugar, slaves and the provision of rations to the navy, his combined fortune was believed to have been worth £166,666, £53,000 of which was invested in his land. His secluded estate, Harewood, lay spread across 4,000 acres of rugged Yorkshire hills, pasture and woodland, eight miles north of the growing industrial centre of Leeds. When he met and married Lady Fleming in 1770, his mind was full of building plans. The construction of his country seat, Harewood House, had begun eleven years earlier and after much disputing and fist-pounding, the schemes of his architects, John Carr and Robert Adam had nearly been brought to completion. It would be another twelve months before the house would make a dignified residence for his wife and two stepdaughters who in the interim passed their time between London and Knaresborough, near to the developing hot-spring resort of Harrogate.

Edwin Lascelles's commanding residence had been constructed on the crest of a hill where its creamy-white stone shone beacon-like in the sunshine. It had been built to attract attention, in the hope of pulling political influence into its gleaming rooms. At fifty-eight, what Lascelles coveted most was a peerage. But the cold magnificence of Harewood alone could not achieve this. Its neo-classical rooms festooned in reds and blues required the expert touch of a sophisticated chatelaine to make both his home and his ambitions come to life. With her 'active temperament, fashionable appearance and wide interests', as well as her occasionally 'saucy' disposition, Lady Fleming brought the vibrancy that Lascelles needed. As a couple who both harboured aspirations they were well matched.

The new mistress of Harewood arrived in the summer of 1771 determined to place herself and her husband at the centre of Yorkshire high society. In an unusual move, she sought to assert her status by retaining her title rather than to take a demotion by becoming simply Mrs Lascelles. She would remain Lady Fleming until her husband was awarded a barony in 1790. In addition to hosting the local gentry in the salons of Harewood, Lady Fleming drew her husband from his estate into the public arena. At the theatre in Leeds her name was attached to numerous benefit performances and at York the couple regularly attended the races, a fashionable haunt even for the grandees of London's *haut ton*. When not enjoying northern society, Lady Fleming was preoccupied with the fine tuning of Harewood's décor. Just as the architects and builders had found her husband difficult to please, they found his wife equally fussy about fabrics and upholstering. As the rooms filled with carpets, lamps, girandoles, mirrors and furniture shipped from the London workshops of Messrs Chippendale and Haig, Lady Fleming was often on hand to inspect the arrangement. Under her direction, cages of chirping birds enlivened the rooms and examples of her own needlepoint were laid over the seats of chairs. When adjustments to the interior were concluded she busied herself with the design of the ornamental garden and the layout of the estate's pleasure grounds. Her role as mistress of a country house carried with it a variety of novel distractions and duties. Now, as Edwin Lascelles's spouse, her obligations were no longer those of a widowed mother of two girls but those of the prominent wife of a powerful landowner whose priorities and agenda transcended the requirements of all else.

Lady Fleming's remarriage was to alter the lives of everyone. Her daughters who had lived for seven years without a father would be expected to adapt not only to Mr Lascelles but to the unfamiliar routines of an alien house ordered by an army of suspicious staff. The move to Yorkshire was a startling change of scenery to Jane and Seymour, aged sixteen and thirteen, who had known only the swaggering manners of Mayfair and the stench of London's streets. Harewood was a two-day ride from the capital through rocky, tufted landscapes and stony villages from which the odd expression of modern technology, a thumping mill or glowing furnace might be seen. The north was a desolate and wild place. From their top floor rooms at Harewood they could hear the nocturnal scream of foxes, while the harsh Yorkshire weather, the ripping winds and curtains of rain made the terrain seem both inhospitable and intriguing.

Lady Fleming's daughters would not have been left entirely to their own devices in this new environment, but they could no longer rely on their mother's supervision. This situation would not be as detrimental to Jane as it would be to her younger sister. As the elder of the two girls, Jane, described as 'an ornament to her sex' fulfilled the feminine ideal in every respect. Pretty and graceful, her delicate features and long, noble nose distinguished her as the more attractive of the Fleming sisters while her impeccable behaviour led Roger Lamb to describe her as 'a pattern, not merely of engaging manners but of the most amiable and virtuous life'. Seymour could not compete with her sister's perfection. She was judged more severely as headstrong and wilful, and was condemned for 'possessing more forwardness than discretion'. In spite of the efforts of her tutors, Seymour's education suffered. Her poorly written letters, riddled with basic spelling errors indicate a lack of regular instruction or of interest in learning. Intellectual pursuits did not appeal to her, instead Seymour preferred physical activities and sport. Access to her stepfather's new stables and expansive estate enabled her to hone her skills as a horsewoman and eventually to make her name among society as 'an equestrienne'. She also excelled at card games. As a teenage girl she not only gained a reputation for being 'very assiduous in calculating the odds at whist and piquet' but also 'distinguished herself in the rooms at Bath with her dancing as well as her personal charms'.

In truth, a sparkling intellect would not have made either Seymour or Jane more desirable as a potential wife. Their knowledge of appropriate etiquette and deportment, their conversational skills and their mastery of the traditional female accomplishments such as music and dance, an understanding of French and elegant penmanship was what genteel society required. In the Fleming sisters' circumstances, as one pundit wrote, had neither girl 'possessed one personal attraction' they 'had at least seventy thousand charms which every fortune hunter contemplated with inexpressible admiration'.

As Jane and Seymour edged towards marriageable age, the inevitable rumours about the size of their respective inheritances had begun to bubble through society. No one was certain of the precise sum. The distended figure seemed to swell with every gasp of astonishment. The London newspapers mentioned that each sister was entitled to £70,000, while Edward Gibbon believed that it was £80,000. The *Leeds Mercury* exceeded all estimations with the claim that it was in fact £100,000. Lady Fleming remained complacently silent on the subject. It was in neither of her daughters' interests to quiet the whispers. The true total, as reflected in family documents was closer to £52,000 each, a gargantuan amount roughly equivalent to £66.2 million today. The majority of this, like most wealth in the eighteenth century, was tied to land and the rents that might be demanded from it. Only a fraction was readily accessible as cash, but this hardly mattered when fortune of any description papered over all ills. Wealth was the century's panacea and the acquisition of it, especially through marriage became one of the period's obsessions. In an age of change and instability, money purchased security. It also unlocked the door to the halls of power. It promised access to comfort, respect, success, and a political voice. A large enough sum offered a life of opulence and the prospect of a peerage. A marriage portion the size of that entailed upon the Fleming girls might buoy up another family's declining fortunes or catapult their husbands into influential realms of government. With such prizes at stake Seymour and Jane would not lack for suitors; their principal concern would be to find gentlemen who could offer them titles in exchange for their riches.

Among the many hopefuls who paid their respects to the Miss Flemings was Sir Richard Worsley. When he announced to Gibbon in 1772 that he intended 'to marry in five months' it was Jane on whom he had set his designs. In spite of the criticisms levelled at him for arrogance and aloofness, Sir Richard had grown into a temptingly handsome man. At twenty-one he was described as being tall, with an 'athletic figure and manly exterior' which 'might prejudice a woman in his behalf'. His boyish features had strengthened into 'an agreeable countenance' and his large grey eyes, full mouth and a firm jaw line were complemented by a head of dark hair. At the time, the rent on Worsley's estates was believed to bring him an annual income of between £2,000 and £3,000, the equivalent of roughly £2.5–£3 million today. In an era when a middle-class man and his family might live in comfort for £400 per year, Sir Richard's assets rendered him soundly rich. With a baronetcy to crown his fortune and a provision of good looks ample enough to sway young ladies and their hesitant mamas, Worsley would have ranked highly on any list of marriage candidates.

The baronet's introduction to Edwin Lascelles and his wife probably occurred in London, as a result of their shared political interests. In the spring or summer of 1772, Sir Richard received an invitation to visit the family at Harewood, where the spacious rooms still smelt of freshly cut oak and clean fabric. At the time, the baronet was contemplating a grand scheme for the renovation of Appuldurcombe and doubtlessly was eager to inspect the recent achievements of Lascelles's architects. The possibility of wooing the eldest of the two Fleming sisters was another motive for undertaking an inconvenient and expensive excursion to Yorkshire. Determined to make an impression on his potential in-laws Worsley equipped himself with 'a new carriage, new liveries, and every external requisite'. Accompanying him was his steward, Richard Clarke, a man on whose friendship and advice he would lean for most of his life. Accounts of his early relations with the Fleming sisters suggest that in spite of his tailored appearance, his impressive brigade of shiny-buckled servants and his shellacked carriage, the object of his attentions failed to warm to him. After several days in his company Jane 'soon discovered the emptiness of her admirer'. However, before his departure Worsley was determined to make a bid for her hand. Unable to read or comprehend her apparent lack of interest, his persistence forced her to 'reject him with disdain,' and 'give him a positive refusal on his outset'.

As this romantic spectacle unfolded, the fourteen-year-old Seymour had been studying its male protagonist with fascination. As Jane's junior by nearly three years, she was still considered too young to enter into the game of courtship, but this did not deter Seymour from youthful attempts at flirtation nor did it prevent Sir Richard reciprocating with playful overtures of his own. By the time the gates of Harewood were opened to Worsley's

London-bound carriage, the seeds for a successful later encounter had already been sown.

It was 1775 when the younger Miss Fleming, aged seventeen, next dropped a curtsy to Sir Richard. They 'renewed their former acquaintance' amid the feathers and fans of the assembly rooms at York Races. Not wishing to hurry either of her daughters into a hasty union, Lady Fleming adopted the strategy of dangling her lavishly endowed girls under the noses of as wide a range of potential husbands as the passing years would permit. A suggested engagement between Jane and Lord Algernon Percy had recently amounted to nothing while Seymour had yet to encourage the advances of any suitor. This was her second spring on the marriage market and having shed the last of her childish figure she appeared before Sir Richard with the confidence of one accustomed to moving in elite society. In recounting the tale of their courtship, an anonymous Grub Street gazetteer records that the two took magnetically to one another, 'he danced with her the whole evening; the next day they were inseparable, and the day after that they were constant companions upon the [race] course and at the assembly'. 'Before the end of the week', he continues, Worsley 'had obtained a promise of her hand'. It is likely that their affections were sealed nearly as quickly as the author intimates. The racing season at York opened in May and by the 17th of June Gibbon writes about a dinner he gave at which Sir Richard announced to the assembled guests that 'He is going to marry the youngest Miss Fleming'. He surmised that his friend was not compelled by passion alone, but rather by 'love and £80,000'.

Indeed, pecuniary issues more than emotional desires played the largest role in dictating when a couple might marry. While fashion now demanded that love or at least an abiding mutual affection should form the foundation of a marital union, a marriage contract which committed to writing the financial expectations and arrangements of both parties always lay at the core. Negotiations between the solicitors and trustees representing Sir Richard and Seymour's respective interests began shortly after the confirmation of their engagement and took several months to complete. As a woman and a minor, Seymour's concerns were represented by her uncles, Francis and Edward Colman who held legal responsibility for her share of her father's estate and for the decisions made on her behalf. By August it had been agreed that Seymour would deliver to her husband on their wedding day 'for his sole use and benefit' a parcel of property and ready cash. From a total of £52,000,

£19,645 11s. 6d. was to be invested in the purchase of lands adjacent to the existing Appuldurcombe estate, a gesture which would expand Sir Richard's holdings and therefore his political influence. At Worsley's insistence, a further £4,789 15s. would be put towards the purchase of an appropriate London town house for the couple. The bitterness of his father's disgrace still lingered in his thoughts. He had learned from Sir Thomas's mistake that an impressive house in town was essential to a gentleman's self-respect. Accordingly, before their wedding the deeds of sale were signed for a recently built property on Stratford Place, a short street off the western end of Oxford Road, near enough to Mayfair to be considered within the pale of fashion.

As the legalities of the impending nuptials were being addressed by the men, Lady Fleming was preparing Seymour for her passage into matrimony and motherhood; that state which was regarded as a woman's *raison d'être*. From her ample marriage portion, £3,000 was deducted for her trousseau, the collection of clothing, linens and ornaments necessary for equipping a young woman for married life. For 'ladies of quality' this not only included night clothing and 'child bed linen' but outfits suitable for public events, ball gowns, sporting attire for riding, and country wear made of sturdy textiles. In the months prior to the wedding, Mr Lascelles's Portman Street house in the capital would have been a scene of scurrying activity as dressmakers and milliners, tradesmen and servants came and went from below stairs ferrying wrapped parcels and bolts of muslin and satin. Lady Fleming would have led her daughter proudly to the shops along Pall Mall and in Piccadilly to purchase gloves, lace, caps and ribbons. In the course of their errands, her mother would not have neglected to trail her before the windows of jewellers and goldsmiths.

Part of Seymour's trousseau was an assortment of twinkling necklaces, earrings and brooches, hair slides, petite watches and dainty bracelets which in her new identity as a married woman would hang from her as a silent proclamation of her wealth. The filling of her jewellery box was a task for her family and her husband. In order to facilitate this and as a token of faith in their union, Seymour was presented with the money remaining from the purchase of her trousseau 'to dispense with at her discretion'. On the eve of her wedding she lovingly awarded this sum to Sir Richard 'for the purchase of jewels on her behalf'. Worsley, who would eventually earn a reputation for spendthrift indulgence, increased the gift substantially with a contribution of his own. It is estimated that £7,000 in total was poured into the hands of gem dealers and goldsmiths, who strung and fastened and moulded the portable fortune that would adorn Seymour's earlobes and *décolletage*.

In the midst of this pre-nuptial excitement there was also cause for serious reflection. Seymour's education, like that of most of her contemporaries would have included moral instruction. Best-selling works such as James Fordyce's *Sermons to Young Women* and Wetenhall Wilkes's *Letter of Genteel and Moral Advice to a Young Lady*, both of which remained in print throughout the second half of the eighteenth century, were given to girls to prepare them for married life. They preached that marriage required level-headed sobriety. Brides were reminded that 'providence designed women for a state of dependence, and consequently of submission'. The duties of a wife were to include 'love, fidelity and obedience to all [her husband's] lawful desires' through the practice of 'meekness, tenderness, patience, and constancy'. Temptation would always beckon, especially within the higher circles. As the moralising Hester Chapone wrote in 1777, a young wife was bound 'to meet with people who will ever endeavour to laugh [her] out of all regards', and although a certain 'dissipated' element of fashionable society might 'find something very ludicrous in the idea of authority in a husband', breaking the hallowed vows of marriage had dire consequences.

But on the 15th of September 1775 under the lightly dappled leaves of early autumn, such foreboding thoughts were far from the mind of either bride or groom. They were married at the ancient church of All Saints on the Harewood estate, a short stroll from the portico of Seymour's stepfather's home. As was the tradition in the eighteenth century, their wedding was a modest, private affair to which only their nearest relations were invited. Edwin Lascelles and his brother Daniel acted as witnesses and later hosted a celebratory feast for the assembled.

That week, the newspapers made public 'the marriage of Sir Richard Worsley of Pylewell in Hampshire, Bart . . . to Miss Seymour Fleming of the late Sir John Fleming, Bart'. Sir Richard's local journal, the *Hampshire Chronicle* extended its congratulations by way of verse in which it boldly exclaimed;

> Tuneful hail the virtuous fair
> Happy, happy be the pair!

> See with graceful mien the bride
> By the happy bridegroom's side
> To the Temple's altar move,
> Call'd by Hymen – led by love!

The anonymous poet echoed the sentiments of those who had bid the pair farewell from Harewood as the newly-wedded Sir Richard and Lady Worsley;

> May their years in pleasure run
> End in love as they've begun!
> May their lives in joy increase,
> And their ends be crown'd with peace!

In their sprung carriage, the rich heiress and her handsome husband bounced down the road toward their contented future together. Were their lives destined to be ordinary, their story would conclude here, in the embrace of a happy ending. But a quiet existence was not intended for the Worsleys and the first act of the drama that was to consume them had hardly begun.

3

Sir Finical Whimsy and His Lady

In September 1775, a previously unknown girl of unexceptional appearance and the son of a backward country squire arrived in London. Following at their wheels came stories of the fortune that had recently exchanged hands. It was enough to arouse excitement and to make those not already acquainted with Sir Richard and Lady Worsley crane their necks in the couple's direction, hoping to inspect them in their theatre box or during a promenade through St James's Park. The newly-weds were the toast of balls, dinners and gatherings, and were trailed about from drawing room to levee, handed between the town houses of Lady Betty Worsley and the Earl of Cork, the man who had placed his signature on his grandson's marriage contract. It was written that during the first few weeks of their union Sir Richard ushered his young bride through the capital 'with the pageantry and pomp of an eastern sultana', and that recently formed acquaintances and intimate friends alike 'were continually striving to outvie each other in attention and politeness' to his rich wife. The ambitious baronet had finally arrived in the situation he had envisioned for himself. The rumoured acquisition of £70,000 had permitted him to step on to society's centre stage.

On the occasion of his marriage Sir Richard had commissioned a portrait of himself to commemorate the momentous event. Painted against a backdrop of Appuldurcombe's rolling landscape, the full-length canvas was to serve as a metaphorical calling card, or a public proclamation of his identity and ambitions. He posed as he wished the world to view him, in the uniform of the South Hampshire Militia; as a gentleman, a landowner, a man of feeling, a soldier. When he entered the studio of his friend, the artist Joshua Reynolds, he was twenty-four and exuded the excessive confidence of youth. In painted form, he stands composed, yet comfortable with his gloves and hat removed, his hands folded in front of him and his feet positioned ballet-like in a practised exhibition of genteel poise. His erect stance speaks of his impeccable breeding, the lengthy sword at his hip a reminder of his masculinity. With his slightly turned head, he regards his viewers with restraint, if not a hint of imperiousness. His emotions, unreadable in his expression, are tucked stoically into the recesses of his mind.

Seymour's image had also been committed to canvas. The commission had probably been proposed by Lady Fleming and Mr Lascelles around the period of her engagement. Earlier that year, Reynolds had painted a full-length portrait of her sister, gliding across an Arcadian scene dressed as the classical goddess, Aurora. The picture of Jane, which hung at the Royal Academy's summer exhibition, had been intended to advertise her charms to the titled bachelors of Britain, but the companion piece featuring Seymour would have been devised to celebrate her wedding. The work, which is now lost, is believed to have depicted the younger of the two Miss Flemings swathed in the coloured robes of antiquity, 'in a repetition of the Diana motif.' The two images with their Roman allusions would have suited the neo-classical interiors of Harewood perfectly, had the portrait of Seymour not been presented as a gift to her husband and sent to hang in his collection on the Isle of Wight.

The creation of these likenesses – of the confident, commanding Sir Richard and his serenely elegant wife – represented their first step in what they hoped would be a steady social climb. Much like Lady Fleming and Edwin Lascelles, the couple were determined to turn the attention they had won through their marriage to their advantage. Together they launched themselves headlong into a frenzy of improvements and activities. For the baronet, the most significant of these was the renovation and extension of Appuldurcombe.

Shortly after his return from his grand tour, Sir Richard had directed his attention to completing the Isle of Wight house. Work began immediately, bringing to fruition the seventy-year-old plans his cousin had drawn up for its edifice. The house, which consisted of a central block flanked by projecting wings, contained a marble-floored great hall with a low ceiling that cried out for lifting. In this period of 'enlightenment' the prevailing fashion was to draw in illumination through the windows and to create open, airy spaces. Accordingly, the great hall was transformed into a bright area for the reception of visitors. To the north and west ends of the house Worsley also added a series of rooms, a spacious kitchen and a broad dining parlour. Beyond these additions, Sir Richard's alterations were mostly cosmetic, but no less particular. While he allowed his cousin's early eighteenth-century designs to dictate the exterior, he had no intention of permitting the heavy, baroque forms of his grandfather's generation to displace the current fashion for light, neo-classical embellishment. In order to make the décor reflect his understanding of high taste, elegant plasterwork in scrolls and swags was added to the ceilings and architraves.

In August 1772, although the interior was not entirely complete, Appuldurcombe with its 'twenty to thirty bedrooms' was deemed comfortably habitable and Worsley, Lady Betty and his sister Henrietta took up residence there. Decorating, mainly in the service wing, would continue until 1782. At various intervals, the existing furniture was replaced with finely crafted objects from the workshops of Chippendale and Haig, the esteemed purveyors who had supplied the halls of his in-laws with their 'split backed japanned chairs' and satinwood tables. By the time he installed his young wife here, Sir Richard was able to survey his schemes and conclude that he had 'much improved upon the original design'. From the house's recently polished interior they could now peer through the windows and note with interest that developments had moved outside into the grounds. These were being dug and reshaped under the direction of Lancelot 'Capability' Brown, the landscape architect who had only recently churned over the grassy meadows of Harewood. For Seymour, who herself had been transplanted from one incomplete country estate to the next, the movement of trees into decorative 'clumps' and clusters, the clearing of vistas and the creation of a sweeping serpentine drive would have been familiar scenes.

This protracted period of renovation did not come without a significant cost. Between 1775 and 1778, Sir Richard's bank account with Hoare's was perpetually in the red. The expenses accrued at Appuldurcombe were matched by the need to outfit his London house. Bills from Chippendale and Haig in excess of £2,000, and payments for china and ceramic ware to both Wedgwood and Spode drained his finances. In 1780, Worsley decided to sell his childhood home, Pylewell to underwrite the cost. The now outdated, compact rooms of Pylewell reeked too much of the manners of awkward country gentry to make for a comfortable home. The modest but valuable collection of books, art and antiquities gathered by his father and his Worsley predecessors were moved to Appuldurcombe, as were the seventeenth-century faces captured by the brushes of Van Dyck, Peter Lely and Godfrey Kneller which lined the walls of the echoing great hall.

Over the years Sir Richard's interest in the small assortment of objects that had fallen into his care had matured into a passion. It was one that had been nurtured under his father's direction and encouraged by Deyverdun. Since his return he had taken his first tentative steps as a patron of the arts by extending his commissions and friendship to Joshua Reynolds. By 1777, he wished to affirm his interest in antiquarianism publicly by becoming a member of London's learned societies. On the 18th of December his acceptance into the Society of Antiquaries was personally signed by its president, who declared him 'a Gentleman in every way qualified to be a Fellow, by his extensive acquaintance with most Branches of Literature' (by which he was referring to the baronet's impressive knowledge of classical texts). The following year he was admitted to the Society of Dilettanti, a type of show-and-tell organisation specifically for gentlemen who had been on the grand tour and who enjoyed a drink as much as they did an opportunity to admire each other's images of Venus, marble priapi and ancient cameos. In March 1778, he was elected a Fellow of the Royal Society, a body with a slightly more serious reputation for scholarship.

Even as a member of these associations, Worsley moved in a very select circle. The antiquarians and art patrons he rubbed shoulders with were in some cases the same personalities with whom he shared his political life. In the year before his marriage the baronet had been elected to Parliament as the honourable member for Newport. Both Sir Richard and his father had been staunchly Tory, a favourable camp in the reign of George III. The Tory party were generally adherents to tradition, they supported the King's authority and the right of the Hanoverians (as opposed to the ousted Stuart pretenders) to sit on the English throne.

It was fortuitous that the baronet's personal convictions, his need for order and hierarchy aligned so neatly with the political philosophy favoured by the reigning monarch. Sir Richard clearly understood his place and duties. He held no radical passion for liberty, no Whiggish interests in serving the public good. His aspirations were to maintain the status quo, always to vote as the sovereign would have him (which the division lists demonstrate he did) and to use political position to increase his own wealth, as was the accepted practice.

Worsley was also shrewd. He understood that the more closely he adjusted his values to that of his monarch, the more ardently he waved the government's banner, the more obsequiously loyal he became, the more likely he was to achieve his ultimate design of obtaining a peerage. Movement upward from the lower end of the titled landed classes into the power-wielding realm of the aristocracy proper would have fulfilled centuries of hopefulness on the part of his ancestors. As George III appeared well disposed toward granting peerages, the current climate was an auspicious one. Sir Richard's strategy was to increase his influence on the Isle of Wight until it spilled over into Hampshire. His recent acquisition of additional land on the island, facilitated by his marriage, was his first offensive move towards controlling a greater share of electoral power. The more of the region he cornered, the larger a political player he became. With such authority, such fortune and such devotion to the throne, Worsley would have believed that his route to royal favour was adequately paved.

Indications that the award of a peerage might be imminent appeared as early as 1777 with his appointment as one of the Clerks Comptroller of the Board of Green Cloth. Two years later he rose to become Comptroller of the King's Household. In this latter role, where he acted as chief accountant to the royal family, Sir Richard excelled himself. A more suitable post could not have been invented for Worsley's organised and mathematical mind. He dispatched his responsibilities with such precision and alacrity that the press dubbed him 'Sir Finical Whimsy'. This dedication to his office paid off handsomely. By the age of twenty-nine in 1780 he had been made a Privy Counsellor (a leading government adviser), and Governor of the Isle of Wight, positions which were rumoured to have brought him £10,000 annually in salary and bribes.

When not balancing His Majesty's books or attending the meetings of the many learned societies to which he belonged, Worsley was buried in another of his long-term projects, the compilation of his *History of the Isle of Wight*. Both his grandfather and his father had collected materials during their lifetimes and Sir Richard regarded it as 'a discharge of a filial duty' to see the book published. In June 1781 when the completed volume finally appeared in the booksellers' shops, he was engaged in fulfilling what he perceived to be yet another familial obligation: commanding the recently re-embodied South Hampshire Militia.

Sir Richard's responsibilities had him in a state of perpetual motion, travelling between London and Appuldurcombe, from Appuldurcombe to Newport, from Stratford Place to Westminster, and then to any encampment in south-west England where his militia regiment might have pitched their tents. Unfailing in his commitment to the King's government, Worsley was never absent for an important parliamentary vote, when his party (and sovereign) might require him. His head was clouded with politics, refurbishments, and the production of the *History of the Isle of Wight*. He was constantly busy, muddled and not always consistent in honouring his social obligations. When the annual 'Club Ball', an exclusive event for the Isle of Wight's 'quality', was held in October 1775, complaints were aired that Sir Richard, the honorary master of ceremonies, acted with exceptional rudeness by 'not making his appearance till 10 in the evening'. With so many distractions it is remarkable that the baronet and his wife were able to share the same room, let alone the same bed for long. However, Worsley's dedication to his dynastic duties always prevailed. In August 1776, within twelve months of his wedding, a son and heir, Robert Edwin was born, but in spite of the rejoicing, all was not well between Sir Richard and his wife. By the end of that year, their relationship, 'like the weather, had grown perfectly cool'.

What precisely had caused this alteration is unclear. In later years, it was reported that Lady Worsley had divulged the nature of the couple's problems as springing from her husband's inability to perform in the bedroom. Her complaint, it was claimed, was that Sir Richard had given her 'the miserable pleasure of keeping [her] virginity three months after marriage', and as a result she had been forced to lie 'in a bed with a man who afforded . . . no other pleasure than that . . . derived from one of our own sex'. There may have been some truth in this accusation. Robert Edwin would have been conceived in November or December, two to three months after their September wedding. In spite of this awkward situation, 'all external appearances were kept up and no one judged there was the least misunderstanding between the baronet and her ladyship'. Contrary to her hopes that the birth of a healthy male heir would have provided 'a further cement to conjugal affection' this was not to be the case. Sadly, 'the fondness that had first reigned between them' was 'not restored'. With the delivery of his son, Lady

Worsley had honoured her obligations to her husband and with this duty dispatched Sir Richard turned his attention elsewhere, to the management of his political life and the pursuit of his many interests. Inevitably, the couple who had hardly known one another on their wedding day began to drift apart.

While Sir Richard was absorbed in his own concerns, Seymour learned to entertain herself and was soon 'seen coquetting in all the gay assemblies in the polite circles . . .' Here her associates were not those of her husband's acquaintance but the voluble and often controversial Whig leaders of fashion known as the *ton*, presided over by Lady Georgiana Cavendish, the Duchess of Devonshire. It is unknown how closely Lady Worsley was affiliated with the Devonshire House set which, in its broadest definition 'numbered more than a hundred people' drawn from the ranks of the aristocracy and gentry and bulked out with notable artists, writers, actors and career politicians. The *ton* enjoyed an exchange of wit and intelligent conversation as much as they did public gatherings, parties, gambling to excess, drinking, flirting, spinning gossip and parading in outlandish fashions. The excitement and energy generated by the company of strong-minded women like the Duchess of Devonshire and her companions, Frances Crewe, Lady Melbourne, Lady Clermont and Lady Derby and her following of louche, droll men like the playwright and MP Richard Brinsley Sheridan and her husband's political opponent, Charles James Fox were difficult to resist.

Seymour had obviously spent enough time among the set to serve (in part) as the inspiration for Sheridan's character Lady Teazle in his comedy *The School for Scandal*. She was certainly among the members of high society who turned out *en masse* to watch themselves satirised at the play's opening night in May 1777. Mrs Crewe was impressed by how shrewdly the playwright had captured the morals and malaise of their elite little world, commenting with a touch of pride that she thought 'the Duchess of Devonshire, Lady Worsley, and I cut good figures in it'. Her remark offers a good deal of illumination of the lifestyle Seymour was leading at this period. Lady Teazle is one of Sheridan's more sympathetic creations, a wife whose wholesome and principled upbringing is challenged by the dissolute habits of fashionable society. Her relations with her husband are strained; she flouts his authority and they frequently argue. Since marrying she has acquired a taste for profligate spending and amuses herself and her friends by proffering gossip. But at heart she as not as corrupt as those who surround her; she is simply bewildered by inexperience.

Unfortunately, unlike her character in *School for Scandal*, Lady Worsley's relationship with her husband did not improve. In fact it conformed more to the description of Lord and Lady Besford's marriage, two of the Duchess of Devonshire's inventions in her novel *The Sylph*. 'We do not disagree because we seldom meet,' comments the cynical Lady Besford. 'He pursues his pleasure one way, I seek mine another, and our dispositions being opposite, they are sure never to interfere with each other . . .' Although it was expected in fashionable society that husbands and wives would each cultivate their own friendships, Lady Worsley may not have anticipated so much indifference from Sir Richard. It was not an arrangement which suited her, and later she would complain of feeling 'slighted'.

During the Christmas and New Year period of 1778–79, Seymour found herself alone once more. There is nothing to indicate that her husband accompanied her to Harewood to spend the season with her family and to attend a New Year's masquerade ball. This was to be an extravagant event to which Lady Fleming and Edwin Lascelles had invited a selection of local gentry and aristocracy. For several days, Harewood radiated with chandelier light and its marble fireplaces rolled with snapping flames. As was often the practice, the owners had arranged for every room in the house to be 'thrown open and made common' so that guests could stroll down the enfilades admiring the handsome décor of dressing rooms, bedchambers and closets. Throughout the night, revellers disguised behind papier mâché faces, were permitted to poke their long noses into the family's intimate quarters, losing themselves in the corridors and upstairs rooms. Masquerades were known to encourage mischief and granting party-goers access to all areas was certain to invite trouble. However, it was not the guests who initiated the misbehaviour at Harewood but the owner's stepdaughter, Lady Worsley. As 'all the rooms of both ladies and gentlemen' were available for free passage, Seymour and 'the two Miss Cramers', the daughters of Sir John and Lady Coghill, seized the opportunity to rummage through the visitors' belongings. Choosing to make the men the object of their antics, they 'threw the gentlemen's cloaths out of the windows particularly their breeches thinking them . . . unnecessary'. In retaliation, one guest, a Mr Wrightson, 'went into Lady Worsley's room, took her caps and band boxes and hung them in a tree in the park where they remained all night'.

While some may have laughed at the impishness of these stunts, they mortified the party's host and hostess, who had also suffered damage to their 'glasses and furniture to the value of £500'. 'I fancy there will be an end of all Xmas meeting at Harewood,' wrote Lascelles's friend St Andrew Warde. The dangerous gossip that such behaviour generated coursed swiftly through the homes of northern polite society. It had the potential not only to damage the reputations of the two unmarried Miss Cramers but to jeopardise Jane's engagement to Charles Stanhope, the future Earl of Harrington whose father had already voiced opposition to a match with the lower-ranking Miss Fleming. Unfortunately, in the coming weeks the situation was to degenerate further. By the end of the month, letters carrying the outrageous story were in rapid circulation.

Francis Ferrand Foljambe of Aldwark Hall could not resist repeating the sordid details of the affair. On the 14th of January, the same troop of troublemakers who had run riot at Harewood had grown restless. With Lady Worsley at their head the 'three heroines desired Lascelles to lend them his coach to go to Leeds, which he refused. They therefore took the cart horses and rode them there.' *En route* the young ladies 'stopt at one of the inns and ordered the waiter to show them into such a room, which he told them he could not do, as it was kept for the officers of the Militia and their colours, etc. were there'. Upon hearing this, Seymour and the Miss Cramers became 'determined to go in and took the pokers and broke open the door, then they heated them red hot and pop'd them into the colours which set them in a blaze'. Worse still, Foljambe writes with amused incredulity, 'How do you think they quenched the flame their own fair selves had caused? They did not call water! Water!, it was more at hand . . .' these three well-bred young ladies, who had been taught to dance, embroider and lisp sweetly in French, lifted their silk skirts 'and fairly pissed it out . . .' The atrocities did not end there. From their vantage in the upstairs rooms, the women then directed their exuberance out the windows. One of their victims, a well-dressed gentleman by the name of Mr Scott, had the misfortune of sauntering by in 'his best coat & wig & laced waistcoat'. As he passed beneath them 'they threw some water, *I really don't know what sort upon him*, and immediately a large bag of soot which covered him entirely over', the correspondent exclaimed. After they had thoroughly raised terror at the inn, the gang proceeded on their cart-horses to Cannon Hall, the home of Walter Spencer Stanhope, where 'they broke open his library, threw all his books about, and . . . took away a pockett book full of Bank Notes'. In the end, Lady Worsley and her companions 'were out three days upon this expedition' and were said to have 'played many more pranks'. St Andrew Warde doubtless expressed the sentiments of many when he claimed that he could not fathom such behaviour in 'the fair sex', 'the whole was too bad for ladies in their right mind. The excuse I have for them is that they were drunk if I may say so . . . they did not know what they did'. Foljambe was more cynical and condemned their conduct as 'a specimen of the wit and courage of the Belles of Harewood'.

What these busy scribblers did not know was that the targets of these acts had not been chosen at random. It was no coincidence that Lady Worsley, who led the charge, levelled her fire against men and more specifically at the symbols of her husband's current preoccupations; the militia and the library. However hard the Worsleys had striven to maintain a smooth exterior on their marriage, the cracks were becoming difficult to ignore.

4

Maurice George Bisset

It had been convenient for all concerned that the baronet was not at Harewood to witness the events of January 1779. Later in the month he travelled north to Stilton to join his wife *en route* to London and also to meet Walter Spencer Stanhope, to whom Seymour owed both money and an apology for the ransacking of Cannon Hall. Presumably Worsley was able to make amends but he remained coldly unperturbed by his wife's reprehensible behaviour. Like most fashionable married ladies of the *ton*, her flamboyant lifestyle would have been subject to disapproving noises from many corners. As an influential member of His Majesty's government and a wealthy landowner, Sir Richard felt that he and Lady Worsley were above the petty dictates of those less privileged than himself. It mattered little to him that 'the world now began to talk freely of her ladyship'. Worsley's response was merely 'to laugh at the scandal'.

By the end of that year, the ever-reliable Sir Richard Worsley was being asked to lend even more time and funds to sustain the increasingly troubled administration of Prime Minister Lord North. When the parliamentary seat for the county of Hampshire unexpectedly fell vacant in November, His Majesty's government, wielding a purse of £2,000, proposed that Sir Richard stand for it in a by-election. This he did, and was duly beaten by those who resented the idea of returning a paid 'placeman' (or a plant) to represent their interests in Parliament. Having contributed a further £6,000 to his own election campaign, the baronet found himself out of pocket but he was nonetheless prepared to rally his resources when, less than year later, the 1780 general election was called.

In the eighteenth century, few things were grubbier and more dishonourable than politics. For all of the era's impassioned rhetoric and pamphleteering about liberty and the rights of freeborn English men, the country's system of government could not, at the time, be regarded as a functioning democracy. By 1800 only 15 per cent of the male population over 21 was enfranchised. The criteria determining who was permitted to vote was haphazard and varied from borough to borough. In some areas a voter had to be a property-owning freeman or a householder who paid the poor rates. In other places, a voter might broadly be defined as someone who could maintain himself independently of charity or who possessed a hearth on which he could boil his own pots. Although enfranchised, these small property-holders rarely had the luxury of casting their votes as their consciences demanded. As cogs in society's great machine, they were more often than not turned one way or the other by the interests of landlords and employers. Open ballots ensured that no man's vote was secret. A signature placed against the local lord might mean that an elector and his family were turned out of their leased homes or, like those in the pay of the Earl of Sandwich at the Portsmouth Docks, told 'if they did not obey his Lordship's mandate on the day of the election' that their master 'would see fit to no longer employ them'. Those who could not be cajoled into casting their votes appropriately could usually be bribed. At the start of any campaign candidates and their supporters prepared a pool of 'election funds' to lubricate the decision-making process in their favour. The King himself participated in this practice and is believed to have spent £62,000 in 1780 securing the seats of those favourable to his Tory administration. At election time, obedient servants of His Majesty's wishes would find themselves, like Sir Richard, rewarded with 'honours, patronage, or court favour'.

On a local level, money and promises exchanged hands for votes just as readily. Men could buy and sell certain electoral privileges or, in advance of a ballot, agree among themselves who they would send as their member elect to Westminster. Such 'pocket boroughs' dominated by the exclusive interest of one or more land-owning patrons and 'rotten boroughs' which contained a meagre handful of voters with a disproportionate representation in Parliament were becoming notorious by the end of the century. The Isle of Wight was a festering nest of corrupt constituencies of both descriptions. The political reformer T.B.H. Oldfield complained that the borough of

Newton alone consisted 'of only a few cottages' which 'paying no more than 3 shillings and 8 pence to the land tax, may be ranked with Old Sarum, Gatton and Midhurst [the country's most infamous rotten boroughs], yet sends as many members to parliament as the entire county of Middlesex!!'

With the assistance of the island's election-fixing Holmes family, an extended network of Worsley cousins were able to reign as the region's dominant political force in all three of the locality's seats. In principle, Sir Richard represented the borough of Newport only, but in practice his relations, James Worsley who held Yarmouth and Edward Meux Worsley the member for Newtown, cast their votes in Parliament according to the baronet's direction. Sir Richard's seat was controlled by a fixed number of approved electors known as 'a corporation', which Worsley could easily manipulate using bribes and coercion. The other two boroughs were comprised of 'burgage tenements', parcels of land to which voting rights were attached. As a burgage entitled its holder to a voice in elections, the often derelict plots to which these privileges were connected were jealously guarded as heirlooms and passed down through the generations. Alternatively they could be sold to the highest bidder. However, more often than not they featured in a pre-election bartering process, where deeds of ownership were unscrupulously distributed among a candidate's supporters who, claiming to be tenants, would then cast their votes accordingly. The conveyances would be remitted to the rightful owner at the election's conclusion in return for a pecuniary reward or compensation of some sort.

These tricks, along with an assortment of other more shamelessly overt tactics were deployed in an unsavoury scramble to grasp the majority of votes. During the 1779 Hampshire by-election, both sides shipped in boisterous crowds of rabble-rousers to intimidate voters and swell the appearance of their candidate's support. On one occasion, 'near two hundred common fellows in carter's frocks, postillion's jackets, and labourer's dresses' were brought to a hustings, having been 'hired for the purpose of huzzaing and hissing'. Additionally, in a deliberate attempt to confuse voters, the traditional polling venue at Winchester was moved without prior notice to Alresford, eight miles away. Later, Sir Richard's opponent complained of unfair practices when 'his champions' were unable to cast their votes. The officials (whom Worsley had bribed) 'had wilfully neglected to provide poll books'. The circulation of handbills stained with vicious accusations, the publication of jeering campaign songs and the intentional misrepresentation of election figures formed only a part of this vastly entertaining but grossly ignoble circus.

Amid the cajoling and the bamboozling, elections also offered an opportunity for celebration and public display. Such events, like executions, festivals and marketing days, gave the general population of enfranchised and disenfranchised alike an opportunity to don their finest apparel and enjoy the spectacle. During hustings speeches and polling days small county towns were rattled awake by the arrival of coaches and cart-loads of strangers. Bands of musicians belted out rousing anthems, while parades of candidates and their followers marched on foot or cantered on horseback to polling stations. Brigades of loyal voters carried slogan-bearing banners and adorned themselves with sashes in the Whig colours of 'buff and blue' or Tory red. The friends of Sir Richard Worsley's cause, both male and female were recognisable among the crowd for their 'red plumes and gold pendants' as well as their flags emblazoned with 'Worsley For Ever'.

While elections legally did not involve women, this did not exclude them from involvement in the campaigning or prevent them from rallying to the side of male relations with unabashed shows of support. Some, like Lady Melbourne, paraded with their husbands while other respectable ladies, eager to demonstrate their enthusiasm but wanting to maintain a distance from the unwashed horde, watched from in their garland-decorated carriages. Others, like Ladies Derby, Beauchamp and Carlisle in 1784, chose to overlook the activities of the hustings from conspicuously placed windows. Most of theses wives, mothers, sisters and daughters were willing to play the role of hostess in a busy round of election entertaining. Candidates were expected to amply reward their supporters, regardless of their social standing. While the candidate's elite coterie would be acknowledged privately with invitations to balls and suppers, all freeholders were regaled throughout the election period at raucous public banquets. Sir Richard, who delighted in advertising his position with grandiose displays, was renowned for the extravagant feasts he spread before his voters. While his opponent hosted measly 'venison roasts', the baronet laid on 'public breakfasts . . . for five hundred persons' who were promised 'tea, coffee, chocolate and a cold collation', in addition to 'three sheep . . . roasted whole', and served up to the accompaniment of 'several bands of music'. It was during the election season, at events such as these that Seymour was drawn to the company of her new neighbour, Maurice George Bisset.

Until that year, neither Sir Richard nor Lady Worsley had met the twenty-three-year-old owner of Knighton Gorges, the estate that lay a mere four miles from Appuldurcombe. Bisset had only recently returned from his continental grand tour to assume responsibility for the property he had inherited from his maternal grandfather, General Maurice Bocland. Unlike the Worsleys or the Flemings, the Bissets were neither wealthy nor titled. George Bisset (as he preferred to be known) was the eldest of five sons and two daughters born to the Reverend Doctor Alexander Bisset, the Archdeacon of Connor in Ireland. His early years had been spent in the parish of Kilmore, in County Armagh, in a rectory house bursting with children. From accounts, Dr Bisset was a devout and compassionate father, an academic man and an influential member of the Society for Promoting Protestant Schools. For him and an increasing contingent of the upper middle classes and lower gentry, education was of supreme importance. Nothing honed both mind and soul with as much precision as the philosophical writings of history's learned men. A devotion to books not only bred civility and politeness but chased away the temptations of idleness, a sin linked to the insidious lures of the card table, the bottle, and fornication. Dr Bisset did not wish to see any of his sons fall victim to indolence, especially his favourite child, George, who due to his grandfather's bequest of land was more likely than his brothers to be lured into its lair. All five of the Reverend's boys were dispatched to Westminster School and at least three of them later matriculated at Christ Church, Oxford. George Bisset did so in 1775 and on completing his university study went on to learn the letters of the law at Lincoln's Inn.

Beyond the basic details of his life, very little is known about the young man who stepped into the realm of inherited wealth while his brothers were left to find their feet in the church and the military. What few images there are of Maurice George Bisset are caricatures which portray him as being quite tall and of a slight build. In some, his nose appears long and sharp, while his small eyes are etched with dark brows. If a brief comment in the *Morning Post* is to be believed, Bisset was not the most conventionally attractive of men. He 'owes but little to nature for exterior graces', the author wrote; however, he was persuasively charming and 'possesses in a great degree the art of captivating by address'. With the exception of this statement, no one, not even his neighbour John Wilkes who befriended him in his later years, passes any remark about his character. When his name first entered into common conversation by way of the events in which he would feature, fashionable society regarded him as a complete unknown.

However, within the provincial circles of the Isle of Wight, George Bisset would have been a recognised figure. The families of 'quality', the merchants of Newport, the villagers, drovers, farmers and harbour men would have respected him as the gentleman proprietor of Knighton, one of the island's most historic properties. With its grey stone exterior 'half-mantled in ivy up to its roof' and its 'plain square tower of great strength and antiquity', the Gothic romance of medieval Knighton could not have contrasted more with the austere, classically tempered symmetry of its nearest neighbour, Appuldurcombe. For centuries a convivial relationship existed between the owners of the two manors. Before the arrival of Knighton's current proprietor, the estate had been let to the Fitzmaurice family, who, along with the actor David Garrick and his wife, were entertained by Sir Richard, his mother and sister in the summer of 1772. As the owner of Knighton had it within his gift to influence his tenants' votes, Worsley's effusive introductions and invitations would have been forthcoming before the dust cloths were so much as lifted from the furniture.

To the baronet's happy surprise, he and George Bisset held more in common than the boundaries of their property. The discovery that the estate's heir was his near contemporary and that they could amuse each other with a cache of anecdotes about their European travels, was enough in itself. As Bisset was also a distant relation of Sir Richard's cousins, the Meux Worsleys he might be called on as a political ally. The baronet found it especially useful that his new neighbour held a burgage claim in Newton which he could command during elections. As the author of *The Memoirs of Sir Finical Whimsy* explained, Worsley 'was always pointing out to . . . [Bisset] the great honours and rewards that were to be procured by a little parliamentary management, and the advantages that would arise to both of them by monopolizing the borough'. At the time, Sir Richard was measuring schemes 'to overpower the parliamentary influence of Reverend Leonard Troughear Holmes' and to establish his absolute primacy on the island. With the combined influence of George Bisset and Worsley's godfather, Sir William Oglander, the achievement of this goal was within his reach. However, the baronet soon found that Bisset had little appetite for politics. Worsley's plotting sounded to the owner of Knighton like 'Don Quixote explaining knight errantry to Sancho Panza, and made about as much impression'. In the end, Bisset required minimal persuasion to lend his support to Sir Richard. At the time of the election, he was far too preoccupied to do otherwise.

When exactly during that autumn the friendship between George Bisset and Sir Richard Worsley's wife ignited into a love affair is unknown. The upheaval of the election period, though it lasted only a fortnight on the Isle of Wight, served both as a screen and a bellows to their simmering relationship. Having pledged his support to Worsley, Bisset was firmly affixed to the baronet's train. In the ever-watchful eyes of the island's residents he had rendered himself 'a very intimate friend and acquaintance of the family'. With the baronet's mind engaged in politicking, much of what passed between Seymour and Bisset would have gone unnoticed. At the time, what Sir Richard failed to recognise was that Lady Worsley was besotted: 'Love alone engrossed all her powers,' states one account. In September 1780, while the baronet and his associates were slipping banknotes into electors' coat pockets, his wife was initiating his neighbour 'into the arcana of love, in which science', it was said, 'he was not only an apt scholar, but soon became a thorough adept'.

On the 11th of September 1780 Sir Richard, who had faced no real challenge from his opponent John St John, found himself re-elected as the member for Newport. For his assistance, the baronet wished to compensate the gentleman who had lately become so indispensable to him as a supporter and as a valued confidant. In return for permitting him to use his burgage tenement, the baronet offered George Bisset a captain's commission in the South Hampshire Militia, when a vacancy arose. As commander, Worsley may have been given an indication that Captain Charles Abbott was about to resign his place in the New Year. This he did on the 3rd of March 1781, and the deeds replacing him with Captain George Bisset were sealed on the 23rd.

Sir Richard's grant of a commission was not merely a gesture of gratitude but was designed to pull Bisset more deeply into his life. In 1780 the country was in a state of high alert. It was anticipated that the war with France currently being waged in America would transfer itself to the coastlines of Britain. In response, the government had raised further funds to expand the militias. For the baronet the coming year would present another cycle of troop movements and dull encampments in muddy fields. The prospect of having a friend at his side would have cheered Worsley considerably. Undoubtedly, Bisset too had reason to welcome these developments. Where Sir Richard would be, there his wife was likely to follow. This was a useful arrangement for a couple who had illicitly fallen in love. Particularly now that Lady Worsley was carrying his child.

5

A Coxheath Summer

In April 1775, five months before Sir Richard and Lady Worsley stood before the altar at Harewood, settlers in the American colony of Massachusetts had gathered on the village green at Lexington and raised their rifles to a troop of British soldiers. This first volley of bullets was the opening round of the American War of Independence, a conflict which was to have enormous repercussions on both sides of the Atlantic Ocean. For the next three years, King George's armies would be engaged in a struggle to put down a colonial rebellion. The intention had never been to trounce their cousins overseas but rather to give the misguided minutemen a bloodied nose and a warning to step back into line. However, by 1778 what seemed to be a manageable family dispute between a mother country and her impertinent daughter assumed the shape of an international war when Britain's neighbour, France, stepped into the quarrel. In February of that year, ships filled with ammunition, cannons and blue-coated French soldiers set sail in aid of the American colonies. Like storm clouds, rumours quickly gathered that Louis XVI's forces also had their spyglasses fixed on the shores of England and were mustering in Normandy and Brittany for an invasion. Suddenly a nation that once had only a passing concern about the distant events of Bunker Hill and Saratoga, sprang to attention at the possibility of a French attack at home. Parliament ordered immediate fortification of the south coast of England and re-embodied the local militias which had been disbanded since 1762.

That summer of 1778, from June until the beginning of November, a network of Kentish fields outside Maidstone became the site of one of the eighteenth century's most impressive military spectacles: 15,000 militia troops had pitched their tents in an encampment that spread for nearly three miles along the pasture grounds of Coxheath. Sir Richard Worsley's South Hampshire Militia had been marched from Southampton, via the Earl of Egremont's estate at Petworth in order to be among them. Their garrison formed part of what was described as 'a miniature city', serviced by local tailors, purveyors and merchants who had closed their shops in the nearby towns to peddle their wares beneath the canopied arches. Surrounded by drilling grounds and makeshift stables, the officers erected their marquees in elaborate compounds comprised of 'sleeping quarters, entertaining rooms, kitchens and servants' halls'. Like the campaign tents of Roman generals, these lodgings were fully staffed and decorated with rugs, silver and furniture brought from home by their wives, who, breaking with tradition, insisted on accompanying their husbands on this patriotic excursion into the field.

The excitement and pageantry of Coxheath enthralled camp dwellers and spectators alike. Morton Pitt, a Lieutenant-Colonel of the Dorsetshire Militia wrote to Lord Herbert to describe the marvel of their encampment, sprawled 'on a ridge of a hill between two beautiful valleys', on which they exercised 'every day and in Brigade generally twice a week'. The Duchess of Devonshire, who had joined her husband at Coxheath, also enthused over the spectacle, writing with childlike excitement about waking early to watch the drills and witnessing the Duke's face 'smart with gunpowder'. The rows of soldiers in red uniform and a collection of 'very handsome' young captains impressed her equally. This exhibition of military might – the fiery blasts of the cannons, the officers galloping on horseback, the parading and bayonet wielding – offered the assembled not only a visual extravaganza but a sense of comfort that Britain was adequately prepared to face the French threat. The scene drew hordes of day trippers to the hills of Kent. Daily, a 'cavalcade of coaches, chaises, wagons, carts, horses' and pedestrians which 'seemed to extend for two miles' filled the surrounding area. One observer wrote in October that 'almost all of Sarum [Salisbury] and its neighbourhood sallied forth' to watch 'the grand review' of the troops by Lord Amherst, the commander-in-chief.

By late summer the country had gone Coxheath mad. The newspapers began 'camp intelligence' columns allowing their readers to keep abreast of developments and gossip. A novel entitled *Coxheath Camp* appeared at booksellers' stands and on the 15th of October Sheridan premiered his new play

The Camp at Drury Lane; an unmitigated success, it ran for fifty-seven performances.

Beyond its obvious draw, what made Coxheath such a source of fascination was the congregation of fashionable society, who had so publicly struck camp there. The fields had become a temporary home for the *ton* and a showcase for their lifestyle. The Duchess of Devonshire, Lady Clermont, Lady Melbourne, Lady Jersey and Mrs Crewe were only a handful of the glamorous women who could be seen striding across the parade grounds. While not a part of the inner circle, Lady Worsley was included in their socialising. The Duchess of Devonshire, her brother Lord George Spencer, Lady Cranbourne and the notorious libertine Lord Cholmondeley were among those who called on her at Sir Richard's tent, which the Duchess described as being 'a very fine one'. With its round of social calls and parties, life continued much as it would have in London or Bath but against an entirely novel backdrop. Whereas women like Lady Cranbourne would have otherwise hosted suppers and card games at her town house, at Coxheath she 'opened her tents to whist and cribbage' instead. Prior to the summer of 1778 it had been virtually unknown for officers' wives to be present in the field or to involve themselves actively in the affairs of camp life. However, for many this was an opportunity to fly the banner of patriotism. The Duchess of Devonshire and Lady George Sutton (whose spouse headed the Nottinghamshire Militia) invented a female version of their husbands' militia uniforms, adapting the regimental coat into a modish riding habit with a trim, practical skirt. The other wives immediately followed suit and by July the *Morning Post* was reporting that 'Her Grace the Duchess of Devonshire appears every day at the head of the beauteous Amazons on Coxheath, who are all dressed *en militaire*; in the regimentals that distinguish the several regiments in which their Lords, etc. serve, and charms every beholder with their beauty and affability.' Not to be outdone, Lady Worsley marched beside them, sporting the red coat and dark blue lapels trimmed with silver frogging that identified the South Hampshire Militia.

Among the coachloads of spectators who visited Coxheath in 1778 was the portraitist, Joshua Reynolds. It is more than likely that while there he met his friend Sir Richard Worsley and caught a glimpse of his wife in her striking red regimental riding habit. The following year, the painter chose to depict her as she appeared on the bright, summer-lit fields of Coxheath, strident and confident. The decision to portray Lady Worsley attired like her husband in his portrait of 1775 was an obvious one, as the images were designed to complement one another. The commission undertaken in June 1779 was to replace the portrait of Seymour intended for Harewood which had instead been given to Sir Richard at the time of their marriage.

As a society portraitist, Reynolds was an exceptionally astute judge of character. The clothing that his subject wears in her picture is as much a reflection of her person as of a specific period in history. The nation was still heated with patriotic fervour when Lady Worsley came to his studio for her sittings in early June, 1779. 'In London one sees nothing but red coats, cockades and recruiting parties,' wrote Morton Pitt of the milieu. 'This country now appears quite military.' Accordingly, Reynolds desired to create a thoroughly contemporary image of a Coxheath 'Amazon', a woman whose uniform distinguished her as a member of the fashionable set, one who pursued her life with the carefree flamboyance adopted by that circle. With a hand on her hip and her gaze directed to the side, she surveys her world with an alert self-assuredness. The masculinity of her dress serves as an alluring counterpoint to her feminine features. White satin-shod feet decorated with ribbons peep from beneath her plain wool skirt. Kid-leather stretches provocatively over the delicate ridges of her hand and a flounce of black feathers sits atop a jaunty rendition of a military beaver hat. At twenty-one the beginnings of a double chin are noticeable above the lace at her throat, while the creaminess of her skin and ruddiness of her lips speaks of a young woman in the blossom of health. Reynolds could never resist the use of iconography, and into Lady Worsley's hand he has placed a riding crop; an allusion to her skill as a horsewoman. When exhibited at the Royal Academy's summer show in 1780, it was this image more than any other that epitomised the stylish woman of the *ton* and the current guise that such personalities had assumed as proud and commanding lady-warriors. Equally, it offered a nod to the prevailing patriotic spirit that had inspired them.

What escaped Reynolds's brushes was the tone of dissipation that ladies dressed *en militaire* came to represent. As the hot summer at Coxheath blazed on, the enthusiasm for the maintenance of decorum wore thin. As Gibbon had observed, the militia environment tended to engender the worst of male excesses: drunken revelry and whoring compounded by a lack of manners and conversation. In the company of ladies, these boorish tendencies were tempered at first but finally the pretences of politeness were dropped. 'Our minds have degenerated into infancy,' the Duchess of Devonshire wrote. 'In the beginning of the summer our evenings were passed in conversation and singing of fine songs, we then got by degrees to Macao, cribbage, whist and catches, and now we are come to the point of diverting ourselves with *"Laugh and lay down"* and *"I'm come a lusty wooer, my dildin, my doldin, I'm come a lusty wooer, lilly bright and shinee"*, and ditties of that sort'. The drinking, pranks and parties raged on through the autumn, presumably worsened by the eventual decampment of the women to rented houses in Maidstone and Tunbridge Wells. Irresponsibility led to accidents; one night of celebrations turned into disaster when carelessness caused a conflagration in a stable block and the loss of six horses. Mrs Greville was also nearly set alight by a giddy Georgiana Cavendish, who like Lady Worsley had found the 'flaming trick' of burning militia banners with red hot pokers an amusing pastime.

The routine at Coxheath had grown boring and the men were becoming indolent. While their fellow officers in America were facing down the Continental Army at the Battle of Monmouth and expiring from heat-stroke in oppressive conditions, they were idling in the Kentish fields. 'I find it a very easy thing to be a soldier,' Morton Pitt wrote from his shady tent; 'it is however, too much of a lounge . . .' Even Sir Richard was becoming fat and listless under a regime of bacchanalian indulgence. His personal physician, Dr Scot was concerned enough to scold him: 'You may fight like Caesar, but you can not drink like Antony. You may write like Pliny but you can not cope with Apicius. You can be all that you ought to be, but you can not deviate; you are severely punished when you descend to the baseness of a toastmaster . . .'

Drinking, dining and gambling were not the only diversions popular among the officers and ladies at Coxheath. Ennui was easily dispelled with a bit of intrigue and adultery. As the Duchess of Devonshire had noted, the camp was bristling with handsome young gentlemen with little more to do than scribble billets-doux, flirt over card tables and visit ladies in their husbands' tents. In the five months between June and early November the Duke of Devonshire took Lady Jersey as his mistress, Lady Melbourne became preg-nant with the Earl of Egremont's child and Lady Clermont aborted a baby she had conceived through a liaison with a local apothecary. Over that summer as well, the Countess of Derby threw caution to the wind and openly pursued a flirtation with the Duke of Dorset, for whom she later left her husband and destroyed her reputation. It is hardly surprising that Coxheath soon became renowned as a cesspit of moral laxity, one which both outraged and titillated the public. In a matter of months, lampoons such as J. Mortimer's *A Trip to Cocks Heath* which featured penis-shaped cannons being admired by sexually aggressive women were appearing in London's print shop windows, ensuring that the licentious behaviour of 1778 was committed firmly to record.

When in 1781 a return to Coxheath was proposed, the prospect must have met with roguish smiles from the officers of the South Hampshire Militia. In response to the continuing American conflict, Sir Richard's regiment had spent the past three years marching around the south of England, from the Isle of Wight to High Wycombe in Buckinghamshire. Only their posting to London after the Gordon Riots of 1780 interrupted their circular progress. It would have been with memories of an earlier, less war-weary summer that they erected their tents on the fields outside of Maidstone for a second time. Once again, Lady Worsley followed her husband to Coxheath. However, on this occasion she was in the third trimester of a pregnancy and accompanied by her lover.

Throughout the period of their encampment, from June through to early November, the recently enlisted Maurice George Bisset was to be found at her side or in the company of her husband. According to the regiment's surgeon Richard Leversuch, the baronet and his wife could be seen 'at the camp almost every day attended by . . . Mr Bisset'. Observers did not fail to notice that the captain and the commander's wife often slipped away together. In fact, the sight of George Bisset 'attending Lady Worsley in riding and on horseback' was so ubiquitous that mention of it appeared in the *Morning Post*. It was quipped that the captain's 'attention to a certain *belle militaire* at Coxheath' had earned him 'the appellation of Lady Worsley's aid de camp'. While these coquettish activities may have raised eyebrows, the true complexity of their triangular relationship remained submerged.

By 1781, the fad for living between canopies of canvas on Coxheath had passed. Instead, the majority of officers and their wives opted for sensible accommodation in Maidstone. Sir Richard hired a spacious house for the summer and insisted that his friend Bisset take 'an apartment' (a set of rooms) within it. This was an unusual gesture, particularly when the baronet might have offered lodgings to his cousin, Thomas Worsley, who was also among his captains. Equally peculiar was his decision to hire an entirely new team of domestic staff for his period of residence there. Traditionally, owners of large households transported a handful of their most trusted servants between their homes, hiring additional help when required, but when the Worsleys moved to Maidstone not so much as a lady's maid or a gentleman's valet was retained. Several months later, when the regiment decamped to winter quarters at Lewes, the entire household was promptly dismissed again. However, in order to lessen the practical difficulties of the move, Seymour was permitted to keep her new maid, Mary Sotheby. Whatever transpired between the baronet, his wife and her lover at Maidstone demanded the utmost secrecy.

It is no coincidence that the arrival of George Bisset in both of their lives heralded a sudden reinvigoration of Worsley's interest in his wife. Far from being ignorant of Seymour's affair with their neighbour, her husband openly encouraged it. The situation provided him with the vicarious sexual thrill of observing another man adore his spouse; of watching a lustful interloper covet and enjoy his possession. The possibility that Sir Richard harboured homosexual longings for Bisset cannot be discounted. The eagerness with which the baronet pulled his neighbour into his life, the intensity and regularity of their companionship which observers described as existing on 'the strictest footing of intimacy', is behaviour unmatched in any of Worsley's other friendships. Whether or not such feelings were reciprocated or acted upon may never be known. In the eighteenth century, the crime of sodomy carried the death penalty and an accusation of an inappropriate relationship between two men was a serious matter. Any unorthodox desires or interactions would have to be painstakingly hidden or repressed altogether.

By inviting Bisset into his home as a lodger the baronet was able to varnish the trio's practices with an innocent veneer, while a household of temporary servants ensured that suspicious tales were never conveyed back to the Isle of Wight. The Georgian elite with their innate sense of entitlement felt free to pursue a sexual code which differed markedly from the accepted norm. Fashionable society was particularly notorious for its liberal attitude. Among the Worsleys' acquaintances, the Duke and Duchess of Devonshire both enjoyed a string of lovers before settling into a state of concubinage with Lady Elizabeth Foster. Similarly, the baronet's friend Sir William Hamilton was later to share his wife, Emma, with her lover, Lord Nelson. Title, wealth and influence often shielded the highly privileged from destructive criticism. It was also to their benefit that society was still of a mind to accept innocent explanations for suspicious situations so long as any incriminating behaviour was scrupulously concealed from view. The drawing of an opaque curtain of discretion across a love affair was considered essential.

Such a curtain had been pulled over the parentage of Lady Worsley's second child. As convention dictated, she left the camp in July to begin her period of confinement in London. On the 4th of August 1781 she gave birth to Bisset's daughter who was baptised twenty-one days later as Jane Seymour Worsley, the acknowledged offspring of Sir Richard. Like many fathers of the landed class who wished to avoid the taint of scandal, the baronet was prepared to accept the illegitimate girl as his own. Five years had elapsed since Robert Edwin had arrived in their nursery and the birth of Jane would quiet speculation about relations between Worsley and his wife. It would also commit their *ménage à trois* to a pact of absolute silence. Unfortunately, their slippery secret was a difficult one to contain amid the prying eyes of Coxheath.

By the time of Lady Worsley's return to camp in early September many had already guessed the nature of relations between Captain Bisset and the commander's wife. With a renewed sense of passion in the wake of their reunion, the lovers were growing careless. Sir Richard himself was among those to note the couple's increasingly blatant behaviour. On one occasion after 'coming rather abruptly into the company of his brother officers' the baronet was embarrassed to discover 'Lady Worsley sitting on the Captain's knee'. He found this compromise of their clandestine agreement alarming. 'You know that Lady Worsley loves you, Bisset,' he reprimanded his friend, 'but you should not take liberties before company, because it will make idle and censorious people talk.' However, as the summer diminished into autumn so did the baronet's insistence on circumspection.

It had been a balmy, lazy afternoon at camp when Sir Richard, Lady Worsley and the captain decided to visit Maidstone's cold baths, which lay on the outskirts of the town. They were in high spirits as they strolled through the sun-burnished landscape. In the distance, harvesters shading their faces beneath straw hats moved through the hop fields. The cool stone bathhouse beckoned to them as they approached through the dust. A male and female entrance lay on either side of the structure, directing the sexes to their respective pools where they could strip off and luxuriate in the water. It was not a busy day for bathing and the three were pleased to find they had the facilities to themselves. The gentlemen escorted Lady Worsley to the women's door before setting off to bathe together in the privacy of the men's side. Once they had finished, they dressed and went to wait for Seymour beside the female entrance.

Lady Worsley had hardly emerged from the bath and slipped on her shift (the basic linen undergarment worn by men and women) when she heard her husband and her lover beside the entrance. 'Seymour! Seymour!' Sir Richard called out to her, 'Bisset is going to get up and look at you!' Suddenly the captain's face appeared in the window above the door. As he smiled at her, Lady Worsley stepped from the darkness of the alcove where Mary Marriott, the bathing woman was helping her to dress. Moving into the full view afforded by the porthole, she displayed herself openly. The baronet held Bisset tightly in place for five minutes, permitting him to savour the spectacle of his half-naked wife as she teasingly drew on her clothing.

Once respectably garbed, Lady Worsley threw open the door. At her appearance, the men exploded with laughter, rejoicing in the audacity of their lark. Seymour soon joined them, their light-hearted mirth ringing through the warm air. The three were behaving with particular smugness. On that day the bonds they shared must have seemed unbreakable.

Their visit to the Maidstone baths could not have lasted more than an hour or so. It was a collection of minutes which Sir Richard would review in his mind repeatedly. The colour of the details would fail to degrade with the years. He would recall it vividly; the words that were spoken, the weight of George Bisset on his shoulders, the heady recklessness of it. Over the next few months he would remember the afternoon with fondness. After that, he would rue it as the most regrettable day of his life.

6

A Plan

The arrival of the chilly rain of October brought change for everyone at Coxheath. As the season began to close its damp grip on the campfires and canvas, the regiment was ordered into winter quarters in Sussex. For several weeks a lengthy convoy of horses, carriages, equipment and wagons wound their way through the muddy countryside to Lewes, a mid-sized coaching town roughly 40 miles from Maidstone. The inhabitants of its steep, cobbled streets watched with excitement as men in scarlet uniforms marched through the thoroughfares. Lewes's stables were soon occupied by the militia's sturdy mounts, while the town's houses were filled by a brigade of strangers: officers, ladies, servants and children. That winter, family residences large enough to accommodate a household of dependants were difficult to find and for the first few days after their arrival, Lady Worsley and Sir Richard were squeezed into cramped rooms at the Starr Inn. Eventually, a suitable house was secured along the fashionable High Street near to their friends, Richard Leversuch and his wife, and Captain and Mrs Isham Chapman. As the Worsleys' new home was more compact than their Maidstone house, the couple's 'lodger', George Bisset, was forced to seek a bed at one of the inns scattered through the town. He managed to secure a set of apartments at the lodging house of Mr Joseph Tubb, near the Castle Green, only a short uphill walk from the Worsleys' door.

This change of circumstance – Bisset's removal to another house and the shift from the lazy routine of the Coxheath encampment – was certain to have unsettled the lovers. In the weeks that passed between the birth of their child in August and the move to Lewes, it is not unreasonable to believe that the couple's feelings for each other had intensified. Undoubtedly Lady Worsley had become accustomed to Bisset's constant presence under her husband's roof where they, along with the infant Jane were able to live as a small family ensconced in a larger one. The new arrangements at Lewes would have come as a jolt and an unpleasant reminder that while Seymour's husband had the authority to dictate the terms of their relations, periods of indefinite separation would be inevitable. Although at the time he permitted their relationship, there might come a period when he would not. As the months progressed, the pair began to contemplate the possibility of cutting themselves free entirely from the baronet's constraints.

It would not have been an easy decision: the elopement of an unmarried man with his friend's wife would be regarded as one of the grossest infractions of morality and honour conceivable. Had their heads not been fogged with passion they might have considered the consequences of their proposed action more closely. While it remained shrouded in discretion, their romantic attachment along with their respectable names might have survived intact, but to abscond together would throw their relationship unapologetically into the public gaze and lay them open to the most pointed ostracism. They would forfeit their reputations as honourable individuals and as a result, lose the goodwill of many friends and family members. To make matters worse, both Lady Worsley and Bisset could expect to be dogged by a range of financial and legal difficulties.

As it was not within a wife's legal prerogative to sue her husband for divorce the lovers would have to weather these risks in order to force Sir Richard to initiate proceedings. This would be an enormous gamble. Ultimately, their hopes would reside on the aggrieved baronet selecting a course of action that accorded with their wishes: a parliamentary divorce. This route had been taken by many members of the landed classes, such as the Duke of Grafton and Viscount Bolingbroke. It was expensive and would involve a humiliatingly public dissection of the Worsleys' private lives by the baronet's friends, political colleagues and rivals in Westminster. It was, however, the only way by which a husband and wife could dissolve a union with a provision for remarriage. It would have been the most amicable of solutions for both parties. The other option, a suit for 'Separation from Bed and Board' through Doctors' Commons was also frequently sought by wealthy husbands wanting to rid themselves of an adulterous wife, though the outcome provided by this type of action would not have been what Seymour and Bisset desired. As Doctors' Commons (based near St Paul's Cathedral) was an ecclesiastical court that dealt with disputes of a religious nature (marriage being among them), its rulings were fixed to Christian doctrine. Through this court, spouses could achieve a form of divorce through a legal separation but remarriage for either husband or wife was forbidden. In the end, the choice was entirely left to Sir Richard. He alone could decide whether to exercise vengeance or compassion.

As Lady Worsley contemplated elopement and divorce, it is more than likely that the Countess of Derby's cautionary tale entered her thoughts. The Countess's misadventure had rattled the tea tables of St James's when it erupted in December 1778. At the beginning of that month the Earl, in a fit of rage, had locked his wife out of their town house. According to furiously circulating rumours he had taken this step to demonstrate that he would no longer tolerate her affair with the Duke of Dorset, a man with whom she had been romantically linked for several years. It was believed that Lady Derby had taken refuge with her lover in the countryside to await her husband's next move. It had been expected that the Earl, who was himself a dedicated philanderer, would deal with the situation affably, that an agreement would be reached and a divorce secured which would free his wife to marry the man she loved. However, this was not to be the case. The Earl refused to apply for a full divorce through Parliament and therefore condemned his separated wife to a ruinous state of limbo where she remained neither respectably wedded nor free to remarry and salvage her damaged reputation. With the hope of sealing their union gone, the Duke of Dorset soon lost interest and comforted himself in the embrace of the opera dancer, Giovanna Baccelli.

In a period when the public contravention of sexual norms was considered unforgivable in a woman the results for the Countess were devastating. Once tainted by sinful behaviour a woman was regarded as no longer fit to interact with virtuous ladies. Concern for their own reputations would prevent them from keeping company with one who had abandoned her husband and children to lead a life of debauchery. Such adulteresses, Lady Mary Coke wrote, 'offended against the laws of man and God'. In order to escape the hail of condemnation the Countess eventually fled to the continent in 1780. Now abandoned by her friends and relations, Lady Derby was looked upon as no better than a courtesan, her name uttered by Seymour's acquaintances with a sneer. Lady Worsley might suffer a similar fate, should her plans fail. It would be her they whispered about. Like Lady Sarah Bunbury, who had also eloped from her husband in 1769, Seymour faced the probability of even being shunned by her own sister, the highly regarded Countess of Harrington. She would certainly no longer be welcomed at Harewood. A fallen woman might expect to find herself entirely shut out.

At the time, Seymour may have believed that her great wealth would shield her. She had come to her marriage as an heiress in her own right, with a fortune tied to the Brompton estate, and invested in West End houses and Appuldurcombe's lands. However, on the day of her wedding any assets were passed directly into the custody of her husband to use and distribute as he saw fit. As women were not legally permitted to hold property, Sir Richard had inscribed his name to the legal documentation as one of his wife's trustees. In the eventuality of his death these possessions would be restored to her and she would be able to nominate another male trustee to safeguard her interests in place of him. The marriage contracts of substantially endowed heiresses often contained clauses which ensured their rights and even an income in unforeseen circumstances. It is probable that Lady Worsley mistakenly believed that divorce, like death would also free her fortune and enable her to remarry as she chose. Regrettably, neither the stipulations of her marriage contract nor the law provided for this. The harsh truth of the situation was that if she chose to leave her husband's protection she would also relinquish access to any funds. The law was constructed so that women were dependent on the largesse of men: fathers, brothers, uncles, husbands and, in widowhood, their sons. Runaway adulteresses, like whores, were expected to live off the charity of their lovers.

An elopement would have tied Lady Worsley's lot to that of the captain and whatever hardships he encountered would also become hers. Although society would stigmatise him less, George Bisset would still face stiff penalties for his behaviour. By absconding with the wife of his senior officer and intimate companion, Bisset would be in breach of a rigid gentleman's code of honour which placed fraternal bonds and the dictates of hierarchy at the very heart of male relations. In future, virtuous women might think twice about receiving him while many of his male acquaintance would be less inclined to trust a man who was prepared to betray a friend and social superior. How his religious family would view his transgression can only be imagined. But in spite of this loss of esteem, scorn would not be Bisset's primary concern. The possibility that Sir Richard might seek satisfaction in the form of a duel could not be discounted altogether; however by the late eighteenth century it was far more fashionable for a cuckolded husband to exact his revenge in court with a charge of criminal conversation.

The offence of criminal conversation, or 'crim. con.' as it came to be known, was no more than a euphemism describing an act of sexual intercourse with another man's wife. Since the religious laws that prohibited adultery had been relaxed in the late seventeenth century, alternative ways of punishing marital infidelity had to be found. The action for criminal conversation evolved out of the civil law of 'trespass', which covered offences of 'mayhem, battery or wounding'. In this case, the 'wounding' had been done to the plaintiff's wife, by 'polluting' or 'defiling' her person and chastity, therefore the suit of crim. con. was about extracting reparations for the damage inflicted on a man's property. As a legal action it stood entirely apart from any additional suit pursued in Parliament or in Doctors' Commons. It was not obligatory for a man to secure a divorce before initiating proceedings for crim. con., nor did the result of a criminal conversation trial necessarily influence another court's decision about the dissolution of a claimant's marriage.

Prior to 1760, the legal expenses of launching an action for crim. con. at the Court of the King's Bench were so unaffordable that most disputes tended to be settled out of court, either by means of a private payment to the injured husband or, in some cases, by a duel. However by the second half of the eighteenth century a general increase in wealth meant that more husbands were prepared to do battle in open court. A successfully prosecuted suit for crim. con. also had the ability to restore a man's injured sense of honour. This was duelling, but by another name.

As might be expected, indignant spouses wishing to salve their dignity brought forth claims for astronomical amounts: £10,000 even £15,000. Spectacular payouts encouraged others to come forward with their complaints. The result was a veritable explosion of criminal conversation litigation between 1760 and 1829. At its peak between 1789 and 1799, 73 cases were heard.[*] The numbers only began to drop when juries became less inclined to hand out large settlements and the action was eventually abolished in 1857, when public sentiment turned against the idea of ascribing a value to a man's wife.

[*]See Lawrence Stone, *Road to Divorce*, table 9.1

It is remarkable that with so many factors to consider and the stakes so perilously high Captain Bisset and Lady Worsley decided to take their chances together. The headiness of romantic love alone guided their instincts. In the early weeks of November, Bisset began laying the groundwork for their escape. His plan was for a sudden flight to London when Sir Richard least expected it. Once there, the couple would lie low and await the baronet's response. For this they would need a liaison in the capital, a trustworthy mediator who would manage their communication with Worsley and defend their interests. George William Coventry, Viscount Deerhurst, 'a particular and intimate friend' of Bisset and Lady Worsley's, was the gentleman he had in mind. The rakish Deerhurst, no stranger to illicit dalliances, had been a confidant of the captain's since the two matriculated at Christ Church, Oxford. He had also been privy to the clandestine attachment between his friend and Lady Worsley for some time. Sympathy for the lovers' predicament combined with an acquired dislike of Sir Richard made him an amenable ally. The Viscount had even offered to arrange a safe house where the pair could shelter: the Royal Hotel on Pall Mall. With the preparations in order, the couple need only wait for opportunity's signal.

Sir Richard's cousin, Captain Thomas Worsley had come from his lodgings at the White Hart Inn for Sunday dinner on the 18th of November. The three were still seated at the table as the afternoon sun began to flicker out on the horizon. The baronet's new butler, a local man of considerable experience named Francis Godfrey, hovered in the dining room, lighting candles. As it had taken some time to replenish their household with servants, this was only Godfrey's second day in employment and he was eager to please his master and mistress. Glasses were refilled and plates cleared at regular intervals. He kept an attentive eye on the party's needs.

Dressed in her 'scarlet regimental riding habit' Lady Worsley listened politely to the patter of conversation between her husband and his relation. Thomas Worsley was a man of few words and Sir Richard was contending with a heavy cold. They were to pass the remainder of the early evening together and later cross the road for a gathering hosted by Richard Leversuch and his wife for 'the married officers and their ladies'. At about seven, Seymour excused herself from the gentlemen's company in order to prepare for the party. Mary Sotheby assisted her out of her rumpled day clothing and buttoned her into a fresh brown riding habit which she paired with a blue hat embellished with a profusion of brown and white feathers. Once laced in and powdered sufficiently, she rang for Francis Godfrey to 'light her across the road to Leversuch's'.

Neither Sir Richard nor his cousin, who had removed themselves to the sitting room, noticed Lady Worsley slip out the door. 'Tell the cook that neither I nor Sir Richard shall sup at home,' she instructed the butler. It was understood that the gentlemen would be joining her later, but as the hours pressed on, the baronet's worsening cold pushed him back into the depths of his comfortable chair.

At about ten, his cousin suggested that they join the party at Leversuch's, but Sir Richard 'being rather indisposed' waved Captain Worsley on, asking him to 'send his excuses' and explain that he had 'gone to bed early . . . to endeavour to get rid of his cold'. He requested a draft of 'sack whey', an eighteenth-century cure-all and afterwards disappeared into his bedchamber.

By the time Captain Worsley appeared in the Leversuch's drawing room, the surgeon and his wife had been entertaining a small gathering for a number of hours. Among the guests was Captain Bisset, who had placed himself attentively at Seymour's side. In spite of gossip, Lady Worsley and her lover understood when to exercise restraint. Indeed nothing that night, their host was later to recall, 'struck him as improper in their conduct'. They were 'chatty and merry together', but not in a manner which attracted curious glances. The couple had become practised at hiding their true thoughts. When Thomas Worsley entered the room offering Sir Richard's apologies, both Seymour and her paramour must have caught their breath. This was the occasion for which they had been preparing. They sat for another hour by Leversuch's fire, sipping tea and waiting.

When supper was called at eleven, the group rose from their seats and went downstairs to the dining room. Bisset moved swiftly to Seymour's side and took her arm. He lingered behind while the chattering wives and finely groomed officers filed down the staircase. Alone, at the foot of the stairs, 'he pressed her hands' urgently and leaning close to her cheek 'whispered for the space of a minute or so'. They would go tonight.

Although no one had seen the signal pass between the two, Lady Worsley's demeanour quickly began to change. Mrs Leversuch's seating arrangements, which placed Seymour between Bisset and Captain Worsley, had flustered her. A cold supper was laid before them, but Seymour's thoughts and appetite were elsewhere. The minutes ticked away rapidly. In what must have seemed a disproportionate span of time, the empty dishes were removed and Mrs Leversuch led her guests into the adjoining room, where Lady Worsley set her eyes on the clock.

As the hands of the timepiece ticked past midnight, Lady Worsley quite abruptly 'got up and made a motion to go'. Leversuch also rose to his feet and, playing the genial host, asked 'if the company was not agreeable to her Ladyship?' 'No,' Seymour answered. What then might they make of 'Her Ladyship leaving them so early?' Those assembled fixed their gazes on her. Lady Worsley's nerves were decidedly rattled. As one 'always remarkable for keeping very late hours', she was betraying herself. In the end it was her lover's words that settled her. 'Don't go yet, my Lady,' he pleaded, taking out his watch and commenting on the time. Slightly chagrined, Seymour 'thereupon sat down again'.

The calm that came over her was fleeting. Hardly a half-hour had elapsed when, 'in a hurry', Seymour 'rather unexpectedly to the company . . . got up again'. This time she was adamant that 'she must go'. Captain Bisset also rose to his feet and simultaneously proposed 'taking his leave . . . in order to see her Ladyship home'.

The distance between the Leversuchs' door and the dimly lit windows of the Worsley's house was no more than a matter of steps. Nevertheless, the surgeon insisted on lighting a candle and escorting his commander's wife to safety. The impatient Bisset followed closely, eager to rid them of the meddling man. In the middle of the road and 'within a few yards' of her home, Seymour stopped her well-intentioned host, commenting 'that he should not trouble himself to go any further'. Accordingly, the surgeon bid the couple goodnight and, at last, retreated with his guttering candle back over the road.

'It was extraordinary,' Leversuch remarked to his wife later that night, after the rest of the party had departed, 'the circumstances of Lady Worsley's breaking up and leaving the company at so early an hour. For at all other times, when the same company spent the evening together in the same kind of way, Lady Worsley . . . never quitted company till two or three in the morning.' Below stairs, housemaids ferried dirty plates and china cups into the scullery. The cook put away the scraps and locked the tea caddy. The household prepared for bed, but no one was to get much sleep that night.

7

19th of November 1781

Standing beside the door to the Worsleys' house, Seymour and Captain Bisset kept very still. On the other side of the wall sat the sleepy Francis Godfrey and Mary Sotheby listening intently for the sounds of their mistress's return. In the stillness of the early hours the lovers watched for the surgeon's shadow to disappear before daring to move. Only after his door had shut did they turn towards the Castle Green and creep away into the darkness. Near to the crest of the hill sat Tubb's lodging house, folded in night. The house, sunk deep in sleep, issued only the faintest glow as the proprietor, Joseph Tubb, slumbered with a low fire in his bedroom grate. They tiptoed up the stairs and stealthily opened the door to the dining room adjoining Bisset's lodgings. Once inside, a candle was lit. It was just after one o'clock in the morning.

Before their departure there were several things they had to do. Bisset took out two sheets of paper. On one, he began a letter to Sir Richard in which he formally resigned his commission as an officer. Before placing a seal on it he retrieved another, slightly larger piece of parchment awarding him his rank of Captain in the South Hampshire Militia. Later, Bisset would hand this to his trusted valet, Joseph Connolly, who would be given the unenviable task of delivering the message to the baronet. Lady Worsley then wrote her instructions to Mary Sotheby, whom she commanded to come to Lord Deerhurst's house on Cleveland Row in London bringing the contents of her wardrobe. Retrieving her infant daughter would be more complicated and would most likely require negotiation with her husband following the elopement.

The letters were sealed and, not wishing to wake the house, the couple then extinguished the light and retired to Bisset's bed. In the handful of hours that remained before their departure, sleep would have been inconceivable. Comfort in each other's arms, however, was not.

At about 4 a.m. there was still no hint of sunrise. Bisset's hearth was cold and the room remained in blackness. During the nervous moments after their arrival at Tubb's lodging house someone had neglected to keep a flame lit. Now, when they most urgently required it, there was none to be had. Without even the slightest glimmer to guide them they would be unable to prepare themselves for their journey. Recalling the sight of Joseph Tubb's illuminated threshold, Bisset jumped from the bed in his nightgown, crossed the corridor and anxiously beat on his landlord's chamber door. Tubb was jerked from his sleep by his 'much agitated' lodger 'requesting that he let him light his candle'. The oddness of the incident piqued him. Afterwards, Tubb crawled back into the warmth of his bed and listened.

From down the hallway he heard the floorboards creak. Someone, or several people were moving about. A loud whisper called out to Joseph Connolly. Fearing that his lodger was ill, Tubb cast off his bed covers and went quickly to Bisset's rooms, where he banged at the door asking if 'he might be of service'. The captain's tense voice responded that he was indeed 'exceedingly ill but that he had sent his man out for something'. The landlord was just about to return to his bed when he heard the murmurings of a conversation. Mr Bisset was not alone.

Tubb did not go back to his bedchamber. Instead he climbed the stairs to the garret and rattled the door of his housekeeper, the matronly Elizabeth Figg. Through the door, her master instructed her to rise and ready herself immediately, since her assistance might be required. The housekeeper lit her own candle and poked the coals in her grate, preparing rather prematurely for a long day's duties. As she dressed in the cold of morning, pulling on her skirts and adjusting her stays, she heard a carriage clatter up to the front of the house. The sound of Connolly in his heavy boots clumping up and down the stairs was replaced after an uncertain pause by Captain Bisset's steps and then by the unmistakable tread of feminine shoes.

Outside in the cobbled courtyard their carriage waited. Connolly, at 4.30 a.m. had been instructed to race across Lewes to the Starr Inn, where a post-chaise and a team of four horses could be hired at short notice. Bisset's chargers and his groom were also staying at the Starr. Claiming that 'his master . . . had received an express from London and was about to set off for that place immediately', Connolly woke Bisset's groom as well as the groom at the Inn, Jerah Thompson, who grudgingly rose from their beds to hitch the horses to the chaise.

Thompson rode with the groom to Tubb's lodging house and waited for Captain Bisset. Within minutes he appeared, accompanied by a lady, whom he escorted into the carriage. In the gloom of early morning, Thompson watched her cross the courtyard in a scarlet and blue cape. She was dressed to travel, in her brown riding habit, the feathers atop her fashionably tilted hat bobbing with the movements of her head. A suspicious Bisset caught Thompson staring. Through the open window of the chaise, he beckoned him round. 'Take care of my horses,' he instructed the groom from the Starr. 'I shall send word for them to be sent on.' Then Bisset shouted to the postilion and the chaise, containing Sir Richard Worsley's wife, jolted off to London.

At 5 a.m., while most of Lewes slept, a carriage shot up the High Street and on to the London Road. As they departed at breakneck speed for the capital, their chaise passed directly in front of Sir Richard's darkened bedroom window, leaving a jangle of noise in its wake. The horses charged down the muddy, rutted roads with only the light from the carriage lanterns to guide them. Bisset and Seymour knew that every minute they put between themselves and the Sussex town they left behind was precious. Tubb would be dressed by now, Worsley would soon be stirring in his bed, servants would be waking and questions would be asked. In London, with its labyrinthine streets, its swarming crowds and countless hostelries, their hired yellow chaise would join a river of traffic and disappear into a stream of urban anonymity. However, while they rode they were vulnerable.

Bisset had ordered his groom (who, in the tradition of a post-chaise was driving the team from astride the front horse) to ride as hard as he could, pushing the beasts to exhaustion before changing them for fresh ones at each stage. For fear of discovery, neither Lady Worsley nor the captain dared move from the carriage. At about seven, their chaise pulled into the White Hart Inn at Godstone, a small coaching village roughly 30 miles from Lewes. As the spent horses were being unhitched from the carriage, Captain Bisset opened the door and stretched his legs. Confident that the most hazardous part of their journey had been accomplished, he paced around his vehicle. At that early hour there were enough enquiring eyes at the inn to notice the presence of a well-attired gentleman and the slightly obscured profile of a lady, hidden behind the panes of the carriage windows.

In roughly two hours they had made considerable progress, but as they neared London, their pace would begin to drag. The roads soon grew dense with north-bound traffic: drovers behinds their herds, wagons of freight, passengers on foot, ungainly mailcoaches lumbering to the capital. They would pass through a series of towns and villages, inching towards the metropolis via the turnpike to Croydon, through the farmland and wooded glades of Mitcham, continuing through the increasingly populated parts of Streatham and Brixton with its collection of hamlets and greens. It was late morning when they crossed Westminster Bridge.

They proceeded through Westminster and the Haymarket to Pall Mall where the chaise stopped outside the Royal Hotel, one of many new, respectable establishments in this, the most fashionable district of town. The Royal Hotel had opened its doors only five years earlier and its proprietor, a Mr Weston, wanted to preserve its reputation among a patchwork of gaming clubs, taverns, tradesmen's premises and Dr Graham's spurious 'Temple of Health and Hymen' with its fertility-restoring 'Celestial Bed'. To maintain appearances, a waiter or footman was always on hand to assist arriving guests. On the morning of the 19th of November, this was Thomas Fort's duty. He came down the steps of the hotel, dressed in tidy livery.

As they sat in the post-chaise, Seymour and Bisset paused to catch their breath. Although their daring escape had been a success it would only be a matter of hours before Worsley, trailing their scent, would be searching every corner of the capital for their whereabouts. Soon word of their elopement would reach London and tongues would be wagging. They dare not venture out until they knew what Sir Richard was likely to do. In the meantime, everyone would crave a sighting of the pair, making it unwise even to pass by an uncovered window. They watched Thomas Fort approach the carriage. He would assist them as they stepped, in plain view, on to Pall Mall. Bisset turned and spoke to Lady Worsley, holding 'the door for a minute or two in his hand as if hesitating and undetermined whether to get out of the Chaise or not'. Having braced themselves, the couple then briskly alighted, rushing through the hotel's entry, 'thro' the passage and up stairs' with the confused Thomas Fort pursuing them.

After a very long, tense ride and a night without rest, Lady Worsley and her lover wanted breakfast. Hotels, taverns and coffee houses had a variety

of upstairs rooms available for better-paying clients who preferred to separate themselves from the establishment's less salubrious patrons when they
dined. The management at the Royal Hotel therefore did not think it unusual
when the pair requested a private dining room. It was about midday when
Seymour and Bisset were shown into the Apollo, the hotel's finest dining
room on the first floor, 'where breakfast was by their order immediately
carried up to them'. As Fort laid the plates of buttered toast and breads on
the table and poured the couple their tea he asked if they would be staying
at the hotel. Lady Worsley answered yes and then requested 'that a bed
chamber be made up immediately for her and her husband'. Fort then rang
for the housekeeper, Mrs Anna Watkinson.

When the capable Watkinson trundled up from below stairs Seymour
explained that she and her spouse intended to hire out the Apollo dining
room for their exclusive use and therefore required a bedchamber 'as near
as possible' to it. Mrs Watkinson settled on the perfect room: number 14,
separated only by a corridor. The bed, Anna Watkinson remarked, was then
'made ready for their immediate reception'.

While Captain Bisset and Lady Worsley were taking their breakfast, two
of the Royal Hotel's housemaids had been inspecting the pair. At twenty-
six and twenty-three, Sarah Richardson and Ann Ekelso had seen enough
to know that not every married couple who slept in their hotel was a
legitimate one. Ekelso's suspicions were raised when she came above stairs
in the middle of the afternoon to find that the two guests had retired to
their bedchamber. She had been ordered to stoke the fire in room 14 but
found the door locked 'and the room shut up'. Furthermore, she noticed that
the curtains had been drawn across their windows. 'It was an odd time of
day for people to go to bed,' Richardson had commented knowingly to her
fellow servant. From then on, for entertainment's sake, the girls resolved to
keep a close watch on the activities of the couple in number 14.

Lady Worsley and Captain Bisset provided them with ample amusement.
At some time after seven o'clock in the evening, the bell rope was pulled
and the two housemaids were summoned above stairs to 'relight the fire and
remake the bed'. The young women revelled in the bawdy scene that greeted
them. With the relish of a tell-tale, Sarah Richardson recounted that the bed
'was extremely tumbled with the pillows and bed cloaths thrown about and
the sheets twisted together and everything in much great disorder . . .' But
more peculiar still, she and Ekelso were compelled to 'put new sheets on the

bed'. This was an 'extraordinary' situation, Richardson added with a hint of coquettish mockery, as she had 'believed the sheets they had first lain in to be quite clean when put on the bed'.

Shortly after midnight, the tinkle of a ringing bell called them to number 14 once more. While the pair were enjoying their supper in the Apollo Sarah and Ann were requested once again 'to make up the bed', a task they had performed not five hours earlier. Lady Worsley took them aside and specifically ordered the girls 'to make it as hard as possible and put [further] clean sheets on . . . the bed'. Incredibly, when the housemaids opened the door to the chamber, the room had been returned to its former state of disarray, with the 'bed cloaths being thrown in a heap and the sheets all in a twist'. These sheets were now soiled like those they had already removed. The bed with its fibrous feather filling had been completely displaced. As a feather mattress required shaping to make it solid, the maids climbed on to this site of debauchery 'and trod it down', though probably not without a lewd jest. With hindsight, and after the details of Lady Worsley and Captain Bisset's story had exploded into the public domain, Sarah Richardson confessed with an edge of acerbity that she and Ekelso had always nurtured 'a suspicion between themselves that they were not really married'. That which betrayed them was simple: 'there appeared a greater fondness between them than is generally seen between husband and wife'.

Unfortunately, the situation that provided such fun for those on the opposite side of number 14's locked door was becoming an increasingly distressing one for the couple behind it. By early evening, Joseph Connolly had arrived at the Royal Hotel. He had come without Mary Sotheby. He did, however, bring the news that Lady Worsley and Bisset were anticipating. Discovery of their disappearance had occurred shortly after dawn. Sir Richard and Captain Worsley, along with Leversuch, Joseph Tubb, the employees of the lodging house and the White Hart Inn, as well as various officers of the South Hampshire Militia, had become involved in a frantic inquest. He regretfully reported that Mary Sotheby and all of Seymour's urgently needed clothing had been shut in the Worsleys' house at Lewes. Connolly had come as soon as he had been able. Before his departure, he had caught sight of Sir Richard. He seemed a man 'in great distress . . . confusion and panic', and capable of anything. The last glimpse that Connolly had of him was when Worsley boarded a post-chaise and set off at full gallop for London.

8

The Cuckold's Reel

When Elizabeth Figg came down the dark staircase to Tubb's basement kitchen she was surprised to find that someone had already lit the fire. Sitting beside it, dressed for a journey was Joseph Connolly. He looked up at her with a fearful expression. In his hands he held two letters ready for dispatch. Unnerved by his appearance, Elizabeth enquired if 'he had known of the cause of the disturbance'. Connolly answered, quite shaken, 'that his master, Captain Bisset was gone off with Lady Worsley and he . . . was to go to Lady Worsley's maid to get her to go with him and to get Lady Worsley's cloaths'. Then he gestured to the packet of papers in his hands: 'the letter', he stated with dread, 'is from my master for Sir Richard Worsley, but I am too afraid to deliver it'. He had been stewing in the kitchen, attempting to fortify his nerve by the warmth of the fire.

As Connolly spoke, Tubb came down the stairs. 'What was this noise I heard in the night?' the proprietor asked. The valet then began to tell his incredible tale again: 'Captain Bisset was set off for London and had taken Lady Worsley with him!' He showed Tubb the letter in his hand and explained 'his master had directed him to deliver it but . . . he feared Sir Richard Worsley should blow his head off'. As Tubb and his housekeeper stood dumbstruck in the kitchen, a shaken Connolly excused himself to pack Bisset's belongings and face the trials that awaited him. For those at Tubb's and for many others in Lewes, this was to be the start of an extraordinary day.

While Connolly and Elizabeth Figg were in the kitchen exchanging gossip, down the hill from Castle Green, Sir Richard Worsley rose from his bed. He had not slept well. Throughout the evening the muted glow from Lady Worsley's dressing room hearth reminded him that she had not yet returned. Mary Sotheby, who had kept a vigil with Francis Godfrey in the servants' room had come above stairs several times to stoke the fire. Hearing the swish of skirts and the shifting of coal, Sir Richard had called out his wife's name, but only Mary Sotheby answered. The clock had struck each of the passing hours and still there had been no sign of Seymour.

At shortly after 5 a.m. a post-chaise with a team in full flight had rattled the windows and jolted Worsley from his sleep. With his empirical, enlightened mind Sir Richard was not normally the sort of man to place much faith in his intuition. Strangely though, this noise, the race of horses' hoofs and bounce of a sprung carriage unnerved him. He pushed aside his bed covers. From the door of his rooms, Worsley shouted to his staff below: 'who is awake?' he demanded. Mary Sotheby and Francis Godfrey replied. Sir Richard seemed perplexed. 'Why has Lady Worsley not returned home?' he called out through the unlit house, but neither the butler nor the lady's maid could offer an explanation. When they climbed the stairs they found him in his nightgown looking 'much surprised' if not confused. 'Certainly,' he said to them, 'she must have been taken ill or some accident must have happened.' He glanced through the window to the house across the road and then turned to Godfrey: 'go instantly over to Mr Leversuch's and enquire for her,' he directed. The butler made haste outside into the cold morning.

Worsley tucked himself into the shadows by his window and observed with stoic stillness. Mary stood beside him. They watched as Godfrey pounded on the door, knocking again and again, the sounds travelling down the High Street. The servant 'had knocked some time' but the Leversuchs' household, fatigued from a night's entertainment was slow to its feet. Growing more anxious Sir Richard turned to Mary and 'ordered her to go over to the Butler and to keep knocking 'til they made somebody answer'. And so she too was dispatched over the road.

After much 'violent rapping at the door', Leversuch in his nightshirt threw open the sash window and stared quizzically at Worsley's two servants. 'Sir Richard Worsley desires that Lady Worsley would come home,' Godfrey announced.

'But Lady Worsley . . . was not there,' the surgeon responded. She had, in fact 'left his house about one in the morning'. She had been in the company of Captain Bisset, who 'had handed her Ladyship over the way and he, himself had lighted them within a very few yards of Sir Richard's door'. This was not the reply that anyone had been expecting.

When Godfrey and Mary Sotheby returned to the Worsley house and repeated the conversation to Sir Richard the last of his solid composure soon melted into 'extreme agitation'. The baronet 'hurried on his cloaths' and shouted for Godfrey 'to light lanthorns'. He was determined to hear Leversuch's story for himself.

He marched Godfrey with his swaying lamp back over the road and thumped once more at the surgeon's door. There, in the drawing room where Lady Worsley had anxiously watched the clock only hours earlier, Leversuch 'gave him the same . . . account he had sent by the butler'; that he 'had lighted her over the way' and had last seen her 'in the care of Captain Bisset'.

Sir Richard stood in disquieted silence for several moments. The surgeon surveyed his expression, observing the incomprehension welling in his features. 'Good God, Leversuch,' he muttered at last, 'what shall I do? I can not tell what to make of it, surely she must be playing me some trick.' He then became 'greatly alarmed', pacing about, 'quite undetermined what to do' and 'not knowing where to go to seek after her'. In fact, Sir Richard knew very well where he might have sought his wife. Leversuch had plainly told him with whom she had departed, but at that moment the betrayal it implied was too enormous for Worsley to accept. The possibility of his wife running away with George Bisset had always loomed, but given his liberal treatment of the affair and the dangerous secrets they shared as a trio, he may have convinced himself that the couple would never have resorted to such an irrational and impulsive act.

After nearly fifteen minutes of fraught deliberation the baronet convinced himself that she must have spent the night at Captain and Mrs Chapman's house, as Seymour and Mrs Chapman 'were very intimate'. He announced to Leversuch that 'he would go and enquire after her' there.

Godfrey strode briskly beside his master, lighting him down the road to the Chapmans' rented house where Worsley believed he might find his wife. But after much anxious knocking and another quarter of an hour passed in Captain Chapman's sitting room, he soon learned that they too 'knew nothing of her'.

Outside on the street, the butler waited. Worsley emerged wearing a stricken face and visibly 'in the utmost agony and distress'. Overcome by 'a state of uncertainty and suspense', Sir Richard now realised that the matter was as grave as he had feared. Which aspect of the situation horrified him the most – the pair's unexpected treachery or the knowledge that they now roamed at large armed with potentially lethal secrets – can only be imagined.

He took Godfrey back up the hill to the White Hart Inn in order to rouse Thomas Worsley from his bed. On learning of his cousin's distress, he too slipped on his clothing and 'after about ten minutes . . . appeared at the house of Sir Richard'. By the time Worsley and his servant had returned home, the dawn had begun to colour the sky. In the glare of daylight there would be further discoveries.

The commander and his cousin were sitting uncomfortably together, when at shortly after 7 a.m. a servant came to the door with a message. It was Joseph Connolly, relieved to deposit his small packet of bad tidings into the hands of Francis Godfrey, another unwitting messenger. Connolly did not linger for an answer. The butler examined the letters with some curiosity 'and finding them to be directed to Sir Richard carried [them] to him'.

Immediately, Worsley recognised his wife's curved, delicate script on the note addressed to Mary Sotheby, and his friend, Bisset's writing on the parcel that bore his own name. He cracked the seal 'and took out a small parchment appearing to be an officer's commission'. Carefully, he unfolded the attached note. Both Godfrey and Thomas Worsley held their breath as their eyes studied Sir Richard's movements. 'Oh,' he looked up and uttered, 'my Lady is found.'

Mary Sotheby was summoned from below stairs. 'Lady Worsley had been found', she was told and Sir Richard required her 'to attend him to the house of a Mr Tubb'. Sotheby had guessed that this trouble involved Captain Bisset. As she followed behind Worsley, moving briskly along the road, an increasing sense of dread began to overtake her, a fear that 'Sir Richard and Captain Bisset might meet and that any mischief might then ensue'. Her trepidation was so great that when they approached the entry to the lodging house she could bring herself 'to follow Sir Richard only as far as the stairs . . . and no further . . . being [too] frightened'.

The baronet mounted the stairway that had led his wife and her lover off on their adventure from Lewes. As he took the steps in his impatient stride, he called out to the floors above, 'Lady Worsley!' Lady Worsley did not answer. Instead Sir Richard was met by Elizabeth Figg, who told him 'that she was not there'.

'Upon your honour,' he demanded, 'can you say that Lady Worsley is not in this house?'

'She is not in the house,' Elizabeth affirmed. She found Sir Richard not only 'agitated' but threateningly aggressive. In an attempt to assuage his temper she added, 'you are welcome to search the house if you think proper'. Worsley continued up the stairs, inspecting the surroundings with acute suspicion.

'Has she not been here?' he asked her pointedly as he reached the top floor. They were standing outside her bedchamber. Elizabeth Figg was feeling intimidated. 'It has been my understanding,' she commented, 'that Lady Worsley had been here and was gone off with Captain Bisset at about five in the morning, but . . . I did not see her.' Then, in an action that 'seem[ed] rather to discredit her', the baronet pushed open the door of Elizabeth's room to ensure that the housekeeper had not been paid to harbour the errant pair. Satisfied, he stepped back and then addressed her one final time: 'Do you know what road they have taken?'

'No,' Elizabeth answered, 'I do not.'

To the housekeeper's relief Sir Richard said nothing more and silently 'turned on his heel . . . and then went away'.

Worsley now had time against him. He returned to his house 'in a violent hurry', bolting through the door and scattering servants in his wake. Urgent preparations were made for a journey to London. Gossip travelled faster than post-chaises. It was possible that the whispering had already gathered speed. He must do what he could to curtail it; to bring her back, to buy her silence, or to begin legal proceedings. Events had happened so suddenly that it is unlikely Sir Richard himself knew what course he would take, or even the situation he might find when his carriage arrived in the capital. He knew for certain that he would require moral support, and looked to his cousin, Captain Worsley, to accompany him.

Another post-chaise and four horses were hired. The baronet took his butler aside and gave him 'strict orders . . . not to leave the house or to admit any one into it 'til he should see or hear from him again'. This message was then impressed upon Worsley's small corps of domestic staff, who would effectively be locked into the house until further notice. This, they were instructed, 'was for the sake of Miss Worsley, [their] daughter who was then there'. Gratefully, their son Robert who remained safely sequestered in the nursery at Appuldurcombe, would be spared the upheaval. Sir Richard had begun to plot his strategy. He believed that if his wife were to return to Lewes on any pretext it would be with the intention of claiming her illegitimate baby. It would not be long, Sir Richard calculated, before the child's true parents began to yearn for her. Should 'Lady Worsley come to the house', the staff were ordered 'not to admit her or to suffer her to come in'. The baronet had publicly claimed Jane as his own and was determined for the sake of his dignity that she should remain so.

The only potential turncoat in his army of captive accomplices was Mary Sotheby. His wife's letter, imploring her servant to come to London had never been delivered into Mary's hands, but undoubtedly the maid was simmering with anxiety, anticipating a command from her mistress. Of all the servants under Worsley's roof, no one would have been more distressed by the events of that morning than Mary Sotheby. Her concerns were not simply mercenary ones, that Seymour's absence would inevitably signal the termination of her position, but genuine worry for the welfare of her lady. It was her responsibility to follow her mistress, to forecast her needs, to soothe her bodily discomforts, to dress her, to bath her and to coddle her emotionally should she require it. The complexities of women's attire and the strictures of a genteel upbringing meant that a lady of privilege was virtually helpless without the assistance of her servant's hands. Their relationship was a complicated one; an association of dependency based on mutual trust, subordination, friendship and sometimes unwavering fidelity and love. As it was Mary Sotheby's occupation to observe her mistress's person completely, she would have been privy to her most intimate secrets: the individuals with whom she corresponded, her private conversations, even the state of her naked body and undergarments. The bond that was forged between a maid and her mistress was often intense. Acts of disloyalty and disobedience could be taken as devastating betrayals.

Mary would have known that Lady Worsley urgently required her presence. With no clothing but the functional brown riding habit in which she had absconded, without so much as a change of linen or stockings, without her jewels, her pomades or powders and without Mary Sotheby's fingers to assist her, Seymour would be as vulnerable as a motherless child. She would be forced to rely on the housemaids wherever she resided, with their catty tongues and thieves' pockets. Without her baby, bereft of her clothing and parted from her lady's maid, both Mary and Sir Richard knew, Lady Worsley would grow increasingly desperate. So it was to Mary that he turned before his departure. He addressed her with sternness, impressing on her the importance of her duties to him, the master, rather than to her wayward mistress. It was the husband, not the wife, who paid her wages. Then, into her care he placed 'Lady Worsley's cloaths and jewels . . . with a strict charge not to let her ladyship have any of these in his absence'. He knew that Mary Sotheby's heart would be burdened and her resolve slippery. Godfrey watched her closely.

As predicted, the first test of her will came shortly after Sir Richard's post-chaise had started for the capital. Out of the dust from his wheels came Joseph Connolly who had been lying in wait, anticipating that Worsley's departure would unfasten the loyalty of his household. Like Lady Worsley's distress for her maid, Bisset would be feeling the absence of his valet; his first line of defence against an irritating world of shopkeepers and creditors who required payment, of affairs that needed arranging and items that demanded tending. Connolly felt the same devotion as Mary Sotheby. He had done as the captain had instructed him and hired a post-chaise which he now had ready to ferry him and Mary to London. As he had received no response to his message, he returned with trepidation to the Worsleys' doorstep and asked for Mary Sotheby. 'It was Lady Worsley's orders that you should immediately pack up her Ladyship's cloaths as well as your own and prepare to follow on to London with me,' Connolly told her, and then explained 'that he had stayed behind to accompany her'. Godfrey stood over her, watching. Mary responded with emphatic regret that she could not perform 'her duty to *her* lady'. As the butler looked on she told Connolly with firmness 'that she was sorry but she could not comply with her ladyship's order', and the Worsleys' door was shut.

9

Retribution

On the western outskirts of London there lay a small, pastoral village known as Paddington. But for the drovers with their bleating herds and the hay wagons that rolled down the Edgware Road, it was a peaceful place. The green at its centre was encircled by a screen of stately elms which shaded the brick-fronted homes of gentlemen as well as the cottages of the area's labourers. Paddington was the sort of location where the wealthy middle class came to retire, away from the noise and stench of the metropolis. It was also where Sir Richard Worsley came to hide from the public.

The afternoon sky had just begun to darken when John Frederick Adam Hesse had an unexpected message placed in his hand. Hesse, an older man in his sixties, was of a convivial temperament. A member of a number of London's more intellectual societies, he had a large capacity for friendship, books and wine. Now that his only son George was a married man with a household of his own, Hesse passed his days between his office at Horse Guards, where he held a position as Secretary and Chief Clerk at the Commissary General of Musters, and his comfortable home on Paddington Green with his wife, Elizabeth. He had been enjoying dinner at the home of an acquaintance when he received word that 'Sir Richard Worsley . . . in a distressed situation . . . was then at his house . . . begging a bed . . . for him and his friend'. Hesse, 'much surprised by the contents of the note', immediately asked for his hat and coat.

It is not known precisely how John Hesse, a high ranking civil servant of the London middle classes came into the orbit of the Worsleys of Appuldurcombe. Although Hesse was closer in age to Sir Richard's father, the two shared a number of interests. Hesse regarded himself as a man of science and letters. In addition to being a member of the Royal Society and of the Society of Artists, his name could be found among the lists of subscribers (or patrons) to a variety of literary works. Certainly by 1781, theirs had been a reliable if not 'intimate friendship . . . for some time past'. Above anyone else, Worsley felt he could turn to Hesse in his hour of desperation.

When John Hesse returned home, he found that his friend 'who appeared to be in the greatest distress of mind' had settled into his drawing room. His cousin, Captain Worsley had accompanied him. Despondently, Sir Richard recounted the harrowing events of the day to his stunned host. Crippled by shame and in fear of London's scandalmongers, Worsley explained that his secrets would soon leak from his Stratford Place town house were he to position himself so conspicuously in the West End. He required a well-camouflaged base from which to operate; a place where he could collect his thoughts, apply for assistance and conduct a clandestine correspondence. No one but those essential to his plotting was to know he was in town. Observing his good friend in such a distraught state, Hesse could not refuse Sir Richard's request. What he could not have foreseen was that, by his act of generosity, Hesse would make himself the lightning rod for Worsley's tempest.

For nearly six weeks, Sir Richard remained under Hesse's roof. During that period, Captain Worsley also lodged with him for a fortnight. Eschewing town and any public places, 'he never once quitted' the house on Paddington Green. Rather than risk showing his face, Sir Richard drew his personal business to him. John and Elizabeth Hesse's entertaining rooms were commandeered as a base from which Worsley's advisers mounted a full scale attack on his wife and her lover. Hesse's opinion was never solicited, nor did he offer advice. Instead he maintained a wary distance. Observing his guest move broodingly between his walls, he and Mrs Hesse silently endured the burden the baronet had brought to them. Morose and overwrought, Worsley took over the spaces of his host's home and bled a dark anxiety into Hesse's life. Worse still, the civil servant found that his guest's troubles were difficult to contain and soon spread beyond the confines of his Paddington residence.

John Hesse's primary responsibilities lay at his office in Horse Guards.

It was here, on Wednesday afternoon, that he was summoned from his desk by a caller. The gentleman announced himself as George William Coventry, Viscount Deerhurst. He cut a grim figure standing in the entryway of the Commission. Deerhurst had once been a very handsome beau, a fast-living member of the fashionable set, but about a year earlier he had suffered terribly as a result of a hunting accident. 'With characteristic imprudence' he had urged his uneasy horse over a five-barred gate. When the beast slipped, he was thrown beneath it. Though fortunate to escape death, 'his right eye was beat into his head, his nose broke and laid flat to his face'. The enduring result of his folly was blindness and disfigurement. After his tragedy, Deerhurst tried to minimise the horror of his appearance by wearing a green silk patch over his mangled right eye. Although equally sightless, his yellowing left eye remained open to view.

The Viscount addressed Hesse with politeness. He had been to his house in Paddington that morning hoping to speak with Sir Richard Worsley. Deerhurst did not reveal how he had learned of the baronet's undisclosed whereabouts, but many would have witnessed the activities and correspondence emanating from Hesse's residence. With enough coin, secrets could be eased from the mouths of even the most tight-lipped servants. Notwithstanding the firm denials which the Viscount received when he enquired for Sir Richard at the Paddington house, Deerhurst was adamant that Hesse was harbouring Worsley. 'I am charged with a message from Lady Worsley,' he declared, 'and I desire that . . . you . . . deliver it to Sir Richard.' Then the Viscount began to dictate it from memory:

'Lady Worsley having for some time past received many slights and inattentions from Sir Richard which she could not bear any longer and as she had for some time had a partiality for Captain Bisset, she has taken the opportunity of availing herself of it. She is so resolved to abide by it that in case Sir Richard should force her back again, which he certainly had a right to do, she would do the same again whenever she could.'

Hesse stared at the messenger's blank eyes in shock. 'My Lord, this is a most extraordinary declaration,' he breathed. 'As this matter may probably come before a Court of Justice, if your Lordship is authorised to say so much, I must entreat your Lordship to repeat it again.'

Deerhurst solemnly imparted his message once more. 'Please communicate the same to Sir Richard Worsley,' he concluded.

Hesse remained stunned, then added after a moment's thought, 'If that was her Ladyship's fixed resolution . . . she had better give her assistance towards obtaining a Divorce.'

Indeed, the Viscount replied, he 'believed that a Divorce was what Lady Worsley wished for'.

Months later, the ageing servant of His Majesty's government claimed that he could not recall any further details of what had passed between himself and Lord Deerhurst. From the instant the words were spoken, Hesse had tried to catch them in his head and went to 'write a memorandum thereof'. He then hurried back to his home in order to relay the information to Worsley.

Although Worsley had landed like a cyclone on Hesse's home, it was not until Deerhurst's visit that Hesse found himself pulled to the centre of the storm. With Sir Richard refusing to speak to the Viscount, John Hesse was forced to become the baronet's intermediary and manage all communication between Worsley and his wife's representative. This much was made apparent when on the following day, Lord Deerhurst's figure appeared once more like a spectre in his doorway. The nobleman came with a further response from Lady Worsley. She had 'authorised' Deerhurst 'to say that a divorce was what she particularly wished for and she would be glad if [Mr Hesse] would recommend it to Sir Richard Worsley'. As he had done the day before, the civil servant committed these weighty words to ink and remorsefully passed them on to his house guest.

Though a painful process, Lady Worsley's open declaration of her desires had the effect of quickly lancing what had promised to become a festering situation. If, in the days since his arrival in Paddington Sir Richard had held any doubt as to how he might proceed in resolving the crisis, the route forward had now been laid in front of him. In theory, if his wife favoured a divorce, she would provide no obstacle to her husband's implementation of it. Such a gesture was further proof of the persistence of Seymour and Bisset's naïve optimism that Worsley would 'do the decent thing', facilitating matters expediently and to everyone's contentment.

Shortly after his appearance at Hesse's home, Sir Richard commenced a campaign of correspondence, begging advice from a number of acquaintances. The most useful of his respondents was a Mr Topham, a solicitor friend. Topham soon found himself sitting in the drawing room at Paddington Green where Worsley, still 'extremely distressed', placed 'the entire management of the matter' into his friend's steadier hands. A day later, Topham returned with someone who was to prove far more useful than himself: James Farrer, an attorney who also was prepared to act as a private investigator. Since the 1770s, James Farrer and his brother Oliver had acquired a specialisation in the prosecution of divorce. To date, Farrer & Co.'s most spectacular case had been the scandal of the previous decade, the divorce of Lady Penelope Ligonier from her husband following her flagrant affair with the Italian dramatist Vittorio Alfieri. It was Farrer who would advise Worsley as to which form of divorce he should pursue. Steaming with rage, the baronet made it clear that he intended to exact the most uncomfortable of penalties for his wife's transgressions.

Of the two most regularly sought avenues for dissolving a marriage, a full divorce or a 'Separation from Bed and Board', Sir Richard chose the latter. Determined to strip his wife of any comfort and future happiness, this option presented the greatest scope for punishment. Such compensations as it held for the wife were paltry. Although she would be allowed to retain her yearly allowance of pin money, this sum alone was unlikely to sustain a lady's lavish lifestyle. If, given her straitened circumstances she was privileged enough to outlive her estranged husband, she would also be entitled to receive her widow's jointure. Negotiated as part of the marriage settlement, a jointure guaranteed a bereaved wife a house and an income suited to her needs. Crucially, a Separation from Bed and Board did not provide any alimony payment, the annual allowance that stood between a forsaken wife and hardship. By snipping the cords of financial obligation, a husband ruthlessly cast his wife into a life of destitution, or reliance on the favours of other men for a livelihood. A 'divorce' of this sort provided little hope of social rehabilitation through a second marriage. It would be, for Sir Richard, a fitting revenge.

But Worsley's appetite for retribution would not be sated by this action alone. His friend must also be held accountable in the stiffest terms possible. His betrayal was unconscionable and Sir Richard would concentrate the fire of his anguish into one lethal shot which he would aim directly at Maurice George Bisset. As an elopement was grounds for a virtually indisputable case of adultery, Worsley had determined immediately that he would prosecute the captain for criminal conversation. It would be a double suit. Farrer agreed to assume responsibility for both cases in the courts, but matters had to be conducted properly. In the eighteenth century, this might entail any number of unscrupulous tricks. Before he could procure the desired results, he needed

Worsley's assistance and that of his entire household in the laying of an elaborate trap.

In the game of suing for criminal conversation, the first move was to lock on to the target, to learn his worth and to prepare one's aim. Through James Farrer a Mr Herne, Bisset's land agent, was approached and asked to ascribe a value to the rents received from the captain's property on the Isle of Wight. Herne claimed that his employer was taking in 'Somewhere about £800 or something more than £800 a year'. To this could be added the income from his other properties in Somersetshire which brought the amount of his total earnings to approximately £1,500 (a sum equivalent to an annual living allowance of roughly £1.9 million in 2008). The actual worth of his house at Knighton, which was filled with works of art and expensive furniture, was not included in these calculations.

In theory, the paramour's ability to pay the damages was immaterial in deciding the penalty a wronged husband might demand from him. If he could not pay, then he might find himself cast indefinitely into the bowels of a debtors' prison, which at least in the plaintiff's eyes was a fitting punishment or 'a retribution for life for an injury for life'. Ultimately, it was held that the husband's claim for damages should reflect the dishonour perpetrated against him. There was no absolute sliding scale, but a number of factors invariably contributed to the tallying of what might be considered a fair sum.[*]

Foremost in the prosecution of any suit was a consideration of the plaintiff's wealth and position in society. Here, the edicts of hierarchy and a rigid class system would have massaged Worsley's conventional prejudices: that an injury done to a gentleman of high standing was greater than one done to a lower-born counterpart. As he stood in a more prominent position and was accustomed to an existence of entitlement, a slight to him was an insult to the established order. Those further down the ladder, who had fewer privileges, would be more accustomed to having less and to swallowing indignities. Legally, their person did not count for so much. A gentleman of stature, due to the quality of his education, was also believed to be endowed with heightened sensitivity and 'more tender feelings than

---

[*]Lawrence Stone's *Road to Divorce* (1992) is one of the most authoritative texts on the subject of eighteenth-century divorce and criminal conversation. He identifies several key components in setting these sums.

the vulgar'. He should therefore receive greater compensation as any injury done to him would be experienced with more acute pain. Wealth, apparently, made one's heart more vulnerable.

Then there were the mitigating factors surrounding the situation in which the act of criminal conversation occurred. A claim for damages might be assessed upwards or downwards when the love triangle and the histories of its three players were examined. As Lawrence Stone explains, 'if the lover was a bare acquaintance of the husband then no breach of friendship and hospitality had taken place'. However, if, like Bisset, 'he had been an old family friend or on regular dining terms and free to stay the night whenever he chose, then the breach of faith was regarded on all sides as very serious'. As a close male friend of the husband the act of adultery 'was regarded as a double betrayal, first of the spousal relationship and second of male bonding'. This especially applied if the husband and the wife's lover had been 'bound together in loyalty' as associates in the same regiment or, more heinous still, as members of the same family. In fact, the more closely the rules of damage setting are investigated, the more clearly they reveal the truth implied in a suit for criminal conversation. At its core, this was not a dispute about the violation of the marriage bed: it was about penalising men who, by breaking the honour code, were perceived to have torn the very fabric of society.

But a criminal conversation suit also was about property and its value. Notionally, legal action was initiated because an interloper had damaged the viability of a plaintiff's chattel; in this case, his wife. In order for justice to be administered, her importance to him, like the worth of a painting or a horse, required appraisal. There were a number of ways in which this could be assessed. By the second half of the eighteenth century, when the ideals of 'companionate marriage' or the love match began to colour society's expectations of matrimony, an injured husband might complain that he had been unjustly robbed of his wife's 'comfort and society', her friendship, company and the pleasures of her body to which he was lawfully entitled. Ascribing a sum to this sort of loss often proved difficult. However, in Sir Richard Worsley's perception, these nebulous measures of worth did not count for as much as did Seymour's value to him in financial terms. Lady Worsley was an heiress in her own right. She had come to him with upwards of £52,000 entailed on her. She and her estate raised his prestige, allowing him to purchase the fashionable town house on Stratford Place as well as properties in Marylebone and on the Isle of Wight. The attention that she and her fortune garnered had pushed them both into the most modish circles. Access to her money increased his influence, and the net worth of this amounted to more to him than an infinite number of tedious evenings spent together sipping tea and shuffling cards. For a man so intent on building a name and power base for himself, she was, in effect, his most precious asset.

In this suit, all three parties bore enormous price tags. In such circumstances, and when factoring in Bisset's breathtaking breach of the honour code, Worsley was certain to apply for an appropriately wounding sum. Before the mid-1780s, it was a rarity for plaintiffs to request damages in excess of £10,000, and even that was a sum reserved for the most exceptionable infractions. In 1730, Lord Abergavenny successfully sued his wife's lover, Richard Lyddel for this amount, an action which in turn ruined him. Like Bisset, Lyddel had been an intimate companion of Abergavenny's and had used his confidence to gain access to his home and Catherine Abergavenny's bedchamber. It did not require much deliberation for the jury to decide that this had been an unpardonable abuse of a close male relationship. A similar decision was made when the case of *Rochfort* v. *Rochfort* was heard a decade later. An unprecedented £20,000 had been demanded and awarded for the worst of all possible offences, a betrayal between brothers. However, spectacular claims such as these were infrequent. Even in the most high profile extramarital scandal involving two exceedingly wealthy parties, the 1770 crim. con. trial of the Duke of Cumberland (the King's brother) for a dalliance with Lord Grosvenor's wife, damages were set at £10,000. As the awards allocated were so bounteous and the crimes committed so juicy, the era's press took to these stories with relish. *Abergavenny* v. *Lyddel* was published throughout the first half of the century as a type of moral parable. The result of *Grosvenor* v. *Cumberland* became household knowledge.

Even before he had taken advice from Farrer, Worsley would have had a strong sense of the sort of sum he might exact. It would need to be large enough to atone for the atrocity committed and to restore his broken authority. Nothing but the complete ruin of George Bisset would suffice. His desire for vengeance demanded it.

10

The Royal Hotel, Pall Mall

For several days, the door to room 14 had remained locked. Its mysterious occupants kept to themselves. Ann Ekelso had tried several times to replenish the fire in the bedchamber but her gentle rapping had met with silence. Only rarely were the housemaids or the butler permitted into the couple's shadowy quarters, where the drawn curtains blocked out the light of midday. Other than a chance encounter, there were few opportunities to gawp at this most peculiar pair. Occasionally in the mornings 'and long before the lady had made her appearance' the gentleman could be seen moving between the bedroom and the Apollo, wearing 'no cloaths whatever but his bed gown and slippers slipped on'. The staff thought it unusual that as soon as he had risen he would then 'return to the bedroom . . . and . . . go to bed again'.

'They were an odd kind of people,' Ann Ekelso had commented to Joseph Connolly, who was often to be found tending to his master's requirements alongside the hotel's staff. What sort of person lingered about 'in bed most of the day' after 'going to bed so very late at night?' she prodded. But Joseph Connolly 'would only laugh'. Neither she nor 'the other servants . . . could discover the Lady or Gentleman's names, or who they were'.

Between the bed hangings and the sheets, Lady Worsley and her lover continued to wait. The hours since their elopement had lengthened into slow, tense days. Although their actions had been designed to provoke a response from Sir Richard, neither could be certain from where it would come, nor the shape it might assume. While there remained any possibility of ambush or violence they were forced to cower in the shuttered and locked rooms of the Royal Hotel. It was within her husband's rights to have Seymour snatched and bundled into a sealed post-chaise bound for Appuldurcombe. Bisset would have been plagued by the spectre of a duel. Sir Richard's where-abouts as well as his schemes were entirely unknown.

Their only succour dripped from Deerhurst's pen and arrived in the form of occasional correspondence. In spite of his visual impediment the blind Viscount was proving himself an indefatigable detective and champion of their cause. Within two days of their elopement, through a combination of bribery and investigation he had located Sir Richard and made the first strategic move towards securing Seymour and Bisset's wishes. But the inter-vals between letters were unnerving. Without a clear view of events beyond their window, the lovers were hostages to fortune.

After the elation of their successful escape, the reality of their situation began to settle in. More than his mistress, Bisset had been prepared for their illicit undertaking, having planned their movements and arrived with servants and clothing. In addition to the emotional strain of separation from her infant daughter, Seymour did not even have a change of undergarments. Although she had set out enthusiastically on this journey, her role was that of a passenger travelling in circumstances now beyond her control. For a third time, a message had been sent to Mary Sotheby, directing her to come immediately to London with Seymour's clothing. The response had not been favourable. 'It was Sir Richard's strict order,' the lady's maid wrote, 'that she excuse herself from coming to London.' As for the coveted clothing, Mary claimed 'it was not in her custody'. To Lady Worsley, this was a clear indi-cation that her husband intended to punish her. Concern over what other reprisals might be lying in reserve caused her great disquiet. Sitting enclosed within the walls of number 14, she could do nothing more than wait and contemplate and worry.

Those of the hotel's servants who attended the couple noted that Lady Worsley in particular 'appeared extremely fearful of being seen'. It was with hesitation that she emerged from the bedchamber for her meals in the adjoining dining room. On several occasions, Ann Ekelso had watched her 'run across the passage . . . with her hand to her face as if to hide it'. At other times, Seymour beckoned Ann to her while suspiciously casting her gaze beyond her doorway, 'What gentlemen were in the house?' she anxiously questioned the housemaid. As requested, the servant would repeat a catalogue of names. 'What apartments were they in?' she insisted. But the answers never succeeded in putting her at ease.

By the third day of her captivity, Lady Worsley could bear her incarceration no longer. Whether or not the couple had been invited to Lord Deerhurst's home, they were determined to see the Viscount in person and escape their restrictive lodgings, if only for an evening. In the morning Seymour pulled the bell rope and summoned Ann Ekelso. The servant opened the door to find her mistress naked and in bed, the sheets wrapped around her modestly. She directed Ann to 'to wash her riding shirt and a pair of stockings and one or two other things' and then explained that as she had no change of clothing or undergarments 'she could not get up' until Ekelso 'had got them ready for her'. For a woman of wealth whose wardrobe contained over 500 articles of clothing, nothing could have felt more compromising than having to swathe herself in bedding while her only pair of stockings were rinsed.

Another anxious day was passed behind a locked door as Lady Worsley's undergarments dried by the fire. When darkness came, the couple prepared themselves for a cautious visit to Cleveland Row. Still fearful of being apprehended they crept from their rooms and 'hurried through the passage . . . afraid of being seen or noticed'. Thomas Fort led them to a waiting hackney coach, whose windows, like those of their lodgings were screened by shades.

That evening, over dinner, Lord Deerhurst divulged the minutiae of his conversations with John Hesse, and any further information he had been able to squeeze from his sources. They learned of Sir Richard's hiding place in Paddington and received assurances that their position at the Royal Hotel remained undisclosed. The Viscount was guarding their interests to the best of his ability. However while Deerhurst was soothing their nerves with his hospitality, Worsley and James Farrer were tying the last strings of their net.

On the morning of Friday the 23rd of November, the tables were turned on Lord Deerhurst quite unexpectedly. Two strangers appeared at his door, asking to see the Viscount. The better dressed of the pair announced himself as James Farrer, the attorney engaged by Sir Richard Worsley. After being admitted into the house on Cleveland Row, Farrer addressed Deerhurst plainly. He explained that he had come to his home to learn the whereabouts of Lady Worsley and Captain Bisset and that he 'apprehended that His Lordship was privy . . . to such information'. Deerhurst hesitated. Farrer further explained that he had 'furnished himself with a writ from the Court of the King's Bench' which he, through the powers of the law, 'intended to serve on Mr Bisset'. The attorney continued. He also had in his possession 'a citation from [the Court of Doctors' Commons] to serve on Lady Worsley'. Then Farrer gestured to the man in his company. Should there be any question as to the authority of this action, he had brought with him 'an Officer to attend serving it to her'. Lady Worsley wanted a divorce and as his visitors were determined to initiate proceedings, the Viscount decided to surrender his secrets.

Deerhurst confessed that the couple had been hiding at the Royal Hotel on Pall Mall since Monday, but that unless Farrer 'pursued a specific set of directions', he would not be granted access to them. As Bisset and Lady Worsley 'were wholly unknown to every body in and belonging to the hotel', Farrer had to enquire for Joseph Connolly, who, through the use of this signal, would show an approved person to the lovers' lodgings.

Farrer was now on the warpath. He and the court officer marched directly to the Royal Hotel and asked 'for the servant, Joseph Connolly'. Connolly cast a wary gaze over the men and was only convinced when the attorney finally added 'that he had come from Lord Deerhurst'. The valet then directed the gentlemen upstairs and into the Apollo dining room, where a startled Bisset rose to his feet.

'Maurice George Bisset?' Farrer asked. 'You are served with a writ from the Court of the King's Bench.' The attorney thrust an article of parchment into the former captain's hand. Before Bisset could offer a reply, Farrer 'then enquired for Lady Worsley'.

'Who asks for her?' demanded Bisset.

James Farrer ignored his interrogator and with an officious tone simply stated 'that it is necessary that I should see her'.

Bisset regarded the man standing beside Farrer and realised that he carried with him the news for which they had been waiting: the launch of Sir Richard's suit for a divorce. 'I shall fetch her,' he said 'and then went out of the room for that purpose'.

Several moments passed before Bisset 'returned to the room with a Lady hanging on his arm'. 'I am Lady Worsley,' pronounced the small but defiant figure.

For a lady accustomed to greetings of deference and curtsies the intimidating stance of the officer of the Court of Doctors' Commons seemed threatening. He stepped up to her and formally served her with a legal citation.

Sir Richard Worsley announced his arrival in fashionable society with this portrait painted by his friend Joshua Reynolds in 1775.

Lady Worsley's mother, Jane, Lady Harewood, around 1795.

Lady Worsley's step-father, the wealthy land owner and MP, Edwin Lascelles (later Baron Harewood), by Joshua Reynolds, 1768.

Seymour's pretty, 'amiable and virtuous' elder sister Jane (later Countess of Harrington), painted by Reynolds as *Aurora* in 1775.

Harewood House, as painted by J.M.W. Turner in 1798

A view of Appuldurcombe in 1834

A Trip to Cocks Heath, by J. Mortimer, 1778, lampoons the summer encampment for its notoriously loose moral tone and for encouraging female sexual aggressiveness.

Captain Jessamy Learning the Proper Discipline of the Couch, by Carington Bowles, is believed to depict Lady Worsley and Captain Bisset at the Royal Hotel. Seymour is shown here wearing a brown riding habit, the only outfit she possessed when she eloped from Sir Richard.

Interior View of Westminster Hall, Showing the Court of the King's Bench in Session, 1808

The SHILLING
or the
Value of A P.. Y: C.......ʀ's *Matrimonial Honor*

The Shilling or the Value of a P–Y: C–r's Matrimonial Honour was the first attack on Sir Richard to appear after the disastrous verdict at the Court of the Kings Bench.

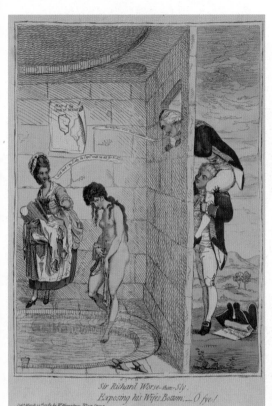

*Sir Richard Worse-than-sly
Exposing his Wife's Bottom – O fye!*,
by James Gillray is one of the
more enduring images to come
out of the scandal. Gillray
was one of several lampoonists
who created 'peeping scenes'
which centred on the events
at the Maidstone bath house.

*Sir Richard Worse-than-sly.
Exposing his Wifes Bottom;__ O fye!*

A Peep into Lady W!!!!!y's Seraglio.
Gillray was the only satirist to
mount a pictorial
attack on Lady Worsley's
sexuality. The image was later
reprinted as the frontispiece
to *Variety*, a set of scandalous
verses about Seymour's
'variegated train' of lovers.

Lady Worsley in her South Hampshire Militia riding habit, which she wore at Coxheath in 1778. Joshua Reynolds painted her in it during the summer of 1779.

Farrer and the court officer left the couple behind the closed door of the Apollo, holding the writs in which Sir Richard's devastating first thrust was couched. The extensive divorce depositions which record in precise detail the movements and behaviour of both parties give no insight into the reactions of either Lady Worsley or Bisset at this decisive juncture; the moment when the consequences of their uncertain venture were revealed: that instant when Seymour opened the documents and realised that she would remain shackled to Sir Richard for the rest of her life, or when Bisset glanced at the paper in his hands and read the charge of criminal conversation.

Like the duellist who aims at the heart, Sir Richard was determined on destruction. He had ensured that his wife and Bisset, his betrayer, would never be free to marry. For her sins against him, and because his sense of honour required it he would cast her off, forcing her to wallow in a state of matrimonial purgatory. It was intended to be a punishment felt by both lovers, equally. However, his friend's unspeakable wrong, his gross violation of an intimate trust and a private agreement required a harsher brand of justice. He should have to experience not only the humiliation and disquiet of the man he had deceived, but a diminution of status and its resulting social disgrace. Worsley decided that Bisset's folly would cost him £20,000 (the equivalent of £25.4 million), or, more plainly, his life.

When considering his social standing and military rank, the position of his wife, as well as the store he set by Bisset's friendship, Sir Richard might reasonably have asked for £10,000, in keeping with conventional practices. This sum, the equivalent of nearly £12.7 million today, would have severely crippled, if not ruined Bisset. But Worsley would take no chances, particularly as juries were known to halve large claims when making awards. The sum of £10,000 was not enough to restore honour. A mere £10,000 could not soothe the stinging humiliation which Sir Richard felt or reconstruct his damaged pride. In order for Worsley to brush off this slight and continue his climb through the ranks of influence he required a very public vindication.

Even for a gentleman of George Bisset's wealth, a claim for £20,000 would be impossible to meet. If his total worth, the complete value of his personal estate, did not equal that amount, he would not be able to make good the debt. In the eighteenth century this meant arrest by a bailiff and imprisonment in the Fleet, the oppressive hole into which insolvents were thrown. Much of Bisset's liquefiable wealth would be placed under the hammer to meet Worsley's demands. The pressure to sell his land would be unremitting. Under English law, a man's property could not be confiscated, but tightened straits could compel him to dispose of it. Throughout the era, estates and their adjoining lands, fertile grazing grounds, farms, stables, and lakes regularly changed hands due to an owner's indebtedness. The sale of his land would mean Bisset's final defeat. His position in society would be compromised. In these circumstances securing a loan or any type of personal favour which might free him from the shackles of his debt would be difficult. Clearly, Worsley intended him to die in poverty and dishonour.

The demand for £20,000 was a highly strategic move on Worsley's part. It is most likely that one of his intentions was to force the sale of Knighton, or at least much of its land. The estate would be the spoils of his victory, a gleaming trophy earned in a bitter rout. The acquisition of this sizeable parcel of property was likely to make Worsley the most powerful landowner on the Isle of Wight. It would be a dramatic resurrection for his injured conceit.

George Bisset now faced ruin. The very contemplation of £20,000 would have been nauseating. He would require lawyers who could build him a sturdy defence, but constructing a convincing case from an indisputable instance of adultery would be nearly impossible. His mistress's position appeared just as bleak. Sir Richard's proposed 'Separation from Bed and Board' read like an edict of banishment, a sentence of exile from the realm of respectability. The last of their misguided hopes for an amicable settlement had been destroyed as well as their foolish belief in the generosity of the baronet's character. The worst was now upon them. How they would contend with a situation turned so starkly against them, if they could salvage anything from their loss, was yet to be seen.

11

A House of Spies

Having successfully discovered the whereabouts of Lady Worsley and her lover and served them with legal writs, James Farrer returned to Paddington, where he explained to Sir Richard that in order to proceed with both the suit for separation and the suit for criminal conversation they must accomplish two important tasks. The first was to positively ascertain the identities of the adulterous pair and the second was to gather 'the most full and clear evidence of the criminality of their intercourse'. The latter was much more straightforward than it sounded. In the eighteenth century it was not considered 'necessary to prove the direct fact of adultery'. A suggestion that illicit sex had probably taken place was all that an indictment required. As adulterers were especially canny about covering their tracks, practitioners of law had long since concluded that if they were forced to produce definitive evidence of guilt there would not be 'one case in a hundred in which that proof would be attainable'. Whether Farrer had burst through the lovers' door and discovered them *in flagrante* or found individuals who could attest to the pair's inappropriate relations didn't matter. Both forms of evidence were equally admissible. However, any accusations would have to be based on actual observation, not hearsay. Malicious below-stairs cant was not admissible. Rumpled and soiled sheets, stained undergarments, overheard moans of passion and hidden love letters, were. The law also stipulated that the testimony of at least two witnesses who could positively identify both parties was necessary 'to conclude that adultery had taken place'. In such matters, there were few better qualified to comment on an individual's private affairs than those who moved invisibly through the lives of the patrician classes: servants.

The Royal Hotel employed an army of such spies. In fact, Farrer assured Worsley that before he had departed from Pall Mall, he had already made some basic enquiries about the situation of the lady and the gentleman in number 14. 'It had appeared from the people of the Hotel,' he told Sir Richard, 'that they passed for Husband and Wife and used and occupied only one Bed.' This being the case, the lawyer continued, it would not be too difficult 'to contrive that some one or other of the servants of the Hotel might go into their bedroom when they were in bed and see them in it together'. Farrer had assembled similar snares for previous clients with unequivocal success. But it was imperative 'that the strictest precautions should be used' so that the couple would 'not have the least ground to suspect that any such step was being taken to procure evidence against them'. One of the surest methods of accomplishing this was to bring in servants from Worsley's household; individuals already known to his wife and whose presence in such strained circumstances might even be welcomed. There were many among Sir Richard's staff who would also be able to positively identify Bisset, a man they recognised as a visitor to Appuldurcombe and to the London house. At the same time, the staff at the Royal Hotel could use these visits as an excuse to gain further access to the lovers' apartments in the hope of observing the couple's illicit behaviour. Farrer suggested that the ideal person for the task was Mary Sotheby.

When Sir Richard had left Lewes the doors of his house were locked behind him. Nearly forty-eight hours had passed before his servants received directions from him in London. Too encumbered by his emotions to write lucidly, Worsley had pressed John Hesse into service as his secretary. It was he who instructed Godfrey to send young Jane, her nursemaid and Mary Sotheby 'to Sir Richard's house in Stratford Place in a post chaise'. Seymour's clothes and jewels were to be packed into trunks and sent with them. Godfrey and the rest of the household were to 'follow in the most convenient manner'. Even before Farrer had advised him, the baronet had recognised the worth of this precious human and material cargo and its potential use as bait. In this developing scheme, Mary Sotheby was to become Sir Richard's next pawn, and the house on Stratford Place an auxiliary headquarters for the operation.

The next challenge was one of logistics. The witnesses had to move quickly, they must not find themselves drawn into conversation, they must observe and leave, all in rapid succession so as not to raise too much suspicion. Farrer himself would orchestrate the exercise, with Mr Topham acting as his assistant. To ensure the seamlessness of events, the recruitment of Mr Weston, the Royal Hotel's proprietor would also be required. Farrer had called on him discreetly the morning before. He had taken him aside and gingerly disclosed to him that his establishment was the scene of an elopement. The unnamed lady in room 14 had run away from her husband with the gentleman currently sharing her bedchamber. The lawyer revealed that 'The gentleman and lady were a Mr Bisset and Lady Worsley', before continuing that he was employed to gather evidence for the divorce and 'desired that it might be so contrived that some of the servants might have an opportunity of seeing them in Bed together and to observe both their faces'. Gripped by the intrigue of the situation, Weston agreed to help with the plan. With the groundwork in place by Friday evening, Farrer was prepared to launch his attack.

The drama began on Saturday morning, long before the lovers' bed curtains were even parted. Anticipating that Lady Worsley and Bisset would rise at a conventional hour, Farrer and Topham arrived at the Royal Hotel shortly after sunrise. At first they established their base in the bar, but as the morning wore into afternoon and hunger strained Farrer's patience, they moved to the ground floor dining room. Here they could pose inconspicuously as diners while monitoring the situation as it unfolded in the rooms above. The previous evening, Mr Weston had addressed his staff and told them the true circumstances of the couple in number 14. It had been decided that Hannah Commander, the brassy twenty-one-year-old barmaid was sharp enough to spearhead the plan. She and the housekeeper, Anna Watkinson would be drafted in as the hotel's principal spies. Farrer instructed them that their testimony would be fundamental in the ensuing crim. con. trial and in the divorce hearing. They must both endeavour 'to see them plainly' as they lay together in bed. Hannah was to address Lady Worsley directly, to concoct a story if necessary in the hope of luring her into disclosing her identity. To ensure that they followed his instructions, he weighted their pockets with a comfortable bribe.

Farrer and his two assistants waited all morning for number 14 to tug on their bell rope. It was not until one o'clock that the bell on the board below stairs tinkled. Hannah and Mrs Watkinson snapped into action. As the couple had only just roused themselves from sleep, the housekeeper could enter their lodgings on the pretext of lighting their fire. While their room remained unheated, the pair were more likely to huddle together in bed, providing Hannah with a narrow opportunity of spying them entwined.

Mrs Watkinson rapped on the door and slipped unobtrusively into the room. As she crouched by the grate, Hannah strode in behind her. Charged by the thrill of flouting the hotel's decorous code of conduct, the barmaid insolently yanked back the couple's bed curtains. The lovers jumped in fright. In the commotion, Seymour 'lifted up her arm . . . and endeavoured to hide the gentleman's face', though she failed to obscure it from the barmaid's fixed gaze. She stared at them as they cowered beneath the bedding. 'With an apology to the Lady for this intrusion', Hannah began, 'Madam, there is a riding habit left for a Lady in this House and there being no Lady in the House but yourself, may I crave the favour of your name?'

'What?!' Lady Worsley asked indignantly.

Hannah 'repeated her message'. Anna Watkinson, using the disturbance as an excuse to peer into the bed, was now examining the pair.

Bisset was furious. 'Ask who it is,' he commanded, whereupon Hannah replied that 'she did not know'.

'Go down and enquire who it is,' Seymour instructed her.

Hannah and the housekeeper scurried from the room, flew down the stairs and appealed to James Farrer for advice. The lawyer returned them both to number 14, with a lie and specific directions that Hannah squeeze the lady's name from her lips.

Unshaken in her resolve to corner the pair, the barmaid reappeared at the bedside. She fed Seymour the invented identity of the riding habit's bearer. Farrer's ruse had unlocked Seymour's guard. 'Might I beg the favour of Madam's name?' Hannah enquired.

'Lady Worsley,' came the voice from behind the bed hangings.

In the ground floor dining room, Hannah relayed her tale to Farrer who listened intently. Not only had she caught sight of the couple in bed and confirmed the identity of the wayward wife, but she had observed further evidence that the pair had given in to their wanton, adulterous lusts. 'The Gentleman's coat and dressing gown were lying on a chair at the bed's foot,' she told the lawyer, 'and the Lady's petticoats and stockings . . . were lying on the floor by the bed's side.' Farrer was pleased with the services of his recruit and would use her again, later in the afternoon in the launch of his rearguard assault.

James Farrer now had to move quickly. After being served with legal papers, the couple in number 14 felt exposed and might view anything unusual as a potential threat. Their suspicions would only be heightened when the suggested riding habit failed to materialise. The lawyer would have to play his final cards under increasingly difficult circumstances.

He and Topham went immediately to Stratford Place to see Mary Sotheby. They interrogated her closely and reminded her of the seriousness of the situation. For a young woman from rural Kent, this entire circus of events in which she had accidentally found herself was disconcerting and over-whelming. Farrer and Topham made it clear that they hadn't much time. They enquired 'whether she should have any objections to seeing Lady Worsley again' and also 'whether she knew enough of Mr Bisset to be certain as to his person upon seeing him'. Mary nodded to both questions. 'Then' the lawyer directed her 'to put up a few of Lady Worsley's most ordinary things to take to her'. In fact, Farrer's orders contained a deliberate barb which Mary Sotheby omitted from her deposition statement. Whether the design of Sir Richard or his attorney, a decision was made to keep Lady Worsley parted from any useful element of her wardrobe. As Mary rummaged through her mistress's boxes, Farrer would have been standing over her, moni-toring her choices. She was to receive nothing of value nor any item which would ease her distress. Lady Worsley later complained at the cruelty of this act, that she was purposely sent 'but very few cloaths . . . and that such as she had received did not amount to a single compleat dress or a hundredth part of her wearing apparel'.

Seymour's maid clutched the small package of mismatched clothing as the two gentlemen escorted her to the Royal Hotel. 'You must not say anything to Mr Bisset when you see him,' he instructed her on the way. 'You must only satisfy yourself as to his person and also as to Lady Worsley's. You must leave the bundle of cloaths for her and then come away.' Farrer knew the difficulty that a loyal lady's maid might have in completing this task when seeing her mistress's sympathetic expression. Mary Sotheby would have been quivering.

On their arrival, Farrer handed Mary into the care of Hannah Commander, who had already grown comfortable exceeding the limits of her domain within the hotel. She confidently showed the maid to the lovers' apartments. Once more, Hannah boldly pushed open the door to the Apollo dining room.

Standing on the threshold, Mary Sotheby came face to face with a surprised George Bisset. Before either could properly draw breath, Hannah pulled Mary away and shut the door. She heard Bisset call out to her, but the barmaid had already pushed the girl across the hallway to Lady Worsley's bedchamber. The door to the Apollo swung open. 'Mary!' Bisset shouted after her, pursuing her to the door of number 14 where he watched her approach Seymour. Mary found her mistress 'at the dressing table' with Ann Ekelso in her rightful place, 'attending and dressing her'. Catching sight of her, Lady Worsley stopped suddenly 'and appeared much startled'. 'I am quite surprised at seeing you here,' she spoke cautiously.

Mary Sotheby could not meet her mistress's glance. Gently, she laid the bundle of clothing on the table. 'I am come by Sir Richard's orders to bring your Ladyship a few things,' she stated.

'Have you any further messages?' Seymour asked hopefully.

'No, Madam. I have nothing further,' she said stonily before retiring, following Farrer's instructions.

As the lawyer had anticipated, this meeting shook Mary considerably. Hannah took her down the stairs, and she left immediately. In her eagerness to escape, she passed by Philip Deighton, the Worsleys' groom, who had unexpectedly appeared in the servants' entry. The two exchanged puzzled looks but Mary said nothing before fleeing down the road.

The encounter startled Deighton equally. Unlike his fellow servant, the groom had been summoned by a cryptic note instructing him to come to the Royal Hotel in Pall Mall. He knew nothing of the role he was about to play in Farrer's scheme.

When hatching his plot, the lawyer had asked Sir Richard whether there was a trusted member of staff among his household who had worked for him for 'a respectable number of years'. Worsley had mentioned Philip Deighton, the head groom of his stables at Appuldurcombe, who not only had 'lived in the service of Sir Richard . . . for upwards of 10 years', but who 'had known Lady Worsley . . . since the time of marriage'. Deighton was also familiar with Bisset whom 'he saw very often visiting the house'.

For whatever reason, Farrer thought it necessary that the groom remain ignorant of his mission until the last possible moment. It was only when he was shown through the door and into the hotel bar that he received his instructions. As she had with Mary Sotheby, Hannah took the groom 'up one pair of stairs' and led him across the corridor to number 14. She opened the door, but Deighton, a male servant and one whose concern was the welfare of horses rather than ladies, recoiled at the impropriety of this uncomfortable situation. In order to confirm her identity, Farrer had instructed him to examine Lady Worsley as closely as he could, but shame held him back and he hovered tentatively at the threshold. To worsen matters, his employer's wife was in a state of dishabille 'with her hair down as if preparing for dressing'. Articles of her clothing were indecently strewn about and he observed 'the room to be very much in a litter'. Deighton had no desire to see a once-respected woman in such an undignified state. He could not even bring himself 'to go far enough to take notice whether it was a bed chamber or not'. However, Lady Worsley caught sight of his silhouette at the edge of the door. 'Philip,' she said abruptly, 'I can not see you now', and at this cue, Hannah drew him away. She then took him to the dining room and sent him inside. Deighton was told to approach Bisset, and this he did, quite literally stepping 'nearly up to the gentleman so as to be perfectly satisfied it was him'. This was a threatening move and one which took Bisset by surprise, rendering him aghast, either at the audacity of the groom for so bold a breach of etiquette or from fear alone. Satisfied, Deighton 'then retired'. Not a word had passed between them.

Downstairs, he was interviewed by Farrer, who wanted confirmation that the groom was 'certain he knew and remembered the persons he had seen'.

'Yes,' Deighton responded, he 'knew them very well'.

'Then I have no further command for you and you may go home again,' the lawyer concluded.

By late afternoon, guests at the Royal Hotel would have noticed that the two questionable gentlemen who had for most of the day fraternised with the servants had at last settled their bill and left. For Farrer and Topham, this had been a profitable excursion, one that they were certain would pay Worsley handsomely.

No sooner had Farrer gone than the Apollo's bell began to jingle. Thomas Fort was sent to answer the call. When he entered the dining room he found Bisset in curling papers, having his hair dressed and pomaded by Joseph Connolly. The captain was incandescent.

'Who was that damned impertinent bitch who had shewn those people into these rooms?' he asked.

'It was the bar keeper, Sir,' answered Fort.

The Scandalous Lady W

'She is a damned impertinent bitch!' he spat. 'If she comes up in that manner again I will shoot her!'

This was a distressing matter. From the moment they woke up he and Lady Worsley had been affronted grossly by hotel staff, by servants taking brazen liberties with their position. Their doors had been thrown open to intrusion, their bed hangings rudely parted, they had been subjected to deceptions and disrespect. Such behaviour from domestic staff would always be regarded as unconscionable but in Bisset and Lady Worsley's perception, these disturbances assumed a sinister shape. By late afternoon the couple knew they had been discovered. Those who had wandered into their rooms unannounced were Worsley's spies. Their presence and their games were intended to cause as much alarm as possible. It was now unsafe to remain at the Royal Hotel and immediate action was required to prevent further mischief. Connolly was ordered to begin packing his master's belongings.

While preparations were being made for their departure, Bisset rang for Hannah Commander to be shown up to the Apollo. There he and Lady Worsley received her with stern faces.

'How,' the captain asked, 'did you come to shew such a person as Lady Worsley's groom up to her bedroom?'

With an unrepentant retort, Hannah answered plainly, 'The Servant had desired it.' She then added, 'And . . . a gentleman below stairs had also desired it.'

Bisset's temper flared. 'You should not have done it and ought to have known better!' he snapped, as if chastening a child. 'I do not know of any reason why you should have done it. It would be of great injury to this House if it was known that persons of quality had been treated here as we have been.'

Hannah swallowed her punishment with at least the pretence of humility. Downstairs, however, the staff were feasting on the enormous portion of gossip Farrer had left for them. Their names were Lady Worsley and Captain Bisset, they repeated to one another, and she had run away from her husband. These revelations were certain to have lightened the mood in the Royal Hotel's kitchens, pantries and laundry but such excitement needed to be managed prudently. Even before Bisset and Lady Worsley had departed, Mr Weston gathered the members of his staff who had attended them – Thomas Fort, Anna Watkinson, Sarah Richardson, Ann Ekelso and the incorrigible Hannah Commander – and gave them a sombre warning.

No servant at the Royal Hotel was to 'mention their names or own who they were', as 'it was more than their places were worth'. This held even if they were to have 'positive orders to the contrary' by any visitor or enquirer who came to the establishment thereafter. Weston must have mopped his brow as he contemplated the coming months and the inevitability of a very public criminal conversation trial. The Royal Hotel would receive a good deal of publicity, but in the wrong sort of publication.

Shortly after sunset, a hackney carriage pulled into the courtyard of the hotel. Connolly loaded his master's boxes and Seymour's assorted patchwork of items into the vehicle before handing the couple into the cab. The shades were drawn and the whip flicked against the horses' flesh. The wheels began to turn as the lovers escaped once more into the darkness.

It is uncertain where they headed. As a member of Lincoln's Inn, Bisset had lodgings at the Inns of Court and it is possible that they retired here briefly until a more permanent address could be found. It is also possible that their departure was planned the day before, as they stared with mounting anxiety at the legal documents. On Friday night, Deerhurst had called upon them and stayed for dinner. In addition to offering an apology for his failures, it is likely that they discussed the future. Now that Bisset would face charges of criminal conversation he and Lady Worsley might consider taking refuge in France, as many fleeing from legal prosecution were inclined to do. However, for various reasons, this option was dismissed. With such a collection of witnesses, Sir Richard held a full house of evidence which he could use against them. The prospect of a trial would have been a menacing one, but in spite of outward appearances, Bisset had a very strong reason for believing that the Court of the King's Bench would laugh in the face of Worsley's legion of lawyers and tell-tale servants. Although it bore the hallmarks of a straightforward case of adultery, there were more strands to this tangled story than even Farrer had managed to unpick.

12

The World Turned Upside Down

In the last months of 1781, gentlemen and ladies across England sat down at their escritoires and breathlessly spilled the latest tattle across their writing paper.

'Lady Worsley has played a flaming prank at Lewes to divert the Sussex Corps,' wrote the diarist Fanny Burney to her literary friend, Hester Lynch Thrale on the 2nd of December. Although her correspondent claimed not to 'care for' the woman in question, she was keen to learn the sordid details.

Four days later, Edward Gibbon scribbled to his stepmother from the House of Commons, 'You have heard of Lady Worsley? Your Old acquaintance, Sir Richard labours with copious materials for a divorce.' After folding and sealing that missive, he excitedly began another to Lord Sheffield, 'Sir Richard Worsley has opened trenches in Doctors' Commons, and cryed down his wife's credit with tradesmen . . .' It seemed that all of Parliament was discussing Sir Richard's affairs. Shortly before Gibbon took it upon himself to disseminate the news, the politician Anthony Storer wrote to Lord Carlisle that 'Lady Worsley is run away from Sir Richard and taken refuge with some gentleman whose name I do not know in the army.'

There was little the baronet could do to tether the scandal; intelligence of the elopement had broken loose. It was not long before word reached the ears of society's gossip-monger general, Horace Walpole. From the cloisters of his pastiche Gothic palace, Strawberry Hill, he dipped his sharp-edged quill into the story:

'Two young ladies are gone off – no, this is a wrong term for one of them, for she is just come to town and drives about London, for fear her adventure should be forgotten before it comes to the House of Lords, it is a Lady Worseley, sister of Lady Harrington.'

Curiously, few of these busybodies could claim to have personally spotted the runaways. Contrary to Walpole's letter, Seymour and Bisset were not only careful to hide themselves but by early December had fled London altogether, and retreated to Bisset's house at Southampton. Within a matter of weeks the story had blown like a storm through London before heading south through Hampshire and across the Solent to the Isle of Wight. Even in the countryside avoiding encounters with those ready to gawp and scorn was difficult. 'Yesterday afternoon I was surprised at the appearance of Lady Worsley and her Gallant Mr Bisset who were together at the Swan in this Town,' wrote one of the baronet's neighbours from an inn at Alresford. 'They came on horseback and set out after dark for Farnham. I pity poor Sir Richard and hope he will never consent to live with such a damn'd bitch. She seemed very shy at seeing me but I did not take the least notice of her as I knew she had elop'd from her husband by a gentleman who brought the news from London.'

As his wife and her lover took shelter in Southampton, Worsley's period of internment at John Hesse's home continued. Unwilling to risk a similar chance meeting with acquaintances, he did little more than stare through the windows, paralysed by his distress. The blow of his wife's elopement and the ensuing anxiety of initiating legal proceedings had debilitated him entirely. His suit for a separation had been filed by the close of Saturday the 24th, a situation which enabled the baronet to resign himself to sleep that evening in the belief that his crisis had been contained. Regrettably, within a matter of hours misfortune would double back on him with another heavy strike.

As it always did on a Sunday, morning broke to a rising chorus of church bells. While the tolling echoes rolled through the capital's narrow lanes and squares, a sea-worn frigate dropped anchor along the Thames. The ship had left the American colonies thirty-eight days earlier burdened with a weighty cargo. A letter was handed to a messenger who tore through the Sabbath streets with an urgent delivery. At midday, Lord North, the Prime Minister was handed the news: General Cornwallis had surrendered to George Washington at Yorktown on the 19th of October 1781. As suggested by the title of the tune played on that historic occasion, the world had turned upside down. For more than a year the Prime Minister had battled against the war's unpopularity in Parliament. The conflict had dragged on with little indication of success or resolution and this latest defeat would only heighten calls for a swift withdrawal. Caught between the King's determination to fight on and a parliament demanding an end to hostilities, Lord North soon recognised that his ministry was doomed to fall. His entire administration would be pulled down with him, including one of His Majesty's most stalwart supporters, Sir Richard Worsley.

In a string of seven terrible days, Worsley's entire personal philosophy, one that he had hewn from the solid precepts of honour, duty and place, had been overturned. A wife destroyed the sanctity of marriage, a trusted friend the inviolability of a fraternal bond, an officer the sacrosanct code of respect and deference, and a band of rebels had dishonoured their King and country. A world which had abandoned its natural structures of hierarchy and its sense of order was an inconceivable one to Sir Richard, and it is likely that he struggled with the horror of this concept as much as he did with the unforgivable actions and their consequences. Worsley would have recognised that this latest calamity held grave implications for him. The political influence he enjoyed as part of North's government would soon crumble. His aspirations, for the time being, would be thwarted.

The final days of a tragic November had given way to winter, but Sir Richard remained frozen with grief, unable to contend with even the most basic correspondence. Until late December all matters of importance had been deferred to the care of his steward, Richard Clarke and the long-suffering John Hesse who had granted him asylum. However, the arrival of a letter in the period before Christmas shook the baronet from his despondent state and forced him to gather his wits. Although Bisset had hired a team of attorneys to begin plotting his defence the couple had privately hoped that Sir Richard's heart might soften towards them. Roughly a month after the elopement their expectations had withered, prompting Lady Worsley to resort to a more extreme tack: blackmail.

Seymour put pen to paper and announced in plain terms to her husband that she had 'resolved to go to all lengths to circumvent his designs'. 'If he persisted in . . . prosecuting the Captain', she warned, he could expect a counter-suit to be launched against him 'for the deficiency of her pin money which he had not regularly paid, and which had occasioned her to apply to many others for relief'. Furthermore, if he was 'still to remain obstinate' she would see to it 'that he was exposed' and made 'the object of universal condemnation'. As the caretaker of his most volatile secrets, it lay in Lady Worsley's power to do precisely this.

Under the shadow of this threat Sir Richard agreed to negotiate. The baronet turned to Hesse and his colleague Richard Leversuch to assist with the bargaining. The proposition issued was simple: Lady Worsley was to end her affair with Bisset and 'return to her conjugal fidelity'. By the 29th of January 1782 the *Morning Herald* was optimistically reporting that 'a Rt. Hon. Baronet has offered overtures of reconciliation of a very affectionate nature to his lady' and that the possibility of this 'desirable and much wished for event' occurring was 'confidently whispered among the *beau monde*'. However, as Lady Worsley had stated in the message Lord Deerhurst had delivered to John Hesse, she refused absolutely to ever return to Sir Richard and the life of 'slights and inattentions' from which she had fled. This being the case and in order to preserve his dignity, Worsley had no choice but to persevere with his suit for criminal conversation and his plans for a separation. Like a gentleman facing his opponent's pistol in a duel, retreat at the point of danger would be seen as cowardice. Instead, Sir Richard would have to stand courageously as he would have on a field of honour and endure the assault aimed at him.

With a trial date set for the 21st of February 1782 and Parliament adjourned for its Christmas recess, the baronet quietly retreated to the solitude of Appuldurcombe. On account of his 'distressed state of mind' and 'most melancholy situation', Richard Clarke watched him closely. He had reason to worry. Within a matter of weeks stories had begun to circulate that once behind the gates of his estate, Worsley's gloom had hardened into rage. In his dangerously black mood, his return to the cold, empty rooms of his matrimonial home had proven too much. 'In an aggregate fit of jealousy' Sir Richard had opened the door to his wife's dressing room, crossed the floor to her vanity table arrayed with its delicate porcelain boxes and figurines and laid waste to it. Once he had 'broke all her china' he turned his savagery on her other keepsakes. He raided her collection of miniature portraits, the small oval faces of her friends and family, and tipped them into the flames of her hearth. Later, he found his own miniature of his wife and 'threw her picture into the fire'. Worrying reports of the conflagration at Appuldurcombe reached the ears of Lady Worsley by the end of January. It was rumoured that 'the whole of her former wardrobe had been literally burnt by the hands of Sir Richard'. This was a distortion of the truth, but not an enormous one.

In effect, the newspapers had combined several pieces of information they had received about Lady Worsley's continuing struggle to obtain her clothing and jewels. Since the day of her elopement, Sir Richard had held on to the things his wife required most for her comfort and peace of mind: her baby and her belongings. The baronet was venturing that his wife's anxiety for her child and lack of appropriate clothing would eventually wear her into a pliable state, rendering her desperate enough to make any concession.

In her time of crisis, Lady Worsley's considerable wardrobe along with her collection of jewellery was the most precious asset she owned. For a woman of Seymour's position, wealth was worn. A lady arrayed herself in the latest fabrics and flounces not merely for the sake of fashion but to demonstrate her social status. The nuances of dress, the breadth and variation of wardrobe, the quality of silk and lace were important indicators of rank. Shabby clothing merited suspicion, disdain or indifference, tawdry over-blown attire indicated a lack of breeding, as did dress inappropriate for specific occasions. Lady Worsley's single suit of clothing, her fashionable but functional brown riding habit, would be wholly inadequate for her needs. Even if she had wanted to flout the rules of convention and appear defiantly in public on her lover's arm, she was ill-equipped to do so. Her state of distress would be apparent from her increasingly worn skirt and jacket and the falling plumes of her once jaunty hat. Without her billowing sacque dresses, ribboned stomachers and twinkling buckles, she was incapable of making triumphant appearances. Sir Richard had not lost control of his wife entirely so long as he held fast to her petticoats.

However, the baronet had other reasons for withholding Lady Worsley's belongings. He did so not merely for reasons of manipulation but out of principle. Worsley understood the value of his wife's wardrobe in financial terms. Of her marriage portion, £3,000 had been converted into the linen and lace of her trousseau, with further acquisitions made in the years following her wedding. Seymour herself admitted that since 1775 she had 'expended various considerable sums in the purchase of other wearing apparel and ornaments'. An inventory of her clothing listed among her holdings more than twenty-four gowns in a variety of styles made from muslin, chintz, silk, satin, calico and tabby, in lilac, orange, black, white, green, bearing stripes, embroidery,

beads and ruffles. The crowning glories of her collection were two exceptionally expensive 'suits of point lace with a considerable quantity of other
valuable lace', probably purchased for wear at court. In addition to this she
possessed endless pairs of gloves in grey and yellow leathers, boxes of feathers
and paper flowers for decorating hats, an assortment of petticoats, tippets,
muffs, aprons, cloaks, twelve riding waistcoats, and nine riding hats. This
comprised only a fraction of the smaller pieces of attire which she could put
on in order to change an outfit's appearance. In just over six years of marriage,
the additions Lady Worsley had made to her wardrobe had increased its value
from £3,000 to between £4,000 and £5,000, according to her lawyers' estimate. When combined with the contents of her jewellery box, believed to
be worth £7,000 alone, the total value of her 'wearing apparel' might be
calculated at roughly £12,000, the equivalent of £15.2 million today.

In Sir Richard's eyes, this tremendous asset belonged to him. He had paid
the majority of his wife's millinery and dressmaking bills and therefore felt
entitled to retain these possessions. He also recognised the collection's practical value to the person who held it. Jewellery and expensive clothing could
be exchanged for ready cash. If he were to relinquish these items Lady Worsley
would have a source of funds at her disposal. She could wriggle free from
hardship or purchase ammunition to deploy against him. Money could buy
attorneys and bribes, it could silence those eager to spill secrets and encourage
timid critics to speak out. It could grease the cogs of the printing presses and
construct lawsuits. The baronet knew it would be foolish to part with this
armoury and guarded it jealously.

Lady Worsley felt far more anxiety over the welfare of her daughter. Since
the 19th of November, the child and her nursemaid had been left entirely
under the direction of Sir Richard, a man with no biological connection to
the girl in his care. Until Seymour's elopement, the baronet had acted
according to the codes of fashionable society, choosing to quietly spare his
dignity by accepting Jane into the Worsley nursery. By pretending ignorance
he had upheld his part of an agreement, but now he was likely to view past
promises as null and void. The little cuckoo in his nest, the progeny of a
spouse who had betrayed him and a former friend whom he despised would
remain a wailing and gurgling remembrance of their deception. However,
like Lady Worsley's apparel, her baby could be used in his strategic game.
The longer he could keep mother apart from daughter, the more inconsolable
and frantic his wife would grow.

By law, as an adulteress, Seymour had forfeited all access to her children, but in spite of this Worsley believed she would stage an attempt to see, if not to seize, her infant. In early December, shortly before she and Bisset left London, Lord Deerhurst alerted the couple that Sir Richard had moved Jane to Stratford Place. Driven by hope, Lady Worsley reacted quickly to this news and went immediately to the town house. Finding the door of her former home locked, she rapped incessantly at it. Eventually Godfrey appeared. 'I have come to the house in order to see my child,' she announced to him, but the butler shook his head and barred the door, claiming that 'he was obliged to refuse her admittance'. Seymour then began to plead with him but the servant remained impassive, stating tersely that he 'had received strict orders from Sir Richard . . . and from Mr Farrer, his lawyer, to forbid it absolutely'. The door was shut against her. She made no further attempts to see the child.

By the late eighteenth century, attitudes to the guardianship of illegitimate offspring had begun to change. A 'growing moral reluctance by wives to pass off illegitimate children as heirs to their husbands estates' may have encouraged Lady Worsley's belief that Sir Richard would be amenable to handing Jane into her care. Unfortunately, the baronet had made it clear that any infant who bore his surname was not legally hers and he did not scruple to use Jane as a bargaining chip in negotiations to secure Seymour's return. In her determination to turn her back on Sir Richard, Lady Worsley was forced to sacrifice her daughter, though she had not anticipated that the outcome of her decision would result in tragedy.

In the week that discussions between Sir Richard and Lady Worsley were abandoned and a battle in open court loomed, the lovers received word that their previously healthy infant was dead. Seymour and Bisset believed the worst, that their refusal to agree to the baronet's terms had prompted the murder of their child. But, grief stricken as they were, their position prior to the criminal conversation trial made their situation difficult. As Jane's true parentage had been masked since birth, unveiling this secret at such a critical juncture would have threatened Bisset's case. Should it become public knowledge that the child had been his daughter, and that he 'had bastardised the plaintiff's issue' the jury would almost certainly push for the maximum penalty. Worsley too would suffer. Not only would he be shamed by these revelations but, given the circumstances of Jane's death, he would be widely suspected of engineering it. For these reasons, there would be no investigation by a coroner or report made to the magistrate. Locked into a position of stalemate, Bisset refused to let the matter lie and instead initiated his own campaign of enquiry.

According to a letter written by Hesse to Richard Clarke, the 'Scoundrel Paramour' began paying visits to those he believed responsible. He first sought out Dr Fenton, the physician who had last tended Jane. 'He asked several impertinent questions for half an hour, suspecting our conduct' and the baronet's 'management', Hesse wrote. Deeply offended by Bisset's suggestions, the doctor responded that 'whoever he was, or whatever his designs might be, his questions and innuendoes were of such a nature as should silence his further speaking'. Dissatisfied with the answers he had received, Jane's father, 'soon after turned upon his heel and decamped, still suspecting the child perchance might not have had fair play'. Hesse reported that Godfrey had also been subject to an inquisition and that he anticipated similar treatment 'in his turn'. The frail civil servant, who claimed to know nothing about the matter, trembled with dismay at these accusations. 'My nerves are at this time dancing like the jacks of a harpsichord,' he complained. 'I leave you to judge the Effect on one of the most tender and cautious of all human nature.'

As his accusations were never turned into a formal complaint, what precisely Bisset was able to learn from his inquisition is uncertain. Whether Sir Richard's hand was behind Jane's unexpected demise will probably never be known. In a time of exceptionally high infant mortality, the child's death would be easy to dismiss as yet another sad but ordinary occurrence. In the wake of the event, Worsley attempted to separate himself as much as possible from the incident, devolving responsibility for the posthumous care of the body to the weary John Hesse. The baronet had plainly expressed a wish to both him and Richard Clarke that Jane should not be interred in the family vault at Godshill. 'You may assure him,' wrote Hesse, 'that I will act in every respect agreeable to his letter concerning the Burial of the Little Infant.' Where Worsley ordered the child to be laid to rest remains a mystery. In addition to being absent from the register at Godshill, her name fails to appear in any of the burial records for London's parish churches.

Prior to the trial, during a period of great antagonism between the two parties, the one concern upon which they could agree was to submerge Jane's death in complete secrecy. Such was the depth of its concealment that neither Worsley nor Bisset's attorneys knew of it. Two weeks after the event, on the day of the criminal conversation trial Sir Richard's legal representatives were still proclaiming in good faith that the baronet and his wife 'have two children, a son and a daughter . . .' Only a handful of individuals knew otherwise.

While this tragedy was playing in the background, James Farrer was handing over the fruits of his investigative efforts to a formidable team of litigators. The assembly of four barristers was to be headed by none other than James Wallace, the Attorney-General himself. Among those due to assist him was Thomas Erskine, the future Lord Chancellor and a lawyer whose name would one day become synonymous with the era's most high profile criminal conversation trials. Erskine had an electrifying courtroom manner which was known to captivate juries. In later years his performances became renowned for their tearful expostulations and swooning fits, although, as junior counsel for the plaintiff, his role in *Worsley v. Bisset* was a less active one. A more senior figure in the proceedings would be John 'Honest Jack' Lee, whose legal aptitude would earn him the position of Attorney-General after the departure of James Wallace. Finally, John Dunning, Baron Ashburton, a man who within a year would be made Solicitor-General, completed Worsley's indomitable collection of legal minds. There could hardly be a more accomplished team. The weaponry of Wallace's forensic skill combined with Dunning and Lee's oratorical capabilities promised to blast Worsley's compelling case to victory.

The baronet certainly required potent advocates to wage his battle by proxy; due to the emotive nature of crim. con. proceedings, the defendant, plaintiff and the plaintiff's wife were all prohibited from giving evidence. It was believed that their passions and biases would make them unreliable on the stand. However, though silent and nervous, Sir Richard and George Bisset would both be present. Lady Worsley would not be. She was not permitted so much as a word in her own defence. As the law regarded her as property, her voice was rendered superfluous to proceedings. No one asked a horse how it felt to be stolen or enquired of a statue why it was broken. In the following century, Caroline Norton, whose husband became embroiled in a criminal conversation suit with Lord Melbourne remarked with frustration that 'a woman is made a helpless wretch by these laws of men, or she would be allowed a defence, a counsel, in such an hour . . . To go for nothing in a trial which decides one's fate for life is very hard.' Undoubtedly, her comments reflected the feelings of many women who, stripped of a voice, were forced to become observers of their own lives.

By contemporary standards, much about the criminal conversation trial and the mode in which it was conducted would fall far short of fair legal practice. Certainly, the composition of the jury and its decision-making behaviour would be among its more questionable aspects. While ordinary juries tended to be comprised of a range of semi-respectable men from the literate middling ranks, crim. con. juries were considered special. The sensitive nature of the proceedings and the money at stake required an assortment of men who more readily understood the implications and value of property, wealth and status. This must be a jury composed not of shoemakers and schoolmasters, but of 'gentlemen of fortune': twelve men selected from the ranks of 'freeholders of substance, knights and urban gentry'. Over the years, many of these jurors gained considerable experience hearing similar cases and became known for the somewhat casual attitude they adopted when deliberating. Crim. con. juries rarely examined or debated the evidence for long. On some occasions they did not even deem it necessary to retire in private before formulating their judgments. Perched in their jury box, they might exchange looks or nods and a few mean sentences before delivering a verdict. Results were usually produced within a few minutes. It was highly unusual if deliberation lasted as long as a half hour. In less time than it would take for a gentleman to button his waistcoat, tie his cravat and wind his watch, a collection of his peers could divest him of all of these belongings, as well as his fortune and his honour.

Sir Richard anticipated with relish the day he could witness his jury do just this to George Bisset.

13

'Worse-than-sly'

Thursday the 21st of February 1782 was not a remarkable day for the majority of the population. The newspapers had little to report. The Duke of Cumberland would give 'a grand supper and ball' for the Prince of Wales that evening. 'A new comic opera', *Vertumnus and Pomona*, was scheduled to open at the Covent Garden theatre. Ordinary people ate their breakfasts, wrote letters, counted their pennies. Sir Richard Worsley and Maurice George Bisset rose from their beds as London's horses and criers stirred outside their windows. Joseph Connolly arranged his master's hair and helped him into his coat. Sir Richard's valet brushed his clothes and cleaned his shoes. Both would be eager to look their best, although neither would be giving evidence. When they passed beneath the arched entrance to the Court of the King's Bench, they would stride on to centre stage. Their previously private dispute was about to become a very public drama.

There was nothing discreet about the arena in which *Worsley* v. *Bisset* would be heard. In the late eighteenth century, the Court of the King's Bench did not even have four walls. It sat in the south-east corner of the cavernous Westminster Hall, divided by a partition from the traffic which passed in and out of the adjacent parliament chamber. Until recently, the stalls of booksellers, haberdashers and milliners had also occupied the space. Although the merchants' bazaar had been cleared away, Londoners continued to regard the Hall as a venue for colourful spectacles and the amusement provided by the Court of the King's Bench did not disappoint.

To the general public who had recently developed a taste for following salacious criminal conversation trials, the performances staged here were moral parables which relayed their tales by way of a titillating narrative. Like the era's best-selling novels and most popular plays its plots revolved on the theme of 'virtue in peril' or temptation and resistance. However, these stories were even more gripping than Samuel Richardson's sagas of masters in pursuit of their servants or middle-class girls tricked into brothels; this was real life. These were stories of human weakness, of revenge and passion which frequently featured known protagonists from the privileged classes. Where entertainment value was concerned, the crim. con. trials at the Court of the King's Bench could rival the productions of Drury Lane and Covent Garden. Better still, there was no admission charge. The courtroom was open to anyone with curiosity and on the 21st of February *Worsley v. Bisset* played to a packed house.

What drew the assortment of bodies into the makeshift room was not just the excitement of viewing a 'reality-drama' but also the promise of scandal. Georgians were fascinated with the behaviour and possessions of their neighbours and friends and greatly covetous of the lives of their social betters. In the race to emulate those with more money and refined taste they became addicted to gossip or any intelligence of how the other half lived. In the early 1780s London had nine daily newspapers and a further ten bi- or tri-weekly publications. The success of at least two of these, the *Morning Post* and its sister paper the *Morning Herald*, could be attributed to their reportage of scandal and the activities of the fashionable *ton*. Grub Street publishers also reaped a small fortune from printing longer pieces of gossip-journalism about the exploits of high society or noted actresses and courtesans. Anything that bore the name of one recently in the spotlight was certain to sell, whether satirical poems, exposés or the transcripts of criminal conversation trials. The public's thirst for such material was seemingly unquenchable.

As Lady Worsley's elopement had already cornered attention in the news-papers, the legal contest between her lover and her husband was hotly anticipated. Anxious to view the next instalment of their favourite running drama, Londoners poured into the courtroom. Mixed in with the throng was a scattering of hacks whose presence would ensure that by the next morning the public were fully apprised of the trial's outcome. With their pencils poised, they waited to record every squirm and nervous tic, every *double entendre* or burst of laughter. Joining their ranks was at least one professional law reporter who earned his wage by taking shorthand notes of the proceedings and peddling his transcripts to Grub Street publishers.

Where the popular press ventured, there also tended to stray many of the women whose escapades helped to sell their publications, namely the capital's upmarket prostitutes. While they undoubtedly harboured a natural interest in the stories of other fallen females, it was good publicity to make an appearance in so public an arena. As long as they made themselves visible there was no danger that the notorious reputations on which they traded would be overshadowed by someone else's scandal. Just as they had hoped, a journalist writing for the *Morning Herald* spotted them in the gallery. Surveying a room peopled by 'the strangest assembly that ever met within the pale of justice', from 'antiquated maidens to simpering misses', the writer noticed 'a large detachment of the cyprian corps headed by Betsy M-y with "Diamond Eyes" in the rear'. Also 'present on the occasion' was 'the recluse', Lady Ligonier, whose own love affair had been the cause of an earlier criminal conversation trial. More than any of the 'sisterhood' in attendance, he speculated, 'her ladyship' was there out of 'a most sympathetic concern'. She had positioned herself discreetly among the mass of spectators, which also included a contingent of well-wishers, family members and servants of both parties.

Sir Richard took his seat in an inconspicuous part of the court, probably behind one of the muslin curtains hung at either end of the room to shield the important players from impertinent stares. Apart from his friends and his legal counsel, no one was aware of his presence or of any disquiet he might have displayed. Although Worsley may have harboured some concern that details of his private arrangements might surface in the course of the trial he would also have felt supremely confident of his assured triumph. His wealth had always purchased him the best of everything, and today he had little doubt that it would buy him the justice to which he was entitled. From his seat the baronet could look out at James Farrer's reassuring presence or examine his extravagant menagerie of barristers, each one an expensive acquisition, draped in their billowing black robes, their heads crowned by rolls of false white curls. This case, expertly assembled and about to be executed by the finest legal minds, would sway the jury with little difficulty. Worsley would also study the jurors' box with calm assurance. The well-attired panel of gentleman who politely hung their hats on the pegs behind them were men of dignity and reason like him. This corner of Westminster Hall with its Gothic surrounds and stone figures of medieval monarchs was a temple to the maintenance of the established order.

At the opposite end of the courtroom, behind another curtain sat George Bisset who, like the baronet, was also able to review his troop of attorneys. Although Bisset was a wealthy man, when it came to choosing his legal team his purse had not been half as deep as Worsley's. As a trained barrister himself, Bisset may have been satisfied that three counsel were as good as Worsley's four, though his collection was not so celebrated as his opponent's. Edward Bearcroft, who was later made Chief Justice of Chester was well regarded at the King's Bench, as was Samuel Pechell, one of the Masters of the High Court of Chancery. They were assisted by Henry Howorth, considered 'one of the First Crown lawyers in practice'. As anyone present might have observed, the legal giants sitting on Sir Richard's side cast a long shadow across Bisset's modest protectors. This was unlikely to be a match fought by equals. Yet the defendant was determined to counter Sir Richard's claims. He had, some months earlier pleaded not guilty to the charge that he,

> ... on the 19th day of November, 1781, and on diverse other days and times, between that day and the 24th of the same month, at Westminster, in the county of Middlesex, with force of arms, made an assault on Seymour, the Wife of the Plaintiff, and then and there debauched, deflowered, lay with, and carnally knew her, the said Seymour, to the Plaintiff's damage of £20,000.

Although the phrasing of the accusation suggested that Lady Worsley played no role in her own undoing, the charge of adultery was an indisputable fact. Nevertheless, Bisset and his counsel came to court ready to do battle. Whether this was an unnerving attempt to bluff Worsley, a desire to demonstrate courage in the face of adversity, or a genuine threat to the plaintiff's case, was to be seen.

The stage had been set and the actors prepared, but the drama could only begin once the Right Honourable Judge, William Murray, the Earl of Mansfield entered the courtroom and assumed his seat. No one person in that arena commanded more esteem than Lord Chief Justice Mansfield, a man whose radical judgments had driven an enraged mob to set his London house alight during the upheaval of the Gordon Riots two years earlier. A reformer and proponent of the abolition of slavery, Mansfield tested the constraints of the arcane English legal code and contributed to the evolution of modern commercial law. The low hum of chatter emanating from the spectators' gallery and from the members of the bar below them was silenced by the bellowed announcement of His Lordship's arrival. The court rose to their feet as he appeared, a mid-sized figure arrayed in the plumage of his office. Hidden beneath a long wig which swung to his shoulders, and the sombre robes of the judiciary, was an incongruously gentle face, whose mouth, when at rest, settled into a natural smile. Mansfield mounted the bench, from which he could preside over the courtroom and monitor the expressions of each anxious witness.

Like a narrator unfurling the first page of a story, Attorney-General James Wallace took to the floor and began to lay down the facts of the plaintiff's case. He described the principal characters and their circumstances, making certain to note the pedigree and 'worth' of the individuals involved. There were no heart-wrenching embellishments to his presentation, simply the facts: that Lady Worsley, the daughter of Sir John Fleming was worth '£70,000 or upwards' to Sir Richard, that their marriage had taken place on the 15th of September 1775 and that they had 'two children, a son and a daughter, the first, born within a year or two after their marriage; and the latter, in August last'. Having established the essentials of his case Wallace's account took a turn of direction. In order to achieve a successful outcome for the plaintiff, it was crucial that the jury be familiarised with details of Worsley and Bisset's friendship; that this was no passing acquaintance but a firmly rooted bond. However, the story he chose to recount bore little resemblance to the truth.

Bearing in mind the history of their relationship – that they had met in the course of fixing an election, that they had lived together in Maidstone and that Bisset had fathered a child by the plaintiff's wife – both parties felt it in their best interests to adjust the information they divulged. Gentlemen were under no obligation to tell all and certainly were not in the habit of incriminating themselves. As the legal system was devised to represent their interests it was also generally willing to indulge their desire to keep secrets. Consequently, the tale Sir Richard had fed to his representatives omitted a number of details and fiddled important dates, many of which were later revealed in private during his separation hearings. However, on that day the Attorney-General was content to relate to the jury the story as he knew it, that, 'the Defendant was an Officer in the Hampshire militia, of which the Plaintiff is Colonel and that he had only been acquainted with him from the end of February, or the beginning of March, 1781'. He implied that the two had no previous dealings or meetings with one another until that time when 'their acquaintance commenced in consequence of a burgage tenure Mr Bisset was possessed of in the Isle of Wight . . . which Sir Richard for parliamentary convenience, wanted to purchase'. At about this time – the end of February or the beginning of March (and well after the general election had taken place) – the two men had entered into a correspondence on this subject and eventually agreed to meet; 'their first personal interview' with one another being facilitated 'by means of Mr Clarke, the receiver of Sir Richard's rents . . .' It followed that 'soon after their acquaintance, Sir Richard gave him the commission in his regiment'. This information primed the canvas on which Wallace then began to daub some colour. He instructed the jury that 'the greatest intimacy subsisted between them' and that 'the Plaintiff had a house at Maidstone, in Kent where the Defendant used to visit whilst in camp at Coxheath. When the camp broke up, they came to Lewes, where Sir Richard had a house, and Mr Bisset took lodgings; and the first attachment subsisted between them, till the unhappy event took place . . .'

With the opening statement completed and a copy of the marriage certificate presented as evidence, the plaintiff's counsel began to call their witnesses. The first of these was Richard Leversuch, now Captain Leversuch of the South Hampshire Militia. With a captaincy vacant after Bisset's resignation, Worsley had been quick to reward the militia's surgeon with a promotion for his selfless assistance. This act of generosity also ensured that Leversuch would give evidence from a script formulated by the baronet. He stepped into the witness box dressed in his brilliant red uniform, prepared to receive John Dunning's questions. Dunning's first tactic was to verify the intensity of the friendship that existed between Worsley and Bisset.

'Had you any opportunities of knowing, whether Captain Bisset had or had not a great friendship with Sir Richard Worsley and his family?' he asked.

'It always appeared so to me.'

'Do you remember their coming to Lewes and the breaking up of camp?'

'Yes, Lewes was the place of the Headquarters,' Leversuch replied.

'I take it for granted that he was a Man of Fashion and kept company?'

'Yes, sir,' answered the captain.

And then, hoping that Leversuch might reveal a bit more about the living arrangements that existed between the married pair and their friend, Dunning enquired, 'In the course of the summer was he [Bisset] ever at Sir Richard's house in Maidstone?'

'Yes, Sir,' he responded through tight lips. There was a pause, but Leversuch refused to say more on the subject.

'During the time Captain Bisset was in his winter quarters, I presume he had lodgings?' Separate lodgings is what the lawyer was implying. But again, Leversuch said nothing.

'Yes; he had lodgings in Lewes.'

'And Sir Richard Worsley had a house there?'

'Yes, Sir.'

Dunning soon abandoned this line of examination and inevitably turned to the events of the party on the night of the elopement, the details of which were certain to cause Leversuch some embarrassment.

'Did you observe them [Worsley and Bisset] frequently together; and do you recollect him and Lady Worsley being together at a party which met at your house?'

'I recollect that perfectly well.'

'Be so good as to tell us the date?'

'On Sunday the 18th of November, they drank tea, and supped at my house,' the surgeon stated.

'Upon whose invitation?'

'Mine and my family's.'

'It was a general invitation I suppose?'

'Yes; Married Ladies were invited, as well as their husbands.'

Dunning walked him through the events of the evening: Sir Richard 'begging to be excused' due to ill health, the appearance of Lady Worsley at seven in the evening and her peculiar insistence that she depart shortly after midnight. 'What became of Lady Worsley after that?' the lawyer asked, and Leversuch explained, perhaps still pained by the memories of letting the couple slip so easily away, that he had lighted them 'within a few yards of Sir Richard's door'.

'And you saw no more of them?' the lawyer confirmed.

'No,' Leversuch answered with regret, 'I saw no more of them'.

The surgeon then described that tense period before sunrise, when Worsley came 'violently rapping at the door' and demanded to know if his wife was inside. Leversuch recalled telling Sir Richard that 'had not seen her since one o'clock'.

Once Dunning believed he had drawn as much from Leversuch as the witness was likely to give he changed tack. The prosecution was determined to prove that Bisset had grossly abused Sir Richard's trust. He had hoped that the surgeon would have attested to this by laying evidence that the captain lived with the Worsleys at Maidstone, but his promptings had failed to produce the information. Instead he brought to the stand a Mr Sadler who was able to positively identify Bisset's handwriting on two letters. The first of these was intended to demonstrate 'the friendship and attachment which subsisted between the Plaintiff and the Defendant'. 'In this letter,' claimed Dunning, 'the defendant congratulated Sir Richard on Lady Worsley's safe delivery of her daughter, and concluded by saying he was much concerned for her health and happiness, and that he wished for nothing so much as her return to quarters.' Also presented was the letter which along with Bisset's commission papers Sir Richard had unfolded on the morning of the 19th of November. The enclosed note asked Worsley to accept his resignation and requested that he send his answer to Lord Deerhurst on Cleveland Row.

Francis Godfrey was next called to the stand and asked to respond to questions framed by Thomas Erskine. It was requested that the butler recount the details of the evening of the 18th of November. He recalled Lady Worsley instructing him that 'she would not sup at home that night' and remembered dutifully 'waiting up' for her 'till between four and five or six o'clock'. Godfrey also explained to the jury that in the early morning he had been sent across the road by Sir Richard to fetch his wife from the Leversuchs' party, but when he arrived there, the surgeon told him 'that Lady Worsley had left the house in company with Captain Bisset about one o'clock'. Erskine was keen to demonstrate that this news and the potential of a terrible betrayal greatly distressed the plaintiff. 'How did Sir Richard Worsley appear? Very much agitated?' he pressed.

'Yes, Sir,' replied Godfrey.

The prosecution, convinced they had established one of their principal points then moved on to the incontrovertible evidence that was certain to guarantee the plaintiff's win: the details of the act of adultery. This would be the meat and potatoes of the legal action, the featured performance which many in the gallery had come to hear. Whilst trials for crim. con. were uncomfortable experiences for both parties at the best of times, this part of the proceedings was the most gruesome for all involved. To have one's private torments and whispered confessions cried through an open court by loyal domestic staff, former friends or family was hideously mortifying. In the process of legal dissection, nothing was sacred. The jury required submission of every detail to confirm in their own minds that an act of adultery had taken place. In order to accurately assess the severity of the crime committed, the diligent spies who had spotted the soiled undergarments and who had pressed their ears against closed doors were required to present their findings in person. The presence of journalists at these proceedings ensured that, once disclosed, reportage of overheard grunts or the couple's undignified position upon discovery would enter into general knowledge.

The ribald element was heightened by the witnesses themselves. Frequently, the servants who had seen the illicit acts were young women, brought blushing and nervous to the stand where they were made to recount to a male audience the minutiae of the lurid entanglement. Louis Simond, a visitor to London in the early nineteenth century remarked that he found it especially 'indelicate and scandalous' when 'Young chamber maids' were 'brought into open court to tell, in the face of the public, all they have seen, heard or guessed at'. Simond condemned this practice as 'another sort of prostitution more indecent than the first'. Moral scruples aside, Wallace, Lee, Dunning and Erskine prepared to roll out their big guns: the staff of Tubb's lodging house and the Royal Hotel. The Grub Street hacks who jostled for space in the gallery must have licked their lips in anticipation.

John Lee called Joseph Tubb to give his testimony. The keeper of the lodging house presented his account of what transpired in the early hours of the 19th of November, when he had been awakened by 'Mr Bisset asking me to let him light a candle'.

'Had you any opportunity of knowing whether Mr Bisset was at that time alone, or whether he had company with him?' enquired John Lee.

'I don't know,' answered Tubb, '. . . when he lit his candle, he was in his bed gown, or morning gown; and . . . went to his own room again. Some little time afterwards he came out, and called Connolly and desired him to go downstairs . . . and a very little time afterwards . . . I think Connolly or somebody else, went out of the door. In about ten minutes, or a quarter of an hour after that, I heard a noise in Mr Bisset's room . . . I got out of bed and went to his room to see if he wanted anything. I rapped at the door and asked him if he wanted any assistance . . .'

At that cue, the gallery erupted into laughter. One of the journalists for the *Morning Herald* suggested that Tubb 'by his ignorance of what had been happening in Bisset's chamber . . . and in the simplicity of his heart' had 'unusually' lightened the mood of the Court of the King's Bench.

Lee, ignoring the disturbance, was eager to continue, but as Tubb persisted with his farcical story of doors opening and shutting and the sound of feet trampling down the stairs, Justice Mansfield began to lose patience.

'This is nothing but travelling a long way about; why don't you come to the point, and bring them to London at once?' he demanded of the prosecution.

Tubb was summarily dismissed and replaced with Thomas Fort, whose evidence promised to be far more-intriguing. The Attorney-General asked the Royal Hotel's waiter to introduce himself and then cut abruptly to the heart of the matter: 'Did you show them to any room in the Hotel?'

Fort described how he had tried to hand Bisset and Lady Worsley out of the post-chaise and said that the captain had, quite oddly, hesitated before throwing open the door and 'going very fast into the house'. He then 'showed them upstairs to a room called the Apollo, a large drawing room; and they immediately ordered breakfast'.

'What did they do after breakfast?' Wallace enquired.

Fort didn't know. 'I carried breakfast upstairs and then I left them.'

'Did they desire you to prepare any bedroom?'

'Yes, as near to the dining room as I possibly could; and I ordered a fire to be lit in No. 14,' the waiter recalled.

'What happened next?'

'I don't recollect anything more,' he answered with honesty.

But this was not enough for Wallace, who was finding Fort a rather impenetrable witness. 'When the bed was made, what did they do then?' he persisted.

'They went to bed,' the waiter responded.

Justice Mansfield was becoming irritable. 'How do you know they went to bed?' he thundered from atop his dais.

The young man, slightly cowed, addressed the bench. 'Because, my Lord, I went to take the things away and they were gone out of the dining room'.

This answer did not satisfy the judge. 'You did not *see* them go into the bedroom?'

'No, my Lord.' The prosecution was not making much progress. The Attorney-General altered his course.

'How long did they stay there?' he asked.

'Four or five days,' said the waiter.

'How did they pass?'

'As man and wife,' Fort stated plainly.

'Did you hear anything to import that?'

'I took them to be Man and Wife,' he explained, 'and I did not hear anything to the contrary.'

Wallace pressed him harder. 'Did you hear them mention one another in any shape, so as to take them to be Man and Wife?'

Unfortunately, Fort could not give him the answer he desired. 'No, I did not.'

'Had they only one bed?' an exasperated Mansfield interjected, grabbing the reins of the cross-examination from the Attorney-General's slack hands.

'Only one bed,' Fort confirmed.

In an attempt to dispatch a now lame and circumlocutory line of questioning, the judge at last demanded, 'How do you know of their lying together, if you never was in the room while they were in bed and what induces you to think they laid in one bed?'

'Because,' Fort answered matter-of-factly, 'there was no other bed in the room, my Lord.'

The gallery, who had been waiting breathlessly for the appearance of a lewd-mouthed and fresh-faced chambermaid, may have sighed with disappointment when the Royal Hotel's matronly housekeeper, Anna Watkinson took the stand. She was John Lee's witness. With no positive confirmation thus far that the couple had committed adultery in room 14, the prosecution was anxious to secure an indisputable admission of some form from the lips of Mrs Watkinson. Lee was determined to know what precisely the housekeeper saw the couple do in the Apollo dining room and between the sheets of the nearby bedchamber.

'Do you know whether they slept in the room, or where they slept?' he asked.

'I don't know whether they slept in the room; I imagine they did,' the housekeeper conjectured.

'What is your reason for imagining, or thinking they did? Perhaps you mean the distinction of sleeping and lying in the room?'

No, Watkinson confirmed, 'I did not see them sleep.'

'Did you receive any orders about it?'

'I received orders to make the room ready, and I got the room ready.'

'Had you an opportunity of seeing the bed afterwards?' Lee continued.

'Yes, Sir.'

'Had anybody been in it?'

'I saw that somebody had laid in the bed,' she commented, hoping that this was the answer the attorney had desired her to produce.

It was. With this statement, Lee had netted his confirmation. Fort had already affirmed that number 14 contained only one bed and that it had been hired jointly by the couple, but Lee wanted to elucidate this fact absolutely to the jury.

'You never saw them in bed, did you?' he asked.

'I *believed* them to be in bed,' Watkinson clarified.

'What was your reason for believing them to be in bed?' he prompted.

'Because I heard them speak in bed.'

Two individuals lying together under the canopy of the bed was enough to conclude that an act of sexual intercourse had occurred. Wishing to leave not an inch for error, Justice Mansfield required a verification of the identities of the post-coital couple. 'Do you know who they were?' he asked.

'Yes, My Lord,' stated Anna Watkinson. 'I did not know who they were when they came in; but I have heard who they were since.'

Mansfield then enquired if the housekeeper had ever heard 'the Lady in the room' called by any name in particular.

'Yes,' Mrs Watkinson stated. When asked, '. . . She said her name was Lady Worsley.'

As Wallace, Dunning, Lee and Erskine were alive to the dramatic possibilities to be teased from a trial, they reserved the testimony of the sassy young barmaid, Hannah Commander for their grand finale. For all of her insolence under Farrer's direction, when placed before the severe faces of the King's Bench, Hannah appeared demure and circumspect. Under the Attorney-General's questioning she presented clipped, concise and slightly nervous answers. Wallace required the barmaid to produce two specific pieces of information: a further confirmation of the couple's names and a statement that she had indeed viewed them sharing one bed.

'Do you recollect Lady Worsley's name being mentioned in the room?' he asked her.

'Yes, Sir.'

'When was that?'

'The 24th, the morning they went away,' said Hannah, recalling the excitement of the day.

'How came that?'

'I introduced two persons, two of Sir Richard's servants, a woman and a groom to Lady Worsley and Mr Bisset while they were in bed.' This was a daring admission.

'How did they take this behaviour from you?' Wallace prodded.

Hannah launched into her account. It was a tale that had almost certainly been committed to the library of legend stored below stairs at the Royal Hotel.

'Why, Sir,' Hannah began coyly, 'in the evening Mr Bisset sent for me into the dining room, and desired to know the reason of showing such persons up as Sir Richard Worsley's groom into Lady Worsley's bedroom; and said it was much against the house to use Ladies of Quality in that manner.'

Hannah had thrown out this arch turn of phrase to the hacks in the courtroom. It was intended to inspire sniggers of derision.

Desirous of bringing the prosecution's indisputable case to a close, Lee continued: 'Have you seen them in bed at any time?' he asked.

'Yes, Sir,' the maid confirmed proudly, 'at one o'clock in the afternoon.'

There was little more that required proving. From the perspective of the handsomely paid prosecution, this case had always promised an especially easy route to padding their purses. At last, Mr Lee rose to his feet and questioned his final witness, Mr Herne, Maurice George Bisset's rent collector. So that the jury was informed of Bisset's wealth and what portion of this might be siphoned from him to compensate Worsley, Herne was asked to confirm that the value of his estate could be approximated at £800 per annum. The conclusion of this minor task brought the prosecution's evidence to a close. The Attorney-General and his indomitable team relaxed into their seats. Worsley must have drawn breath. The worst of the ordeal was over. On what ground the opposition might construct their feeble case was anyone's guess.

Edward Bearcroft, Bisset's leading counsel, rose from his place on the wooden bench and turned to face Judge Mansfield. It seemed as if the defence had been routed and that it was prepared to concede defeat before Bearcroft had so much as put his first point. The attorney claimed that he, Samuel Pechell and Henry Howorth could not 'attempt to make any defence in controversion of the charge exhibited against the Defendant' and that they were 'very ready to admit that the Plaintiff was entitled to a verdict.* The only question which then remained was upon the subject of damages . . .' It was upon this basis and on 'the mitigation' of the award that he would 'defend his client'. Then, like a gambler with a winning hand pressed to his chest, Bearcroft addressed those assembled. He intended 'to prove to the satisfaction of the jury that Sir Richard not only acquiesced under repeated acts of his own dishonour with various persons, but even excited and encouraged it'. Puzzled glances must have passed around the court.

Justice Mansfield's attention had been piqued. 'If a Plaintiff encourages, or is privy to, or consenting at all, or contributing to the debauchery of his Wife, or joined in it, he ought not to recover a verdict,' he commented, citing the law.

Bearcroft, with enthusiasm, claimed that in the case of Sir Richard Worsley, 'he could prove this to be fact'. 'Why', he wondered, had the prosecution 'not called some persons belonging to, or about the family, in order to prove how the parties lived together, a circumstance very material in a case like this?' he questioned, referring to the suspicious omission of any detail about the Worsleys' house at Maidstone. In fact, 'they had only called one person belonging to the family; that was the Butler, who had lived in the house but one day, and who, of course, could not speak to that point'. Sir Richard Worsley was hiding something. Bearcroft was about to unveil it.

He began his story, claiming that 'The licentious conduct of Lady Worsley was so notorious that it had been the subject of common conversation; and that many Ladies of Distinction in the Isle of Wight and elsewhere, had frequently remonstrated with Sir Richard on the subject, and told him, that if he did not attempt to restrain her conduct, her character would be ruined and destroyed.' He continued: '. . . the answer Sir Richard made was, that Lady Worsley liked it, and he chose to do it to oblige her; upon which a very sensible Lady, who had frequently remonstrated [with] him on the subject, replied, *if this is the case, God help you! You are the most contented ——— HUSBAND I ever knew . . .*' Then Bearcroft with all the drama of a showman moved to lift the lid on his most devastating of revelations. This tale was not mere chatter invented to entertain ageing gossips. Lady Worsley, even before her association with Bisset, had enjoyed 'many prior connections'.

*The verdict in this case means a favourable verdict for the person concerned.

Prior connections to such an extent that 'the idea of seduction by the present Defendant was totally done away'.

In the months since November 1781, Seymour had been busy writing letters to those who, like Bisset, had once warmed her bed. She asked them for the sake of her current lover to come to her aid. Outside the Court of the King's Bench awaited three of these faded flames. Somewhere among the town houses of Mayfair and St James, the soft green hills of Hampshire and the Isle of Wight, and along the cobbled roads of continental Europe were rumoured to be twenty-four more.

14

'Lady Worsley's Seraglio'

The baronet was fortunate to be sitting behind the courtroom's muslin curtain, obscured from view when Bearcroft fired his resounding volley across the room. Of all the scribes in the gallery on that day, not one was able to record his expression. This strange counter-attack by the defence took everyone by surprise.

Maurice George Bisset had not been the first of Sir Richard's wife's lovers, merely one among many who had courted her and intrigued with her in a variety of places and circumstances. The defence, with Lady Worsley's assistance, had gathered together a collection of men, who had all conducted some form of relationship with Seymour over the past four years. Bearcroft would parade each of the cuckolders before the jury and the judge. They would sit under Worsley's nose, the stench of their filthy stories airing freely in the courtroom.

The first of these names, that of George William Coventry, Viscount Deerhurst, was cried through the hall of justice. Worsley would not have found the defence's decision to summon him surprising. As the Viscount was the scheming facilitator of his wife's elopement, Sir Richard would have come to revile him nearly as much as he did his former companion, Bisset. There was, however, nothing triumphant about Deerhurst's manner as he was guided to his place in the witness box. Though he could not see the assembled spectators, he must have sensed the weight of their gaze. By 'a particular request from the lady herself' the Viscount had been called to appear as the defence's key witness. In assuming this role he had agreed to disclose the details of his relationship with Worsley's wife in the most explicit terms. Filled with anxiety and shame, 'he appeared . . .', according to the *Morning Herald*, 'particularly distressed at his situation'.

'On what year was your Lordship first acquainted with Lady Worsley?' Howorth asked.

'In the year 1779.'

'Had you occasion to know Sir Richard also?'

'Yes, Sir.'

'Did she receive, during the time you knew him, any endeavour, or attempt, on his part, to check the dissoluteness of her conduct?'

'None.'

'Does your Lordship remember being on a visit to the Isle of Wight, at Sir Richard's House?'

'I do,' replied Deerhurst. Indeed, it would have been difficult for him to have forgotten it.

In the summer of 1779, Lord Deerhurst had found himself in a great deal of trouble. The seeds of his woes were sown many years before but only recently had come into bloom. From a young age, the Viscount, who would inherit his father, the 6th Earl of Coventry's fortune, had acquired a taste for cards, horses and reckless friends. Described as 'tall and elegant' and possessing 'an uncommonly pre-engaging countenance', the Viscount's charms made him a favourite with women. By 1776 at the age of nineteen, his handsome features and 'sprightly and vivacious' character had won the affection of Catherine Henley, the daughter of the Earl of Northington, with whom he stole away to Gretna Green for a clandestine wedding. His father was outraged at his son's behaviour and the embarrassment it brought. Banned from the ancestral home, Croome Court as well as the family's London house, the Viscount spent the next several years of his life begging his stepmother to help him secure a reconciliation with his father. His pleading correspondence rings with desperation and heartache. 'The disgrace at his denial of me,' he claimed, 'renders my life in reality a burthen . . .' '[I] would willingly enter a dungeon' if it would 'recover my father's favour,' he wrote. Deerhurst's anguish was increased by his financial difficulties and intensified further in March 1779, when his beloved wife died in childbirth.

His friend Worsley's invitation to visit Appuldurcombe had come at an opportune juncture. Since Lady Deerhurst's death, the Viscount had shut himself away at Stoke Park with his sister, Lady Anne Foley and her husband. In early September, as debt snapped at his heels and depression ate into his spirit, he wrote to his stepmother that he had not yet 'determined upon any plan for the winter as my sole object is the recovery of my father's favour', but as 'Mr Foley and Lady Anne are soon going to Croome' where he was not welcome, he would instead 'take this opportunity of paying a visit to Sir Richard Worsley in the Isle of Wight'.

It is unknown how long Deerhurst had been acquainted with the Worsleys at the time he accepted the baronet's invitation. *The Genuine Anecdotes and Amorous Adventures of Sir Richard Easy*, which refers to Deerhurst as 'the Lothario of the age' and as a man who 'had already established his reputation for gallantry and intrigue', implied that they had forged a friendship at one of the fashionable sea bathing towns: Brighton or Weymouth. However, it was not until his stay at Appuldurcombe that an attraction developed between the Viscount and Lady Worsley. Deerhurst claimed that his host was not only aware of his wife's allure but had encouraged his guest to make sexual overtures to her. According to the account published in *The Memoirs of Sir Finical Whimsy*, the Viscount and Sir Richard had been examining his works of art when Lady Worsley passed by the window. As their eyes followed her across the landscape, her appearance sparked admiring comments from both her husband and his guest.

'Has your Lordship any recollection of any particular expressions Sir Richard Worsley made use of, respecting his Wife, in addressing himself to you?' Mr Howorth said, continuing with his cross-examination.

'I hope I am not called to betray any private conversation?' the Viscount answered, making a pretence of maintaining decorum. Justice Mansfield confirmed that this would not be the case and Deerhurst resumed his story. 'He did then say, that many young men had tried her to no effect; and that I had his permission to try my chance with her.' But the Viscount, surprised by his host's unusual suggestion, 'took it in a laugh'.

For all that was said openly in Deerhurst's testimony, much more was being implied between the lines. Worsley's pert remark, which the Viscount claimed to dismiss as a joke, was a challenge he would accept. With an invitation to pursue his friend's wife, Deerhurst's affair with Seymour soon took fire directly beneath the gaze of a permissive husband.

Mr Howorth turned to the Viscount in the witness box and pointedly questioned him: 'Do you remember whether Sir Richard Worsley had an opportunity at any time of observing the intimacy and attention Your Lordship paid to Lady Worsley?' Deerhurst hesitated. Howorth led him further. 'And Your Lordship will mention the particular time . . .'

'He found me in her dressing room, adjacent to her bedchamber, at four o'clock in the morning,' the Viscount stated boldly. The jury knew what this implied. There was only one reason why a man would be in a woman's private rooms at that time of night.

'How was Lady Worsley dressed at the time?'

'I don't particularly recollect.' To Deerhurst, this seemed a strange question.

'In a dress,' Howorth groped for detail, 'or undress?'

'I don't remember; I made no observation upon it,' the Viscount claimed. His true concern at that moment had not been the state in which he had left Lady Worsley, but rather that as he had slipped from her separate bedchamber he encountered her husband barring his route of escape. The men were equally embarrassed at their unexpected meeting. Deerhurst had been so flustered that he could only recall Sir Richard's 'astonishment at finding me there at that hour'.

'Do you recollect his expression?' asked the defence counsel.

'He said – Deerhurst! How came you here? And after that I went to my bedroom.' Worsley's guest suggested that he offered no explanation for his conduct beyond that, although the anonymous author of *Sir Finical Whimsy* claims that the Viscount at least made an attempt to excuse the incident 'as an unhappy custom I have of walking in my sleep'. However, Deerhurst's evidence, as it stands, introduces the possibility that Worsley, who was out of bed and lingering in his wife's dressing room in the depths of night had also been caught in a position of compromise, one that he was eager for his guest to forget. In spite of the fact that Lord Deerhurst had clearly emerged from his wife's bedchamber, Sir Richard chose to say nothing more on the subject. It is more than likely that Deerhurst knew precisely why the baronet had been loitering outside his wife's bedroom at 4 a.m.; the keyhole would have provided a luscious eyeful of the illicit activities. In most circumstances the Viscount's behaviour would have been considered a gross breach of conduct but Worsley's guest was neither reprimanded nor requested to leave. Instead, he was encouraged to remain at Appuldurcombe and treated by his host as if the incident had never happened.

Howorth continued with his questioning. 'How long did your Lordship continue there, after that?'

'To the best of my recollection, three or four days afterwards.'

'Do you recollect whether, after that, you were permitted to attend Lady Worsley out upon parties?'

'I was,' he responded.

'To what parts of the country?' Howorth was inching his witness towards another potentially damning admission.

'I don't particularly remember.'

'Do you remember going to Southampton?'

This, Deerhurst did recall. For nearly two weeks, the Viscount had eaten from the Worsleys' table and slept between their sheets. He had admired Sir Richard's collection of art, leafed through the books in his library, and galloped around the perimeters of Appuldurcombe. He had observed Sir Richard and his young wife breezing by one another, their interactions, their exchanged scowls, simpers and words, and learned a great deal about the nature of their marriage. By the time his valet had begun to pack his belongings, Deerhurst had sampled enough of Appuldurcombe to detect an unpleasant tinge in its owner's character. Whatever he had experienced, whether it was the open proffering of Lady Worsley by her husband, or an iciness about Sir Richard, it was enough to turn him with great conviction against the baronet. It was also enough to make him sympathise with his wife. From the date of his visit to the Isle of Wight, the Viscount would unfailingly rally to her side.

To Lady Worsley, Deerhurst represented a means of escape: from unhappiness, from the Isle of Wight, and potentially from her marriage. In the ten days that they had passed together, an affection had taken root between them. Unhappy at the prospect of parting, Seymour began plotting a way to follow her paramour off the island. At the time, the Viscount was planning to return to London via Southampton. *Finical Whimsy* maintains that shortly after he revealed his intended route, Lady Worsley invented a reason 'to set off for town to consult her physician'.

On the day of their guest's departure, Worsley, his wife and Deerhurst set out for Cowes. Sir Richard had no objections to the Viscount escorting Lady Worsley to Southampton. He saw no need to accompany them across the Solent. Riding eight miles with them from Appuldurcombe, he then bid them farewell and turned his horse for home, leaving Seymour and Deerhurst to embark alone. The couple could not have foreseen such a stroke of good fortune.

Mr Howorth appeared quite incredulous at Lord Deerhurst's account, that Worsley would so readily entrust his wife to the care of a man whom he, only nights before, spotted sneaking out of her rooms.

'Was Lady Worsley travelling by herself, unattended, or was Sir Richard with her, or any other person?' he demanded emphatically.

'She was quite alone,' responded the Viscount.

'Did you know of her intention of going?' asked Howorth. Deerhurst's answer hinted at the possibility that this excursion had involved more forethought than chance. 'Yes,' he replied that he was aware that Lady Worsley had been planning a journey to Southampton. From there they had travelled towards London together, stopping for the night 'at Kingston [Hampshire] and afterward at Godalming'.

'Did she sleep there?'

'Yes,' Deerhurst stated frankly.

'Had your Lordship any particular intimacy with her that night?'

The Viscount sensed that he had let propriety slip slightly too far. 'Be so kind as to put that question again,' he responded tartly.

'Was you particularly *connected* with her that night?'

Though a notorious rake, Deerhurst still upheld the gentleman's honour code which barred even the nose of the law from parting his bed curtains. He appealed to Lord Mansfield. 'With your Lordship's permission,' he begged, 'I decline that.'

'Certainly,' the judge defended him. 'You have no right to be asked that.' In one simple gesture, George William Coventry, Viscount Deerhurst and the future Earl of Coventry, asserted his position above that of those who challenged him. In theory, as an aristocrat, he towered above the law. He could choose to abide by it or discard it, to recognise its disciples or to ridicule them. He, like all the men instrumental to this trial, could provide or deny information at his own discretion. These men answered as they saw fit, and the courts bowed in acknowledgement to this. Unwilling to concede anything further, Deerhurst fell silent and Howorth could do little more than dutifully resume his seat.

There was much about his relationship with Lady Worsley that Deerhurst refused to present as public knowledge. From a legal perspective it was essential that he avoid making an incontrovertible admission that he had enjoyed sexual relations with Sir Richard's wife. His evidence had to be folded into an agreed storyline and his answers skilfully threaded through loopholes in order to prevent Worsley from bringing a charge of crim. con. against him as well. The Viscount also found it difficult to participate in a pillorying of Seymour's character, a woman for whom he held an enduring fondness. In September 1779, Deerhurst had washed up on the Isle of Wight in a low state. Rootless, abandoned by his father and still mourning for his wife it is likely that he found support and understanding in Lady Worsley, herself succumbing to a growing discontent. As their relationship had a genuine emotional foundation, eventually sexual desire cooled into a meaningful friendship. Of all her lovers, the Viscount remained, over the years, the most constant in his concern for her. By assisting her elopement and acting as her protector, Deerhurst laid bare his already fragile character to wounding criticism. His confessions at the trial led to a general belief that the Viscount 'had repaid the hospitality of a host by betraying his honour'. This, coupled with his public championing of Lady Worsley and her shameful conduct, resulted in further estrangement from his family. In the wake of the scandal, his aunt, the Duchess of Argyll expressed her disapproval of his behaviour by refusing to speak with him again. For someone who could have opted to remain anonymous during Lady Worsley's ordeal, Deerhurst chose instead to sacrifice himself for a woman he held dear.

Another explanation, however, may exist for his grand gesture of selflessness. When Deerhurst departed for Southampton in the company of Sir Richard's wife, her intentions may have been more serious than the Viscount suspected. A brief visit to the port town across the Solent soon became a progress to London which lasted for three days and at least two nights, taking the pair as far north as Godalming before separating. When Lady Worsley set out, it is possible that she did not intend to return to her husband. However, having already suffered the repercussions of one elopement, the Viscount was not likely to make such a regrettable error again. Though sympathetic to Seymour's situation, Deerhurst had no choice but to leave her; perhaps with a promise that he would aid her in future. Interestingly, in December 1781 as Deerhurst was assisting Seymour and Bisset, he was also orchestrating his sister, Lady Maria Bayntun's affair with Jack Cooper, so that she and her husband might 'obtain a divorce with as little trouble and expense as possible'. Frequent exposure to the unhappily married and a healthy store of guilt had turned a libertine into the defender of malcontent wives.

Although Lord Deerhurst's attractions had been enough to entice Lady Worsley to abandon her husband, it was not the first time that she had been tempted by another man. Her entry into the arena of adultery had occurred over a year earlier, at some point during the late winter and early spring of 1778. Whilst the Viscount had been introduced to Lady Worsley by her husband, Sir Richard played no part in the relationship that blossomed between his wife and the Honourable Charles Wyndham. When they met, the eighteen-year-old brother of the 3rd Earl of Egremont was wavering on the threshold of a fully-fledged career in profligacy. Though the circumstances of their acquaintance are unknown, Wyndham was to be Lady Worsley's first truly passionate love, the man who remained 'foremost in her affection' and who drew her off the path of virtue. Her influence in all likelihood had a similar effect on him.

Wyndham receives little mention in the era's gossip columns until the early 1780s, by which time he had fallen in with a pack of rowdy dissolutes led by the Prince of Wales. By mid-decade, Wyndham's name had been paired with that of the courtesan, Grace Dalrymple Elliott, and proposed as the father of her child. He had also been linked to the Duchess of Devonshire's married sister, Harriet, Lady Duncannon. In addition to earning a reputation for drunkenness and gambling at high stakes, Wyndham was noted for causing a fracas at the town house of the Marquess of Buckingham, where 'all sorts of outrages . . . were committed'. Where Charles Wyndham ventured, trouble followed, or at least impropriety. Walpole complained that the young man and his friends had offended Mrs Keppel, the hostess of a ball by not arriving 'until 10 at night'. 'The violins were ready,' he grumbled, 'but could not play to no dancers.' Throughout the 1780s, little could curtail his dissipation, and by 1791, after impregnating Mrs Anna Sophia Hodges Wyndham found himself the defendant in his own criminal conversation suit.

If the author of *The Genuine Anecdotes . . . of Sir Richard Easy* is to be believed, Lady Worsley and Charles Wyndham's 'first and last interview . . . was in and near Kensington Gardens', the haunt of the fashionable set, who promenaded along the tree-fringed Broad Walk. At that time, the area surrounding the Gardens was known for its discreet establishments where trysting pairs might meet. 'There is a very commodious house not far distant from the palace,' the pamphlet explained, 'where any loving couple may, without ceremony, sacrifice at the altar of the Cytherean goddess.' It was here that Wyndham and Seymour 'often repaired for frequent appointments'. Such locations were not uncommon throughout London. Many upmarket brothels and bagnios (or bathhouses) maintained a sideline in letting out rooms to a wealthy and adulterous clientele, who found it more practical to conduct their assignations outside their matrimonial home or away from the notice of their servants.

Of those who have written about Lady Worsley's liaison with Charles Wyndham, from Horace Walpole to the hacks of Grub Street, all agree that it was an especially heated relationship. Their 'agreeable intercourse', as it was described, 'continued for several months', into the autumn of that year. Emotionally thrilling and dangerous, this illicit romance left an enormous impression on Sir Richard's young wife. Her devotion, described as 'a violent attachment' and 'an extravagant fondness', caused devastation when her lover's military duties required him to go abroad.

In 1777, after the outbreak of hostilities in the American colonies, an ensign's commission had been purchased for Charles Wyndham in the Coldstream Regiment of the Foot Guard. Having entered the Guard in December of that year, with some good fortune he had managed to avoid being deployed for at least another twelve months. 'Ordered for America' in the spring of 1778, Wyndham was back in London by early 1781, drinking with the Prince of Wales at Lord Chesterfield's house and being mauled by a dog after trying to pull out its tongue. Later that year, his antics were still raising eyebrows when he received a letter from his former mistress, requesting that he come to the rescue of her current lover.

Whilst Sir Richard would not have found Deerhurst's appearance as a witness unexpected, it is likely that he regarded Wyndham's presence, and the attendance of a number of other gentlemen, truly distressing. The raffish young man with whom Worsley had only a passing familiarity stepped into the witness box. Henry Howorth was waiting, ready to coax the damning disclosures from Wyndham's mouth. There was one incident the lawyer was insistent that his witness relay to the jury.

'Pray Sir,' he began, 'do you remember, about the time of your going abroad, that anything particular passed between you and Lady Worsley, respecting any particular favour you received in Kensington Gardens?'

'No,' answered Wyndham.

'Do you remember anything respecting a ring?'

'Yes, Sir.'

'What was that?' The lawyer dug more deeply but, like Deerhurst, Wyndham was growing uncomfortable under the spotlight.

'My acquaintance ceased before I went abroad,' he answered.

'What ring was it?' Howorth insisted.

'A gold ring.'

'Was that her wedding ring?'

Wyndham now became quite anxious. 'How can I answer that?' he pleaded nervously to the lawyer. Howorth assisted him:

'She took it off her finger, and made it a present to you?'

'Yes, Sir,' Wyndham was forced to respond.

As they strolled through Kensington Gardens, passing friends and acquaintances on their constitutionals, Charles Wyndham announced to Seymour that he would be embarking for America. The news 'had proved almost fatal' to her. In speculating on their final encounter, one hack claimed that

> In their last interview, to testify to her fondness, her friendship and esteem, she presented . . . [it] . . . to him, as a token of remembrance of those happy hours of amorous dalliance which they had so often experienced . . . she took it off her own finger and put it upon his, to signify that it might be there riveted, as she wished her image might be to his heart. 'Farewell', said her Ladyship, with an involuntary sigh that bespoke the anguish of her mind, 'Farewell' (she repeated) my dear beloved Wyndham; and whenever you look on that ring, remember me, and consider it as a certain pledge of my unbounded love . . .

By all accounts, the conclusion of her love affair with Wyndham was difficult for Seymour to bear and resulted in 'many dreary hours' and 'melancholy reflections'. The couple were not to resume their relationship. At Wyndham's return several years later, much had altered in both of their lives.

In 1778 the ripples created by the conflict in the colonies were felt by a variety of individuals in the most unexpected corners. When the orders came to embody the local militias Edward Rushworth stepped forward to defend the Isle of Wight and the County of Hampshire from the marauding French. Although he was the son of naval captain, Rushworth had not imagined a military career for himself. He was described as a man 'of very small fortune' but one whose 'education and abilities, added to the connections he had formed in life' destined him for a prosperous future. Ambitious and bright, he had only recently completed his training as a solicitor before purchasing a lieutenancy in the South Hampshire Militia that July.

Lieutenant Rushworth arrived at Coxheath camp during the height of the summer excitement. To the regiment's latest recruit, the encampment, with its light-hearted entertainment, its dinners, card parties and balls would have seemed more like a pleasure garden than a military training ground. It was in this carnivalesque atmosphere that Rushworth was introduced to his commanding officer's wife. Unlike her previous lover, Wyndham, the Lieutenant was not a rake, but neither was he immune to temptation. According to the author of *Sir Finical Whimsy*, the duration of their affair was 'of a very temporary date' and did not exceed the period of their encampment in Kent. By the time the South Hampshire Militia had moved to quarters on the Isle of Wight in 1779, Rushworth was preoccupied with other matters. He had fallen in love with the daughter of the infamous election-fixer, Reverend Leonard Troughear Holmes, and was determined to bury his past and establish his name. Within a year he had abandoned his aspirations to practise law and went to study divinity at Oxford. Shortly thereafter he eloped to the continent with Catherine Troughear Holmes (whom he later married again in front of her father on the Isle of Wight) before being elected as an MP for Yarmouth with Holmes's assistance. From the start, Edward Rushworth's successful career had been a tale of perseverance and skilfully managed opportunities. At his death in 1818, the *Gentleman's Magazine* referred to him as 'a truly respectable gentleman . . . of pure and virtuous principles, steadily and zealously attached to the Establishment in church and state and eminently distinguished for a sense of duty in every relation of his life'. It is little wonder that when Lady Worsley requested Rushworth's presence at the Court of the King's Bench, he declined. Unlike Wyndham or Deerhurst, this former flame had neither the family name nor the finances to soften any repercussions of his revelations.

Lieutenant Rushworth had not been Lady Worsley's only acquisition during the warm months of 1778. Among the thousands encamped at Coxheath was George James Cholmondeley, the 4th Earl of Cholmondeley, (later the 1st Marquess Cholmondeley and Earl Rocksavage), who commanded the Royal Cheshire Militia. At Coxheath, Cholmondeley could not have been more in his element. Surrounded by the flirtatious and bored aristocratic wives of his fellow officers, the Earl was like a bee in a garden at full flower. At a period when Wyndham and Deerhurst were still earning their rakes' spurs, Cholmondeley reigned supreme among the roués of his generation. The Earl was already so renowned for his philandering that he had been lampooned the year before in a pamphlet entitled *The Torpedo, a Poem to the Electric Eel*. While the *Torpedo* poked fun at his conquests it also sang the praises of that which was believed to have won Cholmondeley such acclaim among women;

> What tho' Lord Ch——lm——d——ly may conceal
> A most enormous length of Eel,
> Admir'd for its size and bone;
> This mighty thing when lank, depress'd
> A mere noun adjective at best,
> Is useless when alone.

In addition to his rumoured assets, the Earl was tall and athletic and known for his 'great physical strength'. His good looks and daring behaviour inspired feverish gossip. For roughly two years, the London newspapers had been speculating about relations between the Earl and his acknowledged inamorata, the *demi-mondaine* of the moment, Grace Dalrymple Elliott. As their public appearances grew more frequent, whispers of a possible (and deeply unsuitable) marriage increased in volume. However, his connection with Mrs Elliott was by no means an exclusive one. The Earl had never been known for restricting his passions and pursued numerous liaisons, often simultaneously. At any given time, according to one chronicler, he was 'associated with a variety of women without discrimination' and made a habit of engaging in 'intrigue without attachment'. In a perpetual state of motion between the continent, London and his northern estates, Cholmondeley alighted at every racecourse, spa, and centre of diversion between Cheshire and Berlin, making frequent detours to chase a potential amour or placate a sulky mistress. The Earl had a gift for scenting acquiescent women, however coyly drawn to him, whether these were actresses, courtesans or the wives of other men. He could not have failed to notice Seymour, and with his dangerous reputation, she would have found him equally alluring.

Curiously, Lord Cholmondeley's success at intrigue was attributed less to wit or charm than to 'his generosity, attachment and inviolable secrecy where love and honour are concerned', a reputation which made him a particular favourite 'among fashionable ladies' who were eager for illicit romance without arousing their spouses' suspicions. In keeping with the Earl's code of confidentiality the duration and details of his affair with Lady Worsley appear to have been quite closely guarded, though many within a select circle knew of their attachment and that Seymour had become spellbound by him. His uncle, Horace Walpole wrote that Cholmondeley 'has been most talked of for her', while the author of *Finical Whimsy* claimed that he 'cut no inconsiderable figure in the history of her amours'. It was reported that after their separation Seymour found 'his absence insupportable; a confirmed melancholy took possession of her mind,' to the extent that Worsley would 'send for Cholmondeley to *divert her*'. 'Diversions' which, the wag continues, 'became so frequent as to raise the envy and spleen of all the frail sisterhood at the happiness of the poor dejected lady'.

Unfortunately the man whom Walpole thought 'to have the largest pretensions to her remembrance' was abroad in early 1782, chasing the celebrated courtesan, Elizabeth Armistead around the streets and parks of Paris. He had no interest in abandoning the pursuit in order to reveal his assorted misdemeanours.

It is likely that by the autumn of 1779, when Seymour met Deerhurst, her interlude with Cholmondeley had wound down. Her introduction to the Viscount began a spirited new chapter in her adventures. From the end of that year and well into 1780, matters of government held Sir Richard's attention to the exclusion of his private affairs. He was absent for days or weeks at a time, carousing with parliamentarians late into the night. It was at this period that Lady Worsley was drawn into Lord Deerhurst's circle of reprobates. While the baronet scratched out letters on behalf of the government and drank bumpers to the King's armies in America, Seymour lost painful sums at cards and hung on the arms of London's most dissolute gentlemen.

Bisset's attorneys were keen to underline Sir Richard's negligence. His indifference to his wife's reputation implicated him as much as Seymour in the resulting débâcle. As a strategy for Bisset's defence was being assembled, it was probably Deerhurst who suggested that Charles Henry Mordaunt, the 5th Earl of Peterborough and his right-hand man, Joseph Bouchier Smith be brought in as 'anti-character witnesses' who could testify to Lady Worsley's wayward behaviour and to her husband's apathy.

Like his friend Deerhurst, Lord Peterborough had a reputation smudged with scandal. His name had been linked with several actress-courtesans, including the much coveted Sophia Baddeley and the ubiquitously popular

Mrs Elliott. He became involved in the affairs of the Duchess of Kingston, an infamous bigamist, and later in an adulterous relationship with Deerhurst's other sister, Lady Anne Foley. In spite of Peterborough's notoriety for boudoir frolics there is nothing to substantiate rumours that he was among Lady Worsley's lovers. However, the hacks and gossips who scavenged for names to add to her list of paramours were quick to interpret his appearance at Bisset's trial as an admission of guilt. In truth, when the Earl entered the Court of the King's Bench, the crimes to which he was about to attest were not his own.

'Pray my Lord,' Samuel Pechell began, 'what time did your acquaintance with Lady Worsley begin?'

The Earl plumbed his memory for recollections of the season. 'I don't exactly remember. It was at the time Ranelagh opened, in the year 1780, some time in the spring.'

'What was the occasion of your Lordship's first acquaintance with her,' the lawyer enquired.

'I was first introduced to her at Sadler's Wells.'

'By who?'

'By my Lord Deerhurst,' Peterborough replied.

'At that time, had you any acquaintance with Sir Richard?'

'None, either then or after.'

'Then, during the time of your acquaintance with Lady Worsley, you never spoke to him?'

'No,' said the Earl, frankly.

Pechell now desired more colourful details 'What was your Lordship's opinion of her general behaviour? Did it bear the appearance of an affectionate, constant wife to Sir Richard?'

'I made no observations,' Peterborough answered with honesty, '. . . I never saw them together.'

Bisset's counsel allowed the damning evidence of Worsley's detachedness to linger before presenting his next, uncomfortably direct question. 'Do you think,' he asked, 'that she conducted herself as a decent, modest wife?'

'I should rather think not,' he concluded with an almost audible snort.

The Earl was not required to disclose anything further. He quit the witness box having confessed to and been implicated in nothing.

For good measure, Joseph Bouchier Smith was called upon to perform the same service. Like Lady Worsley, Bouchier Smith counted himself among

Lord Deerhurst's broad network of associates, though his connection to the Viscount was more enduring: he was married to Deerhurst's illegitimate half-sister, Emelie. It is unknown how the son of an Oxford don and minor landowner fell in with the likes of Lords Deerhurst and Peterborough, but by 1780 Bouchier Smith had become a permanent fixture in his brother-in-law's life and had managed to make himself indispensable to Peterborough as well, so much so that in five years' time he found himself back at the Court of the King's Bench giving evidence in the Earl's trial for crim. con. with Lady Anne Foley. Bouchier Smith seems to have been the perennial observer, a hanger-on who watched his wealthier friends dispose of their fortunes and reputations while narrowly managing to maintain his own. At court on that day there was no suggestion to contradict this. Joseph Bouchier Smith was regarded by both the prosecution and defence as a man with no amorous connection to Lady Worsley, although guilt by association inscribed his name beside those of her confirmed beaux.

He took his place in the witness box, directly on the heels of the Earl of Peterborough. Edward Bearcroft requested that he recount his observation of events. He was asked to confirm that 1779 was the year when he first met Seymour Worsley. Bearcroft then continued:

'During the time of your acquaintance with her, what was your general opinion of her character and behaviour?'

'I thought she did not conduct herself as a woman regarding her own fame,' Bouchier Smith replied.

'Was that her general character?'

'That is the character I have heard of her.'

'At that time?' the attorney clarified.

'Yes, Sir.'

'Do you remember, at any time, meeting Sir Richard, when you and his Lady were together?'

Bearcroft wanted his witness to recall a day excursion to Blackheath that autumn. Shooters Hill, which rises 432 feet above London, provided a breathtaking view for those in search of the picturesque. The 'vast prospect' afforded a panorama of 'several little towns all by the river, Erith, Leigh, Woolwich etc., quite up to London, Greenwich, Deptford, Black Wall'. By the second half of the eighteenth century, when outlooks and spots of natural beauty were becoming tourist attractions, an entrepreneur had opened 'a hotel on the summit to entertain wealthy travellers' and provide them with refreshment.

A party set out with this destination in mind. It was by no means a private assignation, as Bouchier Smith was anxious to imply. He and Lady Worsley were accompanied by a number of their friends, including Henry Harvey Aston (a noted libertine and cohort of Charles Wyndham) and Caroline Vernon, a lady-in-waiting to Queen Charlotte who had a rather unfortunate habit of featuring in crim. con. trials, having been implicated in her sister, Lady Grosvenor's affair with the Duke of Cumberland.

'. . . Do you remember any particular circumstance, on the occasion of the Shooters Hill party?' the lawyer pressed Bouchier Smith.

'We met Sir Richard, in a phaeton; and Lady Worsley desired him several times to go with her; but he refused and drove off towards town.'

'Did he inquire where they were going?' Bearcroft asked with a hint of disbelief.

'Yes,' responded Bouchier Smith.

'And she asked him to go?'

'Yes.' But Sir Richard, too preoccupied with other matters, had no enthusiasm for an outing.

Although Bouchier Smith later claimed that Seymour's behaviour was irreproachable on that day, his testimony succeeded in exposing her husband's lax approach to chaperoning and offered the jury food for thought.

The defence would soon demonstrate that Sir Richard's indifference to Lady Worsley and the company she kept opened the door for his wife to intrigue with whomever she chose. The next paramour to walk through it in the summer of 1780 was James Graham, the Marquess of Graham (later the 3rd Duke of Montrose). Graham had first been introduced to Lady Worsley in 1779, at a time when he 'was more prominent in society than in politics', but their affair did not begin in earnest until the following year. Like her relationships with Wyndham and Cholmondeley, her romance with Graham was rumoured to be among her most memorable and heartfelt.

Unlike that of her other aristocratic devotees, Graham's life was not centred exclusively on the pursuit of pleasure. Shortly after returning from his grand tour, he appeared in London, intellectually fired by the events in America. Energetic and hungry for a parliamentary seat, he was described by the *English Chronicle* as 'a young nobleman of very promising abilities and admirable address'. For Graham, eager to inflate his influence and make a splash in political circles, this was a thrilling period of party-going and socialising. At some point his trajectory through the drawing rooms and theatre boxes sent him colliding with Seymour, but curiously not with her husband. Again, as in the testimony presented by Peterborough and Bouchier Smith, this was a detail that weakened the plaintiff's case.

Graham was Howorth's witness and the attorney was determined to serve his evidence up to the jury as a veritable feast of revelations.

'When did your Lordship's first acquaintance commence with Lady Worsley?' he asked.

'Three or four years ago.'

'You was not at all acquainted with Sir Richard?'

'Not at all.'

'In your Lordship's acquaintance with Lady Worsley, did you frequently visit at Sir Richard's house?'

'Not frequently,' Graham demurred, recollecting the various instances when he had called on Seymour at Stratford Place. He paused and then amended his statement, 'I believe . . . sometimes I did.'

'What were your Lordship's observations on Lady Worsley's general deportment and conduct, during the time you knew her?'

The Marquess imagined Lady Worsley as he had known her two years earlier in London, unfettered by concerns and left unchecked by her husband. 'She was gay, lively and free in her behaviour.'

'Was her behaviour such that became a modest and married Woman?' Howorth enquired.

Graham's answer echoed that given by Lord Peterborough: 'I think it was not.'

'Was there any absolute impropriety in her conduct?' Howorth would have liked the Marquess to have confessed to scenes of debauchery but Graham disappointed him.

'There was no absolute impropriety in her conduct.'

'Then your Lordship, during the time you knew her, had you no reason to observe that there was anything in her conduct improper or immodest?'

'Not immodest.' Graham was being cagey. He knew where Howorth was leading him and as a gentleman, he found himself reluctant to follow. Like those of Deerhurst his answers were tipped with a hint of contempt, a distaste at the disrespectful tone of the enquiries as well as a subtle desire to remind those assembled of his superior position over them.

'You are speaking of her behaviour and manner?'

'I am speaking of her *conduct* as it fell within conversation.' In truth, what the defence desired Graham to disclose – an anecdote of Lady Worsley's lewd behaviour, a situation where she freely espoused a love of fornication, where she indulged in sexual congress openly, or wantonly exposed her naked flesh – had never happened; at least to his knowledge. Seymour did not behave like a Covent Garden prostitute, sodden with drink, throwing her arms around the neck of her swain. Her outward appearance was almost always circumspect. Her language was polished and guarded. Her sins were committed in private, or at least in the shadows and with a modicum of decorum. Such were the rules of intrigue among her class and she did not break them.

But Howorth required more elaboration. 'What was your Lordship's opinion, as to every circumstance which fell within your observations? Was it, that she was a modest, decent Married Woman?'

Graham sensed the lawyer's invitation to incriminate himself and hastily recoiled from it. 'That part which relates to myself I have no business to answer.'

'Had your Lordship not the occasion to know of her ill state of health, from the care and attention you may have paid to Lady Worsley?'

At this juncture, Lord Mansfield thundered in. Howorth had overstepped the bounds of delicacy and strayed into a potential quagmire. He was, with subtle implication, asking the Marquess to betray a secret. He had offered Graham an opportunity to reveal that, in the words of Horace Walpole's biographer W.S. Lewis, 'his Lordship received favours from the Lady that made a lasting impression . . . the favours were a veneral disease and Graham had conferred them upon Lady Worsley'. Although the Marquess refused to answer, the testimony of a witness who followed him confirmed the suspicions of the jury absolutely.

In addition to several of her lovers, Lady Worsley had also subpoenaed her physician, and what Dr William Osborn revealed during a short stint in the witness box provided more substance to the claims of Seymour's prior ruin than the words of five gentlemen. Normally, eighteenth-century practitioners of medicine were as bound by codes of confidentiality as they are today, but according to the *London Chronicle* Doctor Osborn had received a specific request from Seymour to 'make a point of attending and declare everything you know of me'. The newspaper not incorrectly interpreted this as a desperate *cri de coeur* '. . . which plainly meant, criminate me, as by that means you shall save my lover from the effects of a heavy verdict'.

It was in August 1780, towards the end of her affair with Lord Graham that Dr Osborn was summoned. He had received a request to visit Sir Richard Worsley's wife at their town house on Stratford Place, but had not been given further details of his patient's complaint. As a reputable surgeon and 'man-midwife' who conducted a sideline business in the treatment of genteel 'lady's disorders', Osborn was familiar with the protocol of his profession and what he was likely to encounter on his arrival. The doctor was asked by Edward Bearcroft the year and month in which he first saw Lady Worsley. He then requested that Osborn 'Give an account of the condition you found her in.'

The doctor was not comfortable betraying confidences, and before continuing with his testimony made a point of salvaging his professional reputation by clearly stating that 'Between a patient and a physician there is an implied secrecy; the nature of the case requires it: and that being the state of the case, I should hardly conceive myself at liberty to declare it . . .' Osborn then took a breath: 'But, I have the Lady's permission to give evidence of the truth.'

Bearcroft intended to make this revelation as distasteful and shocking as possible. 'You was not employed by Sir Richard?' he asked.

'No,' answered the doctor, confirming that his call to the Worsley home was not as a result of a husband's promiscuous behaviour passed on to his wife. Rather, it was a case of the wife having damaged her own health.

'In what condition did you find her?'

'Lady Worsley had some complaints on her, which I fancy were the consequence of a Venereal Disorder,' he announced.

'In what state did you find her?' Bearcroft questioned, in an attempt to gain further particulars. But this was difficult as Osborn, in keeping with accepted practice, had not actually performed an examination of his female patient's infected parts. The practitioner explained:

'I believe it was never known; at least I was never asked my idea of the disorder; nor did I think it necessary to mention it. My business was to cure her . . .' Lady Worsley, or perhaps even her servant would have presented the doctor with a description of her symptoms. The word *gonorrhoea* probably never passed either's lips. At a time when many individuals, as Randolph Trumbach writes, would quite literally 'rather have died than have it known' that they bore such an illness, delicacy was of the utmost. Whatever cure Osborn had prescribed, whether this was a daily application of a mercury-based ointment on the affected area or an ingestion of mercury either neat or diluted in a substance, the process was certain to have caused Seymour a good deal of discomfort.

Although the doctor's testimony had come at the insistence of his patient, Osborn remained extremely uneasy about the task he was being asked to perform. Not only was Lady Worsley's reputation at stake, but his own good name. After his last pronouncement, Osborn abruptly informed Mansfield that he chose no longer 'to talk upon the subject, one way or [the] other', whereupon the judge excused him.

If there had been any doubt as to the veracity of the claims presented by Lady Worsley's three lovers and if the character witnesses had not already convinced the jury of Seymour's tattered reputation, then the appearance of Dr Osborn established with scientific authority that Sir Richard's wife had undone herself long before Bisset ever enticed her to the Royal Hotel. Additionally, Osborn's testimony raised some fairly bald questions about the state of the Worsleys' marital relations. Although Osborn was not prepared to speculate on his patient's condition or the possibility that she might have allowed the disease to fester without medical attention over the course of weeks or even months, its implications were obvious: Sir Richard had not been playing his conjugal role in the bedchamber for some time, or, as one wag commented, 'It is somewhat remarkable, that the careless husband never once complained of any injury he had received from his *faithless* wife; a pretty certain proof that he had, by neglecting her charms, left family duty to be performed by substitutes . . .'

It is hardly surprising that shortly after receiving her infection, Graham, 'the substitute', fell out of Lady Worsley's favour. His departure from the courtroom, as well as from Seymour's calendar of intrigues, leaves a gap in the story of her affairs from around September 1780, at about the time of the general election, when she and Sir Richard were to become more intimately acquainted with their neighbour, Maurice George Bisset. However, the gossip-mongers and newspaper men were not content with such an incomplete catalogue of Lady Worsley's conquests. With time, they began to pencil names into the blank spots of her history. This exercise in speculation began shortly before the trial and continued long after it had ended. Subsequently the lines between fantasy and fact began to grow less and less distinct.

By April of 1782, the list of individuals alleging to have passed an illicit evening in the embrace of this 'Messalina of the Modern Age' had swelled beyond any credible proportion. Idle gossip, fanciful boasting and rakish innuendo added a full range of names to her roll of theoretical lovers. Grub Street satirists made use of the opportunity to attach the names of figures from other notorious débâcles to this most recent scandal. The quill behind the anonymous publication, *Sir Richard Easy*, created a tableau of farcical bed-hopping, which paired Seymour with Lord William Gordon (mistaken in the pamphlet for his brother, the instigator of the eponymous Gordon Riots), Sir Charles Bunbury (the husband of Lord Gordon's mistress, Lady Sarah Bunbury) as well as the MP, Satanist and necrophile, George Selwyn and his regular sidekick, Charles 'Chace' Price. Whether these names, and others like them, were included in the official tally of Lady Worsley's lovers can only be guessed.

While Grub Street enjoyed coupling her name with those of other personalities for comedic effect, in some instances men were prepared for reasons of vanity to boast of their (often invented) exploits with Sir Richard's wife. Horace Walpole writes of one ungallant gentleman at the St James Coffee House who after clearing his throat, produced a folded sheet of paper from his pocket and proceeded to announce, 'I have been very secret, but now I think I am at liberty to show this letter . . . I have loved Wyndham, I did love Graham, but now I love only you, by God.' Given the usual displays of decorum surrounding clandestine romances it is doubtful that a bona fide paramour would have been as indiscreet, especially as he also ran the risk of being lumbered with a charge of criminal conversation.

Nevertheless, among the collection of self-proclaimed or gossip-nominated candidates were several plausible additions; gentlemen who had for the most part attempted to keep their secrets from the public domain, though not always with success. Among the publications that appeared filled with stories of Lady Worsley's adventures, *The Memoirs of Sir Finical Whimsy and His Lady* seems quite convincingly to be built on insider knowledge. Its astute and anonymous author makes use of precise biographical and chronological detail that cross-references consistently with other sources. The work's pages contain the names of numerous gentlemen, both notable and unknown, who were understood to have intrigued with Sir Richard's wife. Ranking highly among those who 'have been the subject of tea table animadversion among the ton' was the Earl of Egremont. A prodigious philanderer and the brother of Charles Wyndham, the suggestion that the Earl might be included 'among that number who have possessed an exclusive share of [Lady Worsley's] partiality' would not be entirely unlikely. The Worsleys moved in Egremont's circle and are known to have visited his estate at Petworth in the early summer of 1778, while the South Hampshire Militia were temporarily encamped on his grounds. Equally conceivable is the suggestion that Seymour was intimately acquainted with other officers in her husband's corps beyond Edward Rushworth and Maurice George Bisset. The fabulously wealthy Captain John Fleming, a Member of Parliament for Southampton was cited, as was Captain Simeon Stuart, the son of the regiment's former commander and a man regarded as 'a distinguished favourite among the ladies'.

The list continued. The author added to it the name of George Pitt, later the 2nd Baron Rivers. Pitt, who eventually was forced to sell his ancestral seat, Stratfield Saye to satisfy his gambling debts, was a neighbour of Worsley's as well as a companion of Wyndham's. By 1784 his behaviour had become so reprehensible that his father publicly admonished him in a pamphlet entitled *A Letter to a Young Noble Man on a Variety of Subjects*. Lord Rivers was still brushing the muck off the family crest left by the humiliating divorce of his daughter, Penelope Ligonier, when his son had begun to run wild. A misadventure with Lady Worsley was to become only one sin in a lifetime of errors.

Alongside George Pitt appeared the name of Francis North, a military commander and son of the Prime Minister, Lord North. The author of *Sir Finical Whimsy* writes little about this affair, beyond a remark that it amounted to 'nothing exceeding the common adventures of gallantry', before adding glibly that Sir Richard Worsley had been foolish enough to 'think himself highly honoured by the connection'.

A handful of other, more elaborately disguised identities are fleetingly presented, such as that of Captain E——, with whom Worsley was rumoured to have arranged a wife-swap during an evening under the stars at Coxheath. Mention of an 'Honourable Mr——, son of Lord—— 'is also introduced behind a veil of riddles. He was believed to have 'commenced acquaintance with her ladyship in town' and after running through his 'fortune before succeeding to it' then had 'the singular good luck to be elected for a member of a constituency at the last general election'. The more unlikely the liaison, the greater the author's pretences of discretion, leaving curious readers to scratch their heads at the remaining jumble of indecipherable individuals mentioned only by initials.

From this tangle of acknowledged lovers, whispered names, rumours, conjecture, satirical suggestions and dubious sexual boasts, a log purporting to contain the sum total of Lady Worsley's paramours was created. No one, however, could agree on the actual number. The author of *Sir Richard Easy* exaggerated the scandal by citing the existence of 'a list of about three score gallants'. Walpole wrote with barely contained relish to Horace Mann on the 25th of February that 'she summoned thirty-four young men of the first quality' but later revised this to twenty-seven. He had probably got his information from the newspapers; the *Morning Herald* had been asserting that 'no less than twenty-eight were subpoenaed at her own express command'. After the initial excitement of the February trial had flickered out, numbers were readjusted downward. *Finical Whimsy* suggested a more reasonable fifteen while the cartoonist James Gillray's lampoon, *A Peep into Lady !!!!y's Seraglio* depicted her with eleven supposedly identifiable admirers.

There is nothing to suggest that any of these assertions are correct. Since the time of the couple's elopement, a stream of gossip had leaked into the facts and diluted them beyond recognition. Perhaps one of the greatest errors made, not unintentionally by those twisting the truth, was to mistake the tally of those subpoenaed with the notches on Lady Worsley's bedpost. In the formulation of Bisset's defence this list of men included those like Peterborough and Bouchier Smith familiar with Seymour's reputation, as well as others privy to personal information such as Dr Osborn, who had never seen the inside of her bedchamber. Undeniably, others who had, such as Cholmondeley, Rushworth and possibly the Earl of Egremont, Simeon Stuart, John Fleming, Francis North and George Pitt, would also have been called. But it is here that the true problem of assigning a precise figure to Lady Worsley's catalogue of lovers encounters its stickiest corner. Seymour's name was linked to numerous gentlemen, but how many among them committed categorical acts of adultery with her is unknown.

A married lady's character was a fragile thing. As the historian A.D. Harvey comments, 'among the most sophisticated classes a woman's reputation for chastity generally depended on her ability to maintain an appearance of being entirely uninterested in sex'. As it was believed that a woman's physical desire was ignited by the loss of her virginity, recently married women of the leisured classes were especially prone to suspicion. In the airtight observation tank of high society, the scrutiny of pretty young wives by scheming matrons became one of the period's favourite pastimes. Who would be first or next to waver and who appeared disenchanted or suffocated by the ennui of marriage were the subjects of many ladies' daily correspondence. It required little more than a hint of coquetry, one too many turns on the dance floor with the same partner, or a stroll in the company of a man not one's husband, to excite a twitchy eyebrow. Lady Sarah Bunbury found herself the subject of unrelenting gossip long before she had committed her indiscretion with William Gordon. On a visit to Paris with her husband, the couple were joined by Lord Carlisle. Only a handful of unchaperoned sightings of Lady Sarah with her 'cicisbeo' (or male admirer, as he was called) were required before news of a 'flirtation' had reached London. Back in England, her socialising and friendship with the womanising Duke de Lauzan sent the hacks leaping for their scandal-filled inkwells. More than a year before her elopement with Gordon, while Lady Sarah virtuously dodged the advances of de Lauzan and Carlisle, Grub Street intelligence was eagerly brewing tales about her lascivious adventures. A married woman need only display the slightest hint that, in the words of Madame du Deffand, 'she seeks diversion' to set the machinery of gossip spinning.

In Seymour's case, she had done far more than hint at a desire for diversion. Instead she had publicly cast off her cloak of virtuous pretence and proclaimed herself a whore. In the view of Grub Street, she had placed herself in the stocks and openly invited her character to be pelted with any dirt their publications chose to hurl at her. As her self-denouncement was shocking, so the invented tally of lovers had to be equally jaw-dropping. In practice, the reality of Lady Worsley's relationships with men was likely to be somewhat at odds with the reputation she had acquired. Given Grub Street's ability to exaggerate, it is doubtful that Seymour had sex with the majority of the twenty-seven plus attached to her name. Even accomplished gallants such as Fleming, Stuart, Pitt and Egremont, whose involvement with her seems more plausible due to their own sexual histories, may have enjoyed no more than a light-hearted flirtation. As in Lady Sarah Bunbury's case, many rumoured liaisons were likely to have been based on observations of suggestive body language, over-attentiveness, or sightings of two individuals enjoying each other's company. Even in less innocent situations, not every flirtatious encounter ended in the bedroom. Seymour could be discriminating. Some of her pursuers may have found that their name and hers were the only parts of their persons to be coupled.

Aside from Bisset, there is compelling evidence to suggest that Seymour had affairs with five additional men: Wyndham, Rushworth, Cholmondeley, Deerhurst and Graham. The possibility will always remain that there were more, but in keeping with the intriguer's code of secrecy, it is probable that some of her paramours preferred to take their stories to their grave rather than tell them to a hack. Ultimately, identifying all of them was never the objective of Lady Worsley's contemporaries. The prurient curiosity of the masses was easily distracted. What mattered most was that from the day of the trial society viewed Seymour as a deviant, and capable of any sexual aberration.

As the number of letters mentioning the events of her elopement suggests, those of Lady Worsley's class followed the unfolding of events with a sharp interest. Unlike the censorious middle ranks and the press that pandered to them, the disapproval in the correspondence of those such as Walpole and other members of the gentry was not necessarily of Lady Worsley's sexual appetite but of her conduct. The twelve jurors, men chosen for their knowledge of the world, were not ignorant of the morality of the age. Nor would they have viewed Lady Worsley's behaviour as unusual for a woman of her position; adultery among the 'better class of wives' was 'rather esteemed a fashionable vice than a crime'. As her lover's criminal conversation trial was being heard, other ladies of their acquaintance, the Duchess of Devonshire, the Viscountess Melbourne, the Countess of Jersey, the Countess of Clermont, and the Countess of Bessborough, were entertaining inamoratos of their own or involving themselves in the clandestine amours of their friends. Where Lady Worsley fell foul was by acting on impulse, by breaking with received practice and then compounding her errors by kissing and telling. By casting open the shutters of a private club, she risked exposing the quiet immorality of all its members. As the Duchess of Devonshire explained in her novel, *The Sylph*, condemnation must be heaped on those ladies 'who are enslaved by their passions, and bring public disgrace on their families by suffering themselves to be detected'. Such thoughtlessness was a betrayal of them all. She continues that the punishment for this was ostracism, as those who had offended were worthy of nothing but 'our scorn and ridicule'.

Although Lady Worsley was not present at the trial, it was she who had given the most in the course of the proceedings. She had relinquished her entire character in order to save her lover. As yet, this gesture in itself was no guarantee of success. In the end, the sacrifice of her reputation might still count for nothing. Either way, should the defence succeed or fail, Seymour would pay an enormous price to be levied in stiff penalties for the remainder of her days.

15

The Verdict

In the months before the trial, Bearcroft, Pechell and Howorth had been busy creating a defence volatile enough to explode Worsley's suit. Together, they had assembled a strategy which they believed would save Maurice George Bisset from an impending £20,000 bondage.

From the action's outset Sir Richard's collection of smug lawyers had concluded that the defendant would have little room for manoeuvre. When Bisset appeared in court he was, in their view, no better than a criminal come to receive his sentence. But while there was no refuting the charge of adultery, the factors that governed it, the mitigating circumstances that first brought Lady Worsley to Bisset's bed, would be the springs that freed Seymour's lover from her husband's trap. As the defence was proving, there was much more to this story than Worsley was willing to divulge. Midway through the trial, as a result of their endeavours, the hidden truths had only just begun to seep out.

Bisset's defence had been honed into two exceptionally sharp prongs. The first had been designed to spear the plaintiff's argument by proving that the worth of Sir Richard's wife had been seriously compromised long before the Captain made off with the spoiled goods. Bearcroft, Pechell and Howorth would have recognised that this was an extremely unconventional approach which might raise a number of objections, particularly from Lady Worsley. To undermine Sir Richard's case, Seymour would be required to publicly defame herself and to relinquish any lingering hope of resuscitating her reputation by permitting a number of her male associates to attest to her corrupted character. The logic behind this plan of attack would have been laid bare to her. Bisset faced complete ruin should the jury favour her husband and, in the end, Seymour would suffer doubly at the loss of her only protector. It was essential for the jury to understand that, contrary to belief, Sir Richard had not lost something of great value. As she herself had claimed, he had been indifferent to her, she had 'received many slights' from him and therefore her elopement had not deprived him of her 'comfort and society', as the law might argue. Worse still, Sir Richard was partially to blame as he had been remiss in shepherding her conduct. Bearcroft, Pechell and Howorth required witnesses who would regale the stunned jury with tales of her debauchery. Most importantly, the jury must also be convinced that any child Lady Worsley might bring into the Appuldurcombe nursery would be of questionable paternity. Her husband could not even trust her womb to secure his dynasty. The jury should not view her as one whose now soiled character commanded £20,000 in damages, but as an object in her husband's collection whose value was worth far less.

The defence had formulated a proposal for obtaining the vital information. With assistance from her trusted friend Deerhurst, they asked Seymour to compile 'a list of . . . gallants, to whom she acknowledged having been perfectly liberal with her favours'. She also 'enclosed Doctor Osborn's account with the recipes prescribed for her' so the public would know how 'liberal' her husband had been. The impropriety of this measure was clear, both to Lady Worsley and to the men to whom she was to write. No honourable gentleman would ever consider publicly destroying the name of a lady of quality or his own reputation by betraying her confidences or by revealing details of their love affair. This was considered not only a disreputable act but one which posed a serious threat to the ordering of society. By virtue of her position, the wife of a baronet was entitled to deference, but respect for an individual and the class they represented might be easily eroded by the exposure of their moral flaws. The recipients of Lady Worsley's pleading letters would have had serious reservations about appearing as witnesses. For this reason, it is likely that those who refused to testify outweighed the list of those who eventually did.

It is unknown whether or not Lady Worsley consented to having her character ruined. She may have required some convincing before giving up the remnants of her reputation to her lover's legal team, but they would have reminded her that where her name was concerned, she had nothing more to lose. Through the narrow lens of those who judged her, it would not matter whether she had committed one public transgression or a multitude: she was no longer respectable.

The second point of this attack was even more vicious. Once they had finished shredding Lady Worsley's character, they turned their knives on Sir Richard's. Worsley had entered the courtroom with the confidence of the indomitable, with a certainty of his position as a titled landowner, a gentleman, a commanding officer, and as a member of the establishment. Irrespective of any possible mitigating circumstances, these fundamental factors would weigh more heavily in favour of him than they would for those who had subverted the laws and natural order of society. As Worsley had been the victim of a moral outrage perpetrated against him by a man of a lesser rank, the court of law had an obligation to punish the malefactor. But as Bearcroft, Pechell and Howorth would demonstrate, there were circumstances which challenged this assumption as well. The lovers were not the only ones who had violated the codes of honour and duty.

The privileged classes had a weak spot which handicapped them severely where matters of privacy were concerned. Since birth, they had been trained to be blind and dependent. When surveying a room they saw only the bodies of those who mattered. In most cases, this excluded virtually everyone of a lesser social standing. As a result the privileged classes frequently forgot themselves in front of a theatre of labourers and staff, whose presence they failed to acknowledge. Such negligence was the undoing of many, especially where matters of law were concerned. In Sir Richard's case, his ruin would be the ageing, callous-handed bathing-woman at Maidstone, Mary Marriott. Worsley would not have seen her as she had helped his wife in and out of the plunge pool, but Mary Marriott, insignificant in her functional shoes and muslin dress, knew he was there and witnessed what he did.

Mary Marriott had been deemed so unimportant by the court that her name had not even been granted the courtesy of a prefix; the requisite Mrs or Miss, which denoted a woman's all-important marital status. She was simply a worker, a drudge. On that day she was not present to give her testimony in person. It had been reported to the jury that 'the bathing-woman was ill', but whether this was the true reason for her absence is questionable.

The secrets Mary Marriott carried were heavy ones and it was not in the best interests of the plaintiff that she haul them to London.

As she was unable to attend court, the bathing-woman was asked to swear affidavits before a lawyer attesting to what she had seen. Accordingly, an agreement had been struck that both parties in the suit would send their attorneys 'down to the place for the purpose of taking the affidavits'. Unfortunately for the defence, Worsley's wily solicitor, James Farrer was the first to arrive in Maidstone.

Farrer had wanted to ensure that no aspect of his client's case was left to chance. Every avenue demanded investigation, and delicate information required safeguarding, where necessary. If the defence was to call on the bathing-woman, he would travel to Kent before them in order to receive her statement. If she produced something incriminating, he would be poised to catch it and mitigate its impact. So Farrer rode to Maidstone and located the cold baths. In midst of winter, he followed the pathway down to the neo-classical temple. At some point, he found Mary Marriott, who unknowingly carried on her a vital and volatile piece of information. He spent some time with her, drawing out the account which was later read to the court. Farrer took her story down as follows;

> . . . Lady Worsley used to come to the cold bath near Maidstone to bathe, and that she [Marriott] used to attend her; that Sir Richard and Mr Bissett [sic] were generally with her; and that the last time she came, which was about noon, in September last, and at the latter end of hop-season, Sir Richard and Mr Bissett staid at the door without, while she bathed; that after she had bathed, she retired into a corner to put on her shift, as Ladies usually do after bathing, and then returned to dress herself, and sat herself down on the seat: that there is a window over the door of the building in which the bath is, and which is the only inlet for light into the bath, and from which any person, who is sitting down on the seat, may be seen, but not when retired into the corner; that when she had almost finished dressing herself, Sir Richard tapped at the door, and said 'Seymour! Seymour! Bissett is going to get up to look at you', or words to that effect; and looking around, she saw his face at the window: that he continued there about five minutes; and that she did not see the plaintiff on the outside, but believes he must help the defendant up; and that after Lady Worsley had dressed herself, she went out, and they all were merry and laughing together: that, excepting this, she

*never saw any improper conduct or behaviour in the said three persons,
unless what is above stated may be thought so.*

The corrosiveness of the bathing-woman's recollections must have grown
evident as Farrer transcribed them. It was a veritable admission that Sir
Richard had played a role in his own undoing. Farrer studied Mary Marriott's
assertions closely, searching for the holes in her story. After some consideration the lawyer returned to the structure of the bathhouse. He examined
it, both inside and out. He paced before the window and looked at the small
balcony above the door. He took measurements and made notes in his pock-
etbook. Then, discovering a chair on the outside of the building, he dragged
it to the entryway and hoisting himself up to the inlet he peered through
the glass. He would argue that Bisset might have done the same, without
the assistance of Worsley.

In order to counter Mary Marriott's claims, the baronet's lawyer, Attorney-
General Wallace was eager to have Farrer spell out his findings for the jury.
Between the rational judgements of an educated professional man and the
stories of an illiterate woman of the labouring class, Wallace knew to whom
the benefit of the doubt would be given.

'Did you see the place, on which Mr Bisset got to look into the Bath?'
Wallace asked Farrer. 'And do you think he could do it without the assistance of Sir Richard?'

'I believe he might do it with a great deal of ease, and without assistance,'
he responded succinctly.

'What is the height?' Wallace continued.

'It is about breast-high; there is an arm-chair on the outside; and when I
was on the chair, I could raise myself up to the window very easily.'

'How many feet high may it be?'

'About four feet,' Farrer claimed.

But this description did not seem correct. Mary Marriott, who knew the
building better than most, had clearly stated that the window was situated
above the door, and doors were not likely to terminate at 'breast-height'.
Nor did it make much sense to suggest that, once on a chair, Farrer was able
to scramble a further four feet above him, and while hanging from the edge
of the balcony manage to hold his position there comfortably for five minutes.
The solicitor had either pressed his nose to the wrong window or found his
evidence by looking through the glazed panes of his imagination.

Farrer's scheme and his race to Kent had been anticipated by the defence. Bearcroft, Pechell and Howorth knew that he would be determined to bury anything incriminating. When he took Mary Marriott's sworn statement he had been far from impartial, and so, at the request of the defence who had arrived at Maidstone after Farrer, she gave a second affidavit. In it, she reiterated and clarified her earlier claims. She also confirmed the obvious, that an inlet above a functional entryway could only be reached with difficulty, and therefore 'Mr Bisset could not have got up to the window, unless he had been assisted by Sir Richard, or stood upon his shoulders . . .' More importantly she made a point that not even Farrer could refute. Mary Marriott may have been a humble figure, she may have been poor and illiterate but she was not simple-minded and she knew the ways of human nature as well as any lawyer. It was on the observations of this small individual that the entire case of *Worsley* v. *Bisset* would turn. In her affidavit she insisted that it was immaterial how Bisset came to gaze through the bathhouse window; what mattered was 'that Sir Richard might easily have pulled him down if he pleased'.

When read out in court, this sentence was one over which the jury was certain to linger. Irrespective of whose testimony was actually correct, the learned observations of a solicitor or the disclosures of a bathing-woman, one fundamental and inescapable fact emerged: Bisset had peered through a window at Lady Worsley's naked body in the presence of a husband who offered no objection. No decent, self-respecting gentleman would ever goad another man with the flesh of his own wife.

By the time the defence had rested their case the jurymen had only to roll together this evidence with the lurid stories of the Viscount Deerhurst, the shameful confessions of the Marquess of Graham and Charles Wyndham, the words of the character witnesses, Lord Peterborough and his friend Joseph Bouchier Smith, and the statement reluctantly put forward by Dr Osborn, to see the weakness at the heart of Worsley's suit.

Judge Mansfield was convinced of it long before the jury began to murmur. Before handing the decision to Worsley's peers, this panel of wealthy bankers, shipbuilders and landowners, he reminded them of their task. However they chose to rule, they were not there to contest that an act of adultery had taken place but to determine just how serious this incident of criminal conversation had been. Mansfield addressed the jury;

There arises upon this evidence a serious question for your consideration. – The nature of the action is such, that the Defendant cannot confess the Verdict, because this is between the Husband and the Wife and the Adulterer; and further proceedings may be had: therefore the Verdict you give must be out of the truth and justice of the case, and the Justice of the Evidence.

Now the single question is. Whether Sir Richard has not been privy to the prostitution of his Wife? Assenting to, encouraging and exciting even this Defendant? And, if he is so, upon your opinion of the Evidence, he ought not to recover this Action. – If he is not, why then the only question remains, is upon the subject of Damages; upon which I will not say a word to you. You are the best judges of that.

The judge then turned his attention to the evidence he felt to be most compelling in this trial;

This woman, for three or four years, has been prostituted with a variety of people; that is extremely clear, and extremely plain. A stronger instance than the Doctor's appearance this day, and what he has said, need not have been brought. – In the year 1779 Lord Deerhurst knew Lady Worsley; she was very profligate, and no step was taken by Sir Richard to prevent her: he continued in the Isle of Wight ten days, and he has mentioned a conversation that passed between him and Sir Richard, which ought to be laid out of the case, because it seems to be ironical: 'That many young men have tried her, without success; and that he might take his chance with her'. But he says, once the Plaintiff found him in Lady Worsley's dressing-room at four o'clock in the morning; and he only says to him, 'Deerhurst, how came you here?' And there is no further explanation or examination between them. Is it not extraordinary to find a Gentleman in his Lady's dressing-room at four o'clock in the morning, and nothing further said? All is well; they are all good company the next morning and some few days afterwards Lady Worsley is going to Southampton; he stays there twenty-four hours, and she stays three or four days: – yet there is no appearance of jealousy in the Husband!! This evidence deserves your consideration.

Another piece of evidence, is the evidence of the Woman at the Bath at Maidstone; and the Woman at the Bath swears, she believes it was impossible for Mr Bisset to have got up the height of the balcony, to look into the

Bath, unless he had stood upon Sir Richard's shoulders: but this is a matter of belief; and they have called the Attorney, and you have heard his evidence: he went down there to take the affidavits: he says he got up with a great deal of ease, and without assistance; that he got up first on an arm chair which stood on the outside of the Bath, and then it was only four feet above him; so that, if he had not stood upon Sir Richard's shoulders, he might easily have pulled him down if he pleased; instead of which he only taps at the door, and says, 'Seymour! Seymour! Bisset is looking at you.' And when she is dressed and comes out, she joins them, and they are all jolly and merry, and laughing, and go away together.

Mansfield then took the opportunity to reiterate a matter of law which had been mentioned several times in the course of the trial. The scales of justice had to be calibrated on one essential point: if the jury believed that Worsley had in any way encouraged the act of criminal conversation, then he was as guilty as the defendant and they, as a jury, could not rule in his favour.

This is the evidence which they have given; and if upon that evidence you think the Husband was privy to, consenting, and encouraging this debauchery, he ought not to have your Verdict; but if you think he is intitled to your Verdict, then the only point for your consideration is. What Damages you will give. – You will consider your Verdict, and give what damages you think proper.

Lord Mansfield turned to the jury. Not unreasonably he might have expected their decision within a matter of moments. If the circumstances of the case had been presented plainly enough, many jurors saw no need to so much as leave their box before alighting upon a verdict. However, *Worsley* v. *Bisset*, from the moment the damages were set until the last witness had climbed from the stand, had been an exceptional legal action. Recognising this, the twelve gentlemen entrusted with producing the verdict chose to retire outside the courtroom in order to closely consider their pronouncement.

Richard Gildart, the sugar magnate, Henry Kitchin the alderman, Marmaduke Langdale the investor, Barrington Buggin the owner of a fleet of ships, George Wheatley the banker at Drummond's, and seven others of similar status sat in seclusion, pondering the morality and responsibility of both parties. This was not a straightforward decision. An act of criminal conversation had been committed; the staff at the Royal Hotel had witnessed Lady Worsley and Captain Bisset sharing a bed. This was not a point for dispute, but the degree to which Sir Richard had played a role in precipitating the situation formed the mainstay of their debate. The baronet's behaviour had been far from exemplary; he had ignored his wife on some occasions and on others, virtually thrust her into the embrace of friends and strangers alike. He had proffered her like a pimp. His behaviour had been untenable and immoral. But the wife, some of the jury may have argued, had taken to debauchery with zeal, had loved her way through a number of rakes and infected herself in the process. Worsley may have been remiss as a husband, but he had not plotted his wife's elopement with his friend and military subordinate. The questions would have flown back and forth.

For the better part of an hour the jury remained confined in their quarters, rapt in deliberation. The unusually slow progress of proceedings must have caused both Worsley and his opponent excruciating anxiety. As Lawrence Stone writes, even in 'the most complicated and bitterly contested of cases, the jury rarely took more than "a short time" or "a few minutes" to make up its mind on a figure, and in all but a handful of cases, the longest time taken was a half hour'. By the time the jury filed solemnly back into their box, the impatience and tension in the courtroom would have simmered to boiling point. They had taken longer to consider their verdict than a jury in any other criminal conversation trial in history.

Such was Sir Richard Worsley's arrogance at the outset of his suit that he had deemed Bisset's insult to him worth £20,000 in reparations. In setting these damages so steeply he had publicly registered his moral outrage. He had wanted to assert the integrity of his character over that of the unprincipled man who had committed an abominable crime. But in the end, the jury did not view it this way. After reviewing the details of the case, £20,000 far exceeded that which they felt was due to him. Worsley was not the paragon he presented himself to be. In fact, the baronet's behaviour had been appalling throughout. The jury would acknowledge that a breach of legality had occurred when Maurice George Bisset had escaped to London with Sir Richard's wife, but they would do so in the most condescending and humiliating way possible. In criminal conversation cases it was common for juries to award half of the damages requested. The panel of twelve in this trial might even have granted Worsley a cursory thousand or so in acknowledgement of his loss. However, in their concerted opinion, his claims were not even worthy of this. Instead, bearing in mind the circumstances of this dishonour, they awarded him what they felt he deserved: a total sum of one shilling.

For the price of a pound of soap, a muslin neckcloth or a roast beef dinner, Worsley had sold his wife and his honour to George Bisset.

16

'The Value of a Privy Counsellor's Matrimonial Honour'

William Clarke, one of the two brothers who managed Sir Richard's affairs on the Isle of Wight, had been sitting in the gallery of the courtroom on the 21st of February. He had come especially from Newport to offer both practical and moral support to someone he considered a friend as much as an employer. Just before two o'clock, he found his seat on the benches and there remained, stewing in embarrassment and 'truly real concern' for the next three hours. By the time the decision was read, 'a doubt' had been 'long sustained that the jury would not find a verdict . . . for the Plaintiff'. 'However,' Clarke wrote with anguish, 'a verdict *was* found with a *shilling* damages.' 'Think what I felt!' he exclaimed. 'Judge what *all* his friends felt!'

Compelled by both astonishment and sympathy, Clarke pushed his way through the commotion of black robes, hats and strangers towards where he could view Worsley surrounded by his counsel. As he approached him, Sir Richard appeared blanched and visibly unwell. Shock had rendered him 'too agitated to speak'. 'What effect this will have on him, I know not,' the steward wrote to his brother; 'he will be miserable at his friend's triumph.'

After this fraught encounter, a rattled William Clarke left Westminster Hall with the intention of later calling upon Sir Richard at Stratford Place. But the baronet did not return to his town house that evening. After several hours of enquiries, Clarke sat down with pen and paper to report the trial's nightmarish events to his brother. At 11 p.m. Sir Richard Worsley was still missing. 'I know not where he is to be found,' the steward wrote anxiously, 'but I shall find him and see him.'

Sir Richard did not want to be found. He had vanished without explanation and remained lost until the following week. In all probability he had returned to Hesse's doorstep in Paddington, imposing himself once more on his beleaguered friend.

It is unknown how Worsley solaced himself in the bleak hours between his disappearance on the evening of the 21st and his re-emergence on Wednesday the 27th. The promise of an easy legal victory which had sustained him through the miserable months since November had proven empty. Having suffered a humiliating public disgrace he was now, at least in his own mind, a completely ruined man. What he had endured as a result of his wife's elopement was a light penance when compared to the burden of ridicule he would be forced to carry. As the author of the *Cuckold's Chronicle* surmised, Worsley not only faced 'the contemptuous pity of his friends' but 'the indignation of the Public and the sentiments of his own mind'. 'The impartial Public would not hesitate in giving their judgement,' he warned, while echoing Sir Richard's darkest concerns that 'all posterity' would 'hear of the curious discussion' and 'find no difficulty in delivering an adequate decision'.

The shame of the trial's outcome literally sickened Worsley. The following day, he could not even bring himself to face his parliamentary duties, despite the Prime Minister's urgent need for support. Since the announcement of the defeat at Yorktown, Lord North's administration had hung from a thread. The King would not permit North to resign and so his government limped on until the Whig opposition could take it down, and in doing so end the war with America. In this time of crisis, His Majesty required as much support as could be mustered from his regulars: Tories like Worsley who would cast their votes obediently. The absence of even one loyal party-man had the potential to topple North and foil the King's plans.

No one in the government could have predicted that the peculiarities of Sir Richard's private life would play a role in the defeat of North's ministry. As the Prime Minster scanned the chamber for his supporters on the 22nd of February, the unexpected absence of Sir Richard Worsley alarmed him. In his years as a politician the baronet had never missed a parliamentary vote. When enquiring after Worsley's whereabouts, North was reminded of his colleague's recent misfortune, 'Oh,' he is said to have replied with a nervous smile. 'If all my Cuckolds desert, I shall be beaten indeed!'

Worsley's absence had not gone unnoticed by the Whigs either. North was one man down and the opposition took this as a signal to strike. Before the session came to an end a motion was tabled asking for '. . . An humble address be presented to his Majesty, that . . . the war on the continent of North America may no longer be pursued for the impractical purpose of reducing the Inhabitants of that country to obedience by force . . .' The Whigs, joined by the ranks of the disenchanted from across the floor, wanted this to be a vote of no confidence, a clear message to the King that the war must be ended.

The motion failed by only one vote. The administration remained on its feet, but only for another five days. It was a narrow escape for Lord North as well as for Worsley. Had the Prime Minister been unseated that day as a result of his absence, Sir Richard's folly at the Maidstone bathhouse would have been committed to history as the sex scandal that granted America its freedom.

When North's ministry finally fell, the last of the baronet's potency was stripped away from him. Every aspect of the public image Worsley had so meticulously constructed for himself was collapsing. By the end of March he was no longer a Privy Counsellor and had resigned his position as Governor of the Isle of Wight. Emasculated by the judiciary and denuded of his influential status, he and his ordeal became ripe targets.

As he emerged reluctantly from his second period of retreat, Worsley had to steady himself for a pelting by the press. Already the hacks had spilled the contents of their notebooks on to the pages of the London newspapers. For days after the trial, the *London Chronicle* and the *Morning Herald* ran extracts from the proceedings. A lengthy summary of the case was even printed in Sir Richard's local gazette, the *Hampshire Chronicle*. His neighbours would all be informed of his dishonour. However, the worst was yet to come.

The court reporter who had been sitting among the hacks on the 21st of February was a man known as Robert Pye Donkin, a self-professed 'expert brachygrapher'. In spite of mishearing several of the witnesses' names, Pye Donkin had studiously recorded in shorthand the detailed transactions of the trial. Immediately after he took his last note, the witness testimony, the arguments of both parties, as well as the comments of Justice Mansfield, were handed over to a publisher and set in type. Within forty-eight hours, *The Trial with the Whole of the Evidence between the Right Hon. Sir Richard Worsley,*

Bart. and George Maurice Bissett, Esq., Defendant, for Criminal Conversation with the Plaintiff's Wife, ironically priced at one shilling, appeared at the book-sellers' stalls. When word of the spectacular verdict reached the drawing rooms and tap rooms of London, demand for the pamphlet became insatiable. On the morning of the 23rd, the Fleet Street bookseller George Kearsley was virtually under siege. The *Morning Herald* reported that an 'unprecedented demand' for the work 'occasioned its being out of print a few hours after it was published'. Not wanting to miss an opportunity to line his pockets, Kearsley was pleased to bring to general notice that 'two presses are now employed in working off a sufficient quantity to gratify the curiosity of the public'. He was not the only bookseller to spot a potential profit. The transcript was published in both London and Dublin, and in 1782 alone ran to at least eight editions. By 1783 copies could even be purchased in the newly formed United States of America. In addition to 'a pair of handsome and Fashionable spurs' and '10 pounds of the best hair powder' General George Washington listed among his requested supplies for the week of May 15th an edition of '*The Trial between Sir Richard Worsley and Maurice Bissett*'.

Pye Donkin's trial transcripts and the accounts in assorted newspapers were the beginning of a sustained campaign of destructive lampooning in both written and pictorial form. Sir Richard and his wife received equal treatment at the hands of illustrators and pamphleteers, though in the immediate wake of the verdict, Worsley, due to his more conspicuous profile, suffered more acutely than Seymour. Ridicule was a potent form of popular entertainment in the eighteenth century, and as the poet Mark Akenside expressed it, 'fools who are ignorant of what they ought to know' were considered among the most worthy objects of satire.

Before pictures accompanied newspaper stories, the images which appeared in print sellers' shops allowed the population to feel a part of current events. Almost as soon as reports of the latest political crises, scandals, and sartorial fads were set in type cartoonists had transformed them into lively and often subversive parodies. Animal-shaped politicians roared and clawed at each other while the bug-eyed King ate boiled eggs. Mountainous hair-styles caught alight, respectable ladies' skirts flew over their heads, and fat bottoms filled chamber pots. No person's misfortune was too tragic to portray, and not even the Royal Family was granted immunity from the satirist's stylus. This side-show was updated on a daily basis and drew a constant audience to print sellers's windows. Those who jostled for a view were 'of high and low birth alike'. Oliver Goldsmith commented that among such crowds, 'the brick-dust man took up as much room as the truncheoned hero, and the judge was elbowed by the thief-taker; quacks, pimps and buffoons increased the group, and noted stallions only made room for more noted strumpets'. Sir Richard Worsley had everything to fear from this army of illustrators and print pedlars who would soon pepper the windows of London with his disgrace.

In addition to his other misfortunes, the baronet's life had been plagued by bad timing. On the 27th of February, the day he chose to re-emerge into the public arena and resume his seat on the parliamentary benches, William Humphrey, a New Bond Street print seller decided to hang the first of many Worsley caricatures in his shop window. With a ruthless flourish *The Shilling; or the Value of a P——Y C——R's Matrimonial Honor* portrays Sir Richard's moment of degradation. From across a table where the plaintiff sits, a be-wigged James Wallace, holding a copy of the charges, tosses his client a shilling while ruefully commenting, 'They would not believe you possess any of your contrivance for his peeping has ruined your cause.' Worsley, looking over-fed and florid grasps his chest, his eyes rolling heaven-ward, his mouth gaping as if in the throes of a coronary. 'O Lord O Lord no more than one shilling for my lost honour,' he exclaims while dropping his sword (a symbol of masculine virility). From his head, a full rack of cuckold's horns, the tradi-tional emblem of the deceived husband, has sprouted, with each point bearing the name of a witness. Above this scene floats Lady Justice with her scales. As she points her sword at the damned baronet she utters a curse-like procla-mation: 'Take away that badge of distinction, Shame may transfer the colour to his face.' As a representation of the judicial ruling, this first stab at Worsley's character was a deep one. It played mercilessly to the gallery, that laughing mass who collected under the eaves of Humphrey's shop, pointing and guffawing at Worsley's freshly printed image while its subject, himself on view that day in Westminster, struggled to retain his dignity.

Like a battery, the invectives followed in rapid succession: *A Bath of the Moderns* on the 4th of March, *The Maidstone Whim* four days later, *The Maidstone Bath, or The Modern Susanna* on the 12th and the *coup de grâce* of this collection, James Gillray's *Sir Richard Worse-than-Sly, Exposing his Wife's Bottom; O fye!* which arrived at the print sellers on the 14th. Unlike *The Shilling*, these works chose to focus on what became the defining inci-dent of the scandal: the moment of Sir Richard Worsley's self-ruin at the bathhouse. Nothing had captured the public imagination more than the events at Maidstone. The very act of a husband lifting his rival to the window had come to summarise all that was thrilling about this case; the folly, the titillation, the scandal, the corruption. It represented the instant that the Worsleys' lives had tilted off their axes. The satirists immediately recognised the Maidstone bath as the crucial turning point of the Worsleys' narrative. It was the breath-sucking moment of impact, when the fates of three individuals collided; the excitingly erotic first glimpse of an unclothed woman and the point of no return for one who had just committed a vital error. Each of the cartoons that appeared between the 4th and the 14th of March depicted this scene, and of the three individuals whose lives were irrevocably altered on this occasion, Worsley universally fared the worst.

There was no mistaking the identity of the fat, compliant and foolish figure in the lampoons. Sir Richard is dressed as he appears in his dignified portrait by Joshua Reynolds, in the distinctive uniform of the South Hampshire Militia. But these images are not the glorified depictions of a soldier-philosopher, and he wears the emblems of his office with disgraceful irony. In *The Maidstone Whim*, he simpers stupidly as Bisset climbs on to his shoulders before planting a foot on the rack of horns springing from his head. As in *The Shilling*, this additional headgear bears the names of his wife's various lovers. As Bisset hangs on to the balcony below the window, Sir Richard shouts out, 'Seymour, Bisset's looking at you', echoing the words that Mary Marriott reportedly heard. *A Bath of the Moderns* offers a similar scenario but with a dollop of coarse bawdiness. The viewer is presented with a cut-away of what resembles more closely a country cottage than a bathhouse. Inside Lady Worsley dresses and her breast carelessly tumbles out of her bodice as she pulls her stockings over her exposed thighs. On the outside of the structure is Sir Richard with Bisset astride his shoulders. The dialogue is steeped in slapstick ribaldry: 'Captain, do you see the whole Garrison?' Worsley asks. 'Only the Breast work and the cover'd way,' his friend answers. Lady Worsley, meanwhile confides in Mary Marriott, 'Blis.it, he goes to all lengths to please me,' while the bathing-woman, sighting the lover at the window shrieks, 'Lord, my Lady, I believe the Captain wants to be in the watering place!'

For those who found this sort of mocking too vulgar, *The Maidstone Bath, or The Modern Susanna* offered a more aesthetic alternative. Its anonymous author wanted to create a realistic picture of the transactions at the bathhouse, drawing on two well-known ancient stories. The Susanna to which the title refers was a Babylonian maiden, who after being spied in her bath by two elders was forced to submit to their lust, while the inscription, *Candaules Invenit*, which appears along the side of the image, ties the players to the drama of King Candaules who opened the door to his destruction by inviting his servant Gyges to admire his naked wife. From behind the wall of the bathhouse, this contemporary Candaules assists his friend to a port-hole where he can gaze on Lady Worsley, a Susanna, modestly posed like the Venus di Medici, standing in a plunge pool.

The most iconic of these bathhouse pictures was created by the young cartoonist, James Gillray. *Sir Richard Worse-than-sly Exposing his Wife's Bottom; O fye!* presents the same arrangement of characters and setting; Sir Richard squats down outside the building while Bisset, in a conquering pose stands on his back.* Inside, a completely naked Lady Worsley is tended by Mary Marriott. Here, Seymour says nothing but coyly exchanges glances with her lascivious spectator, as her husband helps him to the view. 'My Yoke is Easy and my Burden Light,' Worsley says, while Bisset, playing the militia captain reports to his commander, 'Charming View of the Back Settlements Sir Richard.' Only Mary Marriott, in accordance with her trial statement, appears startled. 'Good lack!' she exclaims, waving her hand in the air, 'My Lady the Captain will see all for Nothing.' But the three parties are too preoccupied with indulging their whims to take much notice.

Bribery was the accepted way of silencing the printing presses, but if Worsley attempted to take such measures there is no indication that he was successful. According to historian Vic Gatrell, in the face of such a barrage it was traditional for those subjected to the engraver's mockery to 'maintain a contemptuous silence rather than to stoop to challenge gutter products'. Outwardly they might express only fleeting disdain. Those such as politicians who were more accustomed to lampooning readily shrugged off the images as jests, or, as William Pitt deemed them, 'the harmless popguns of a free press'. But for individuals like Sir Richard Worsley, who found themselves attacked for their personal failures rather than their polit-ical ideologies, the assaults from the printing presses could be genuinely wounding. As the fashionable classes were slaves to vanity, gossip and

---

*In a rarer version of this same scene, Gillray has rearranged the figures of Bisset and Worsley; Worsley is standing upright with his friend sitting on his shoulders. Both versions were published on the 14th of March.

scandal could be lethal weapons in bringing down a reputation. No punishment was dreaded more than public demolition of one's character. Relentless satirisation drove men like William Cobbett and Richard Payne Knight to despondency. Goldsmith expressed the fear of many who sat in the expensive theatre boxes when his character Charles Marlow in *She Stoops to Conquer* trembled at the thought of being 'laughed at all over the whole town' and being 'stuck up in caricatura in all the print shops . . .' Featuring in the print seller's window was tantamount to appearing in the public stockades. For one accustomed to respect and deference, there could not be a more humbling experience.

Worsley's ruin occurred on a number of levels. The trial and its revelations exposed his weaknesses, the press and the print shops then disseminated them. Their writings and engravings helping to consolidate all of Georgian England's assumptions and prejudices about men of Worsley's position and about Sir Richard as an individual. They universally condemned him as an arrogant fool but also as something much worse. Among the most shocking revelations to emerge from *Worsley v. Bisset* were the acutely mortifying details of Sir Richard's irregular sexuality. What became apparent to all of society was that the baronet was a voyeur.

On its own, voyeurism offered no great offence to eighteenth-century sensibilities. 'Keeking' or secretly spectating on the sexual act or on unclothed women, while not encouraged, had a place within the spectrum of ordinary erotic experience. Exposure to the human body in unexpected and accidental circumstances was common. A general lack of physical privacy and a greater acceptance of bodily functions meant that one was likely to encounter uncovered flesh on a fairly regular basis. Before the widespread introduction of reliable indoor plumbing this might include frequent sightings of men and women urinating, defecating and washing on street corners, in alleys, in streams, pools, gardens and hedgerows. Neither the rich nor the poor had complete privacy. Servants were constantly moving through the rooms of their masters, while the poor bunked together or huddled into close living quarters. Under these conditions sexual pleasure had to be taken without concern about its visibility. Lovers of all classes copulated in corners, behind buildings, against trees and in the camouflage of the undergrowth. Prostitutes pleasured clients in shared beds, married couples made love behind curtained mattresses from which their children, parents or household staff might hear their sighs. Country dwellers stumbled across courting couples in the fields while Londoners cavorted in the metropolis's parks and pleasure gardens. These sights were so common that they were likely to be most of the population's first exposure to sex. In adulthood these experiences might take on voyeuristic dimensions as they often did in the era's erotic literature and art. The majority of the eighteenth century's most infamous works, including *Fanny Hill*, *A Dialogue between a Married Lady and a Maid*, and *Venus in the Cloister* incorporate at least one incident of voyeurism, where a couple or an individual are unwittingly observed by a third party. Engravings, usually created to accompany salacious publications, are also replete with images of the voyeur. Clergymen peek through grates at scenes of carnality in *Histoire de Dom B—* as bawds; Roman gods and putti observe the rutting taking place in the popular sex manual, *Aretino's Postures*.

While voyeurism in itself may not have been considered deviant, using one's wife for the sport was. It contravened not only the traditional morality that governed married sexual behaviour and notions of female modesty, but also the dictates of common sense. As one moralist wrote, the deliberate exposure of a woman's body was 'an unpardonable crime . . . an offence against nature' and should a man subject his spouse to the gaze of another 'many inconveniences may arise from it'; not least, as the fabled King Candaules learned, a wife's 'wish for vengeance against such ill treatment'. Even to those willing to wink at the indiscretions of voyeurism, Sir Richard's fetishistic interests would be considered a shameful abnormality and a step too far.

Worsley's secret would have been acknowledged only among his most intimate companions, gentlemen such as Lord Deerhurst and George Bisset who were honour bound to maintain their silence. However, after the sensational verdict revealed his foibles to the public, stories otherwise safeguarded began to circulate. In the months following the trial the popular press regaled readers with additional incidents said to have been whispered about town. Sir Richard's practice of displaying his wife was rumoured to have begun shortly after marriage. Worsley's vanity was cited as the root of his undoing. For a short period and much to the groom's conceit, their union of wealth, youth and attractiveness had been the subject of fashionable society's admiration. Sir Richard, it was claimed, 'was not a little pleased at the *fancied envy* which he supposed himself the object of' and as a result 'never seemed so well pleased as when he could introduce his friends to a participation of his happiness'. The first opportunity for this arose during the winter of 1776 when Worsley hosted a hunting party at Appuldurcombe.

The baronet was said to have enticed his guests with the promise of 'a sight of the most beautiful woman in the world' before 'taking them to a glass door that communicated from his study to her ladyship's dressing room'. There 'while the unsuspecting beauty was disrobing [he] presented them with a *side glance* of the toilet'.

Like the situation that Deerhurst had described in his testimony, it was alleged that these sorts of 'presentations' were commonplace entertainments for Worsley's friends. A similar viewing was said to have been staged for Lord Cholmondeley, who at the time was already involved with Sir Richard's wife. The spectacle was believed to have been the result of a wager. Cholmondeley, noted for his extensive knowledge of the female form, was invited by Worsley to examine his wife's naked body and to judge for himself whether she was not one of 'the finest proportioned women in Europe'. According to the author of *The Memoirs of Sir Finical Whimsy*, it was unknown to Cholmondeley that the baronet 'had communicated the whim to his lady', who prepared to titillate both her lover and her husband with an exhibition of her flesh. Under the direction of Sir Richard, Seymour was to disrobe, wash and then dress herself with deliberate slowness. Rather than performing this usual morning routine in her dressing room, she was to move to the parlour where Worsley and Cholmondeley could observe her from behind a sham door disguised as a bookcase. Together, Sir Richard and his guest squeezed into the aperture and awaited the peep-show. Lady Worsley did not disappoint them. In order to give 'the umpire a fair opportunity of making an impartial decision' she 'displayed herself in the several postures, which the nicest virtuoso could have required: first sitting in front of the book case to draw on her stockings, and then setting her foot on the chair with her back the same way to tie on her garters'. It was purported that after the performance, and much to Worsley's satisfaction, Cholmondeley was forced to 'confess his wager lost'.

As this distasteful aspect of the baronet's personality came into sharper focus it opened the door to further conclusions about his character. To many, his voyeuristic habits were to be expected from someone so interested in artistic connoisseurship and collecting. Sir Richard defined himself as part of the cognoscenti; the intellectual elite. He allied himself with scholars of the classical world as well as acknowledged arbiters of taste, men who immersed themselves in the detailed study of artistic beauty, who debated its principles and dissected its components. In its pursuit, they ogled the round bottoms and firm breasts of marble Venuses, admired prostrate goddesses spread naked in bucolic landscapes, stared at disrobing Susannas, bathing Dianas and seductive Europas. However, as true connoisseurs they aspired to be unmoved by these shows of classical flesh. In the practice of evaluating beauty, they prided themselves on their dispassionate stoicism and strove to unplug their animal reactions. It was a type of behaviour that many critics believed to have a detrimental effect on a man's sexuality. A connoisseur's 'dry aestheticism,' John Brewer explains, appeared 'to undermine his virility'. In relying exclusively on his gaze, the connoisseur 'risked becoming merely a passive spectator in the thrall of feminine beauty'. It was argued that 'looking took the place of anything more active'.

This could be a genuine problem where the connoisseur's wife was concerned, particularly as these men frequently 'failed to distinguish between canvas and flesh and blood'. According to the moralist, Hannah More, the connoisseur had an unfortunate habit of regarding his wife as merely another valuable object for display. As he might with an antique urn or a painting, he delighted in sharing her beauties with his associates, permitting her to 'escape to the exhibition room' where she could be shown as if she were not 'private property'. Just as Sir Richard Worsley had, his good friend and fellow antiquarian Sir William Hamilton fell into this trap. Renowned for his collection of art and artefacts, Hamilton also acquired an exceptionally beautiful mistress, Emma Hart who later became his wife. Emma, described by William Beckford as 'a breathing statue', was regularly placed on display at the collector's villa in Naples. Hamilton would invite his guests to a spectacle where his mistress, through an artful use of shawls, expressions and postures transformed herself into classical goddesses and heroines. Hamilton, so pleased with his animate *objet d'art* eventually created an appropriate display case for her, consisting of 'a chest . . . its front . . . taken off, the interior painted black and the whole set inside a splendid gilt frame . . . large enough to hold a standing human figure'. Given her exposure, it came as no surprise to anyone when, like Worsley, Hamilton became a willing participant in his own cuckolding by his friend, Admiral Lord Nelson.

These and similar incidents demonstrated to the eighteenth-century public that connoisseurship emasculated men. It detached them from the practical world and enslaved them to beauty. Overawed by women, they were incapable of discharging their masculine roles and performing sexually. As Thomas Rowlandson presented them in his cartoons *The Collectors* and *The*

Cunnyseurs, these were impotent fetishists, only able to admire and observe but not to please. The connoisseur may be a learned man, but he is also a confused buffoon, unable to grasp or admit that he delights in the unclothed female body. Worsley's identity as a member of the cognoscenti when coupled with his behaviour at the Maidstone bath instantly qualified him to be counted among these feeble and sexually dysfunctional specimens of masculinity. Accordingly, the lampoonists who attacked him embellished their depictions with references to his deficiencies. As Sir Richard treats Bisset to a view of his naked wife, the creator of *The Maidstone Bath, or The Modern Susanna* has strategically positioned a water spout shaped like a drooping penis at the height of the cuckold's crotch. The artist behind *A Bath of the Moderns* is even more explicit. By including the caption 'Lately discovered at Maidstone, by Sir Cuckledome Worse-Sly, Fellow of the Society of Antiqueerones', he draws a direct correlation between the 'queer' or sexually base activities of the Society of Antiquarians to which Worsley belonged and the behaviour of one of its Fellows.

To literate middle-class England, the connoisseur was a figure of suspicion and derision and Worsley's behaviour encouraged their preconceptions. To them he was a man with irregular sexual leanings, a deviant, an impotent, possibly even a homosexual. In their view he was so stupefied by his love of art and beauty that the dangers of displaying his wife as he might a painting or a piece of marble were entirely lost on him. For committing such a crime against common sense Worsley was regarded as an idiot, 'a block-head' with so little wit 'that it should be wondered how . . . horns could sprout from such barren soil'. Not only was he a cuckold but 'the sower and cultivator of his own towering antlers', a man who for his own stupidity should be 'naturally pitied'. In a period when the very essence of masculinity was defined by a man's ability to perform sexually and to beget children, these pictorial attacks tore into Worsley's dignity. Furthermore, in the mass consumption of such images Britain absorbed an entirely new impression of Sir Richard Worsley. Not only was it one that counteracted all that he had striven to correct since his father's death, wiping away years of skilful politicking and reputation honing, but it introduced his name to those who would not otherwise have known it. Infamy, not greatness, had projected him into the public consciousness.

If this was not devastating enough, the baronet was made to endure one further splash of mud. There were those sceptics who would always believe that Worsley had played some deliberate role in his wife's elopement. In spite of the fact that the jury had found to the contrary and decided in the plaintiff's favour – that he had not been 'privy to or consenting at all or contributing' to Lady Worsley's actions – many refused to accept this. A number of pamphlet writers when referring to the events of the case assumed a mocking tone, 'commiserating' that one with such 'an immaculate bosom', 'such an amiable man should suffer by fraud and deception'. How did it come to pass, questioned the author of *The Cuckold's Chronicle*, that on the night of the elopement, 'at this very crisis, poor Sir Richard finds himself indisposed and is necessitated to remain at home' and then 'waits till five in the morning . . . with a patience truly exemplary' to enquire as to his wife's whereabouts. The incredulous suspected connivance, possibly even collusion. As a result he was made to wear the additional epithet of scoundrel as well as that of cuckold and to bear the unjust accusation that he had attempted to defraud the justice system by arranging the entire event. One hack railed that for his 'vile compliance' he 'should be damned'. Many theorised that although he 'pled ignorance', Worsley had intentionally set up Bisset, his dear friend, for the purpose of extracting £20,000 from him. In the aftermath of the trial the public was willing to believe the worst.

But the public did not know the entire story. The scandal that had been loosened from its moorings at the court of the King's Bench was only half of the drama. The gossip-mongers thirsted for Lady Worsley's words. So far her lips had remained firmly sealed, but since the end of the trial, attention had turned in Seymour's direction. The public eagerly awaited her account of events.

17

'The New Female Coterie'

At the end of February, a plate of polished metal was affixed next to the door of a house on Harley Street. The brass square was so large that it was plainly visible to anyone passing down the road. A correspondent of the *Morning Herald* noticed it and, amused by its appearance, thought it worthy of mention. The sign suggested to him that 'the celebrated Lady Worsley was preparing to crow over her victory'. No longer 'resolved that her place of rendezvous be kept a secret' she had ordered 'an oval brass plaque as large as the panel of a coach' to be bolted on to her place of residence. On it appeared her name, boldly 'engraved in letters many inches long'. More than an indicator of her new address, this was an announcement to the world that Lady Worsley was unrepentant.

To the ordinary English woman, the seamstress bent over her stitching, the grocer's wife boiling puddings for dinner, the banker's daughter thumbing her way through the pages of *Pamela*, Lady Worsley would have seemed a perplexing creature. Whilst the act of eloping with her dashing lover may have captured the secret sympathies of the nation's novel-reading women, the revelation of the affair's sordid details would have disgusted even the more romantically minded. Seymour Worsley was a far cry from the pure-hearted heroines of books and plays. Instead, Lady Worsley, an heiress and the wife of a wealthy baronet, who led an existence to which the majority of the newspaper-devouring public aspired, had cast aside morality, comfort and dignity. More baffling still, she never once displayed a hint of regret.

At a time when convention governed every facet of a genteel woman's behaviour from her turns of phrase to the outward turn of her toes, Lady Worsley's indifference to notions of feminine delicacy was considered utterly indecent. As one anonymous moraliser wrote in 1780, the 'offence' given to society by a highborn woman's tumble from grace was much greater than that bestowed by any other female, as 'from her station' it had been 'incumbent upon her to have been an example of purity to the rest of her sex'. In the aftermath of the criminal conversation trial it was expected that Seymour would retreat from the public stage to weep privately for her lost character in a foreign cottage or the draughty rooms of some forlorn family estate. In the manner of Lady Sarah Bunbury and, later, Lady Mary Cadogan, she was meant to swallow disgrace like bitter medicine. Withdrawing from respectable company and its lavish entertainments, she was to wear her shame and mourn for the loss of her honour. Quite contrary to this, Lady Worsley displayed no intention of withdrawing from fashionable London life.

The denunciation of Lady Worsley's character which echoed from the courtroom of Westminster Hall heralded her initiation into the sisterhood of the 'fallen fair'. The final sentence of *Finical Whimsy* made it abundantly clear to readers where Seymour's future lay. By the end of February, she had 'already received the compliments of Lady Harrington, and Lady Grosvenor'; two women whose names were synonymous with intrigue and wantonness. Banished from polite society, Lady Henrietta Grosvenor reigned as the empress of the *demi-monde*, or 'half-world' as it translated from the French. Noted for her illicit amours, Lady Caroline Harrington presided as a queen 'demi-rep', a lady who barely clung to 'half of her reputation' by remaining married. Unlike *demi-mondaines* who 'dwelt on the fringes of respectable society' and were 'supported by wealthy lovers', a 'demi-rep' was, as Henry Fielding defined it, a woman of 'doubtful character', 'whom everybody thinks to be what nobody chooses to calls her'. They were among the select few of their sex who by virtue of their high birth could slip between the drawing rooms of the *haut ton* and the shadowy underworld.

The *demi-monde* existed as an alternative society, the establishment's polar opposite. Comprised of enchanting courtesans, coquettish actresses and divorced wives, it teased, intrigued and infuriated the virtuous world by mirroring everything that was celebrated in it. It rivalled its respectable counterparts, with its own beauties and fashion icons. The chaste daughters of shopkeepers and the wives of clergymen were just as likely to style their hair like the actress Ann Cateley and copy the gowns of the courtesan Mrs Robinson as they were to follow the trends set by the Duchess of Devonshire. Much to the fury of moralists, the homes of these Cyprians were as expensively furnished with Turkish carpets and polished silverware as the town houses of the elite. They had the temerity to charge through the streets of London in their own silk-lined coaches, in colours designed to flatter their complexions. Butlers and housekeepers opened their doors, liveried servants ordered their homes and lady's maids straightened their skirts. They made themselves as conspicuous as possible, flaunting their lovers' gifts, which glittered on their necks and ears as they sat in their theatre boxes.

The mix of envy, curiosity and po-faced horror which the *demi-mondaines* inspired fuelled the sales of newspapers. Henry Bate Dudley, founder of the *Morning Post*, one of the most successful publications, recognised the public's desire to reap more than just information from their daily paper. To the disdain of his competitors, Dudley filled his columns with gossip, reviews, poetry, sport, anecdotes and smut. When in 1781 his lucrative profits allowed him to launch a second publication, the *Morning Herald*, he single-handedly forced a revolution in British journalism. All other newspapers rushed to revise their content. The hunt for scandal and anecdotes to fill the sheets of newsprint became fierce. Not a day elapsed without some report of the caprices and movements of the *demi-monde* appearing in print. Their decisions to take lodgings in Bath or to set off for the continent, the costumes they wore to masquerades, the money they squandered at gaming tables, even the details of their lovers' tiffs, were all catalogued in the dailies. Much like modern celebrities, the *demi-monde*'s shamelessness accounted for much of its allure. Its inhabitants basked in their publicity and felt no compulsion to apologise for their excesses, since their lives were entirely underwritten by the titled, wealthy and the powerful; men like the Earl of Derby, the Duke of Dorset, the Duke of Grafton and the Prince of Wales.

Relegation to the outskirts of respectable life did not always end in abject ruin. Eighteenth-century instructive literature was unequivocal in its threat of a dark and dejected fate for those women who 'turned out off the right path'. Disowned by their beloved families and cherished friends, without the comforts of a home and bearing the scars of a sullied soul, a fallen woman was guaranteed to experience 'a great torment of guilt and misery' for abandoning her duties to both her husband and her children. Having 'lost the peace and happiness of their whole lives' they were certain to 'languish away and die most wretchedly'. John Fordyce in his *Sermons to Young Women*, one of the most widely read moral tracts, suggested far worse. Such debauched figures would in the eyes of society transmogrify into monsters, who smiled 'only to tempt' and 'tempted only to devour'. 'Their hands,' he wrote, 'are the hands of Harpies. Their feet go down to death, and their steps take hold on Hell.' Needless to say, having crossed the Rubicon into this sinister other world, many found this not to be the case. The scope for a woman to recover from a fall from grace was largely dependent on her financial circumstances and social standing, and those with titles often found themselves shielded from the full blow of complete disgrace. By far the most heart-wrenching experience in the tumble from honourable woman to *demi-mondaine* was the segregation from family and friends, especially close female associates whose company and counsel formed the backbone of an eighteenth-century woman's existence. In an era divided by gender, tightly bonded female communities were essential lifelines and channels of support. Mothers, sisters, cousins and aunts offered vital information about uniquely female experiences which not only encompassed advice on the physical body, pregnancy, sex, childbirth and hygiene, but intimate wisdom on personal relationships, etiquette and the trials and joys of life. Not surprisingly, the close circles that existed among women in the respectable realm were duplicated in the *demi-monde*. As Lady Worsley was to experience, intimate friendships were formed between members of the 'fallen sisterhood', who leaned as much on one another as they had on their now estranged family and friends. In Seymour's case, these new female companions were no less high-born than those she had left behind.

After her disgrace, the one woman of her extended family group who continued to receive Lady Worsley was the notorious but socially acceptable Caroline Stanhope, 2nd Countess of Harrington, her sister Jane's mother-in-law. Undoubtedly, the friendship offered by the much senior Lady Harrington was a comfort to Seymour, who was frequently seen in her company. By the 1780s, the Countess was entering the twilight years of her life. Known in her prime as the 'Stable Yard Messalina' and considered 'one of the *haut ton*'s most profligate toasts', she had led an existence steeped in sin. The least of her transgressions was that she used her home, situated near St James's Palace as an unofficial gambling house, even on Sundays, when the aristocracy and members of the royal family could be found gathered around her tables. The Countess was also known for 'making introductions' and acting as an unpaid procuress to many of her wealthy contemporaries. When not counting gaming chips and pairing peers with expensive prostitutes, she took lovers. *Town and Country* boasted that she had entertained so many paramours, 'from a monarch down to a hairdresser', that their names alone would have filled an entire page. When arranging for discreet places of rendezvous, the Countess had called on the services of Mrs Prendergast, the keeper of one of St James's most elite brothels on King's Place. Over the years, Sarah Prendergast proved to be a trustworthy friend, both to Lady Harrington and to her husband, who was known to society as 'the goat of quality' for his 'exceptional immorality'. It is believed that, between Lord Harrington's four times weekly visits to Mrs Prendergast's establishment and the retainers paid by his wife for use of the bawd's rooms, the couple almost single-handedly supported her enterprise.

Although the pair's reputation for lechery was widely acknowledged, respectable society was prepared to wink at their misbehaviour. Lady Caroline was the daughter of the Duke of Grafton and a member of one of the most influential families in Britain. Her husband, William Stanhope, a military hero and a politician, held the title of Viscount Petersham before succeeding to his father's earldom. The Earl and Countess moved in the highest circles, attending state occasions and royal functions. Regardless of Lady Harrington's misdemeanours, even the condemnatory and prudish, such as Horace Walpole and Lady Mary Coke, saw the advantage in coming to play loo in the Countess's drawing rooms. The merits of Lady Caroline's position spoke loudly enough for Lady Fleming and Edwin Lascelles to permit Seymour's sister to marry the Countess's son, Charles Stanhope. So long as Lord Harrington agreed to maintain her as his wife, Lady Caroline's character remained intact.

Lady Harrington enjoyed 'a frequent association with demi-reps' and other questionable characters whose companionship led to many 'injurious insinuations against her reputation'. As propriety barred her from receiving these acquaintances in her own home, the Countess made use of Mrs Prendergast's plush premises. Here she hosted a regular gathering of *demi-mondaines* who were dubbed 'The New Female Coterie'. The title, which was either self-appointed or given by Grub Street, was, with a pinch of irony, a reference to the Ladies' Coterie or Female Coterie, an exclusive club for 'women of quality' which met weekly in hired rooms at Almack's. Although the group admitted men by ballot, its founders were six 'fashionable ladies': 'Mrs Fitzroy, Lady Pembroke, Mrs Meynell, Lady Molyneux, Miss Pelham, and Miss Loyd'.

Quite bravely, the founders had decided to blackball Lady Harrington from the outset. According to Horace Walpole, the association came together 'every morning, either to play cards, chat, or do whatever else they please'. Dinner was provided if required and 'a supper to be constantly on the table by eleven at night', after which the assembled 'played loo'. Mrs Prendergast's undoubtedly offered a similar arrangement and variety of activities. For excluded women like Seymour, the opportunity to associate with others from similar backgrounds was invaluable. In ordinary circumstances, no respectable lady would be seen entering a house like Sarah Prendergast's, but the soiled reputations of Lady Harrington's guests liberated them from convention. Inside the sumptuously furnished abode, decorated with expensively uphol-stered chairs and sofas in the acidic greens and pinks of the Georgian era, this 'New Female Coterie' – whose core membership included the infamous Lady Henrietta Grosvenor, Lady Penelope Ligonier, Lady Margaret Adams and later Lady Derby, Lady Anne Cork and the Honourable Catherine Newton – sipped tea and champagne, laughed and gossiped.

It was through the introduction of Lady Harrington that Seymour formed an almost immediate affinity with Lady Grosvenor, a vivacious brunette who for nearly twelve years had lived as a social outcast. Henrietta Vernon had met her future husband, Richard Grosvenor, then the 1st Baron Grosvenor, in a rainstorm. A romantic but tumultuous married life awaited her. Within a month of their introduction in 1764, the couple were wed. Her father, Henry Vernon, an ambitious MP and Staffordshire landowner, heralded the union as a triumph, though in his haste to off-load one of his daughters to an aristocrat he neglected to study Lord Grosvenor's form for gambling and whoring. Considered 'one of the most profligate men, of his age, in what relates to women', not even matrimony could slow his progress through London's brothels. His appetite for vice extended to the gaming tables and racecourses where it is believed he lost in excess of £250,000.

It did not take long for the newly wedded Lady Grosvenor to realise that she had made a terrible error in tying herself 'to such a mate . . . for the sake of rank and title . . .' Disconsolate and feeling 'ill used', she eventually began an affair with Henry, Duke of Cumberland, the brother of the King. Unfortunately, the couple's elaborate schemes of letter exchange and illicit meetings were uncovered by the cuckolded baron. His pride trampled by a member of the royal family, Grosvenor asserted himself by bringing a charge of crim. con. against the Duke, which, after the publication of the adulterous pair's explicit correspondence, won him damages of £10,000. Much like the Worsleys' matrimonial dispute, Lady Grosvenor's battle with her husband did not conclude amicably. Determined to reveal Lord Grosvenor's hypocrisy, she sabotaged his plans for divorce by 'going into bawdy houses and other places to search and procure witnesses' who would testify to her husband's infidelities. The Grosvenors were officially separated in 1771. She was granted an annual allowance of £1,200, an insubstantial sum for a lady of the leisured class who allowed money to dribble through her fingers. Unskilled in the management of their finances, dispossessed women of her rank lived in a constant state of need which they could ease by accepting the sexual advances of wealthy men. Through the years Lady Grosvenor had become adept at padding out her living, while permitting onlookers to believe she was perfectly content with her carefree lifestyle. Frequently, the *Morning Herald* hinted at another reality; as it quipped in 1783, 'Lady Grosvenor has these several nights past been spotted in the green boxes with no fewer than three different beaux which our correspondent judges to speak as much of misery as it does of variety'.

The shared experience of public defamation through a criminal conversation trial drew the two women together. Ladies Grosvenor and Worsley were seen often 'in amorous league together', strolling arm in arm at the Pantheon or perched high above the throng at the theatre. Gossip sheets suggest that Seymour had a similar friendship with Lady Penelope Ligonier, another disgraced divorcee of Lady Grosvenor's acquaintance whom the *Morning Herald* spotted at Westminster Hall watching *Worsley* v. *Bisset*. Like Seymour, she too had been swept up in a passionate affair which ruined her marriage and her good name. Before the Worsleys' matrimonial dispute dominated the press, the affairs of Lady Ligonier and her ill-fated marriage to Edward, 2nd Earl of Ligonier had occupied that position. It was in Paris that the intellectually and musically gifted daughter of Lord Pitt Rivers met Captain Ligonier, the heir to a Surrey estate and a military man with a promising career. They were married in 1766 and returned to England shortly thereafter. While abroad, the Ligoniers made many distinguished foreign friends whom they later entertained at their home, Cobham Park. Among them was the Italian dramatist and poet, Count Vittorio Alfieri. In his memoirs Alfieri does not reveal the details of his relationship with Penelope Ligonier, only the adventure involved in the consummation of it. The Count's story is not lacking in romantic embellishment; he writes of furious rides from London to Cobham Park, of broken limbs, scaled garden gates, a jealous servant's betrayal and finally of a duel with an outraged Lord Ligonier. Alfieri escaped the fracas with a minor wound, but his mistress was not as fortunate. Ligonier proposed to divorce her, which he promptly did, but Alfieri refused to marry her and resuscitate her reputation because of rumours that she had taken her coachman to bed. With her reputation in tatters, she departed for France in 1771 and Alfieri 'most gallantly and politely accompanied her', along with her mother and, curiously, her loyal sister-in-law, Frances Balfour. Twelve weeks later, Lady Ligonier returned to England without the Count. On her father's request, she quietly took up residence in a cottage, a 'lonesome and dreary retreat' on the perimeter of the family estate. With an allowance from her husband of £600 per year, Penelope Ligonier settled for a quieter existence than her friend Lady Grosvenor. However, much to the satisfaction of the newspapers she also made regular appearances in London with a new lover, a Yorkshire landowner by the name of Locke. By 1784, two years after befriending Lady Worsley, she was again married, this time to a Captain Smith, 'a trooper in the Blues'.

What linked Lady Ligonier with her once respectably married sisters was a complete absence of remorse for her conduct. Twenty years after the conclusion of her affair with Alfieri she described the shape her life had taken in a candid letter to him. She expressed her gratitude to the Count for delivering her from the constraints of 'a world in which I was never formed to exist' and that she 'never regretted' abandoning 'for a single instant'. Throughout their affair she claimed to have been entirely sensible of her actions and to have foreseen the consequences of them: 'I thank Providence for having placed me in a more fortunate situation,' she wrote with hindsight. Freed from the restraints of convention she professed to 'enjoy perfect health, increased by liberty and tranquillity' and to seek 'only the society of simple and honest people, who pretend neither too much genius nor to too much knowledge, who blunder sometimes, and in default of whom I rest satisfied with my books, my drawings, my music, etc.' Although a life outside the boundaries of polite society held numerous disadvantages, the sentiments expressed by Lady Ligonier also attest to its merits. As Ladies Worsley and Grosvenor experienced, the loss of reputation closed many doors, while also opening others through which fulfilment might be found.

Due to a significant surge in criminal conversation suits and petitions for divorce, the disgraced but well-bred woman who roamed at large was becoming a more common figure in the late eighteenth century. Convention branded all women who had broken the prescribed sexual norms as whores, but fallen ladies of the landed class managed to float above the other members of their untouchable caste. Accordingly, the anonymous author of A *Congratulatory Epistle from a Reformed Rake*, published in 1758, placed 'Women of fashion who intrigue' at the top of his hierarchy of harlots, reigning far above the streetwalkers, expensive prostitutes and filthy beggars, who were thought to share an equally corrupt nature. More importantly, the possession of a title as well as a small maintenance allowance or alimony sum prevented disgraced former wives from being called courtesans. When describing the *bal d'amour*, a salacious masquerade held at Mrs Prendergast's brothel, the author of *Nocturnal Revels*, a chronicle of the sexual underworld in the late 1770s, is very specific about the differences between the two. Although the event was attended by a variety of celebrated 'votaries of venus', including Ladies Grosvenor and Ligonier, the author is quick to state that these 'Ladies refused any pecuniary gratification, and by that means distinguished themselves from the *Grizettes*'. Practically, however, the position of Ladies Grosvenor, Ligonier, Worsley and others tainted by separation or divorce differed little from that of the women beneath them. True security could only come from a gentleman's purse, and the pool of gentlemen willing to dispense their cash for sexual favours did not distinguish between a courtesan and a disowned baroness.

In the early 1780s, disgraced married women dominated the pricier end of the mistress market. Apart from the titled group of divorcees, three of the era's four most celebrated courtesans – Grace Dalrymple Elliott, Mary 'Perdita' Robinson, Gertrude 'The Bird of Paradise' Mahon, and Elizabeth Armistead – had entered into their profession as a result of ruined marriages. Grace Elliott, who later became a firm friend of Lady Worsley's, had been the young wife of an established physician before her romance with Lord Valentia sent her husband to Parliament petitioning for a divorce. Mary Robinson was the spouse of a debt-ridden lawyer who had taken to the stage and then to her pen in order to survive. The much sung Bird of Paradise, who had been born Gertrude Tilson, was the pretty niece of Lord Kerry who had shamed herself in a dubious marriage to the Irish gambler, Gilbreath Mahon. When too many rolls of the dice had worn through his money, Mahon abandoned her and fled abroad. Of the four, only Elizabeth Armistead had followed the conventional route; she rose to prominence through the exclusive 'nunnery' brothels of King's Place. With more obscure origins, these women and a constantly changing list of other names formed the corpus of the *demi-monde*. As a select division of the 'Cyprian corps', they were the true 'courtesans'.

While the membership of the New Female Coterie appears to have been restricted to previously married ladies of title, it welcomed the participation of these other 'sincere worshippers of . . . the loose rob'd Goddess of Delight and Tender Dalliance', especially Mary Robinson, who was currently in demand as a theatrical luminary. Such a congregation of controversial women was bound to excite the imagination of Grub Street and to pique the fear of respectable society. Catchpenny publishers slavered for tales of their deeds and records of their conversations. The author of a work entitled *The Court of Scandal* assumed that the *demi-mondaines* simply sat about exchanging lurid stories of their conquests. Others knew differently. Thomas Robertson, a friend of Lady Ligonier's and a hack who wrote for the salacious *Rambler's Magazine*, provided several months of copy on the Coterie's exchanges. Claiming to have been present at one of the 'assemblies', he described the gathering as a type of philosophical society, not unlike those which flourished among the learned middle classes.

In keeping with the traditions of Mrs Prendergast's house, these 'Cytherian Discussions', alternately chaired by the association's madam-president, Lady Harrington or by her protégée, Lady Worsley, were concerned predominantly with the subject of sex. From the mouths of Mrs Newton and Mrs Elizabeth Williams, a fellow adulteress and one of the guests of the society, came well measured philosophy with feminist undertones. During several meetings which Robertson attended, the members debated a number of rhetorical points, discussing the merits and demerits of marriage and posing questions which cut directly to the heart of the inequities of the male–female relationship. The group argued a case for situations in which adultery might be excused, such as in the procreation of children when 'our husbands are not competent to the purpose for which marriages were instituted'. The question of whether 'taking one lover constitutes a lesser crime than committing that faux pas with many' was also raised. However, most gatherings were likely to have been more frivolous, revolving around gossip and friendly chat and it was this light-hearted aspect that interested the newspapers most. The scandal sheet readers were more captivated by the public escapades of these doyennes of dissipation and their badly behaved admirers than they were by wider-ranging philosophical issues.

One of the many hypocrisies that underpinned the eighteenth- and nineteenth-century double standard was the custom which permitted gentlemen to mix freely with tarnished women while ensuring that their unblemished sisters never did. Lady Worsley's elopement shut off relations with respectable female companions but the names of her fashionable male acquaintance would hardly have altered at all. If anything, Seymour's fall drew her more tightly into the circle of the Prince of Wales. Along with titled *demi-mondaines* and courtesans, gambling blacklegs, scheming Whig politicians, actors, ageing roués and the dissolute sons of the landed classes flocked to the future George IV. Lady Grosvenor's former lover, the Duke of Cumberland, who was held responsible for corrupting the Prince, was a constant fixture in his nephew's life. He was joined by the alcoholic brothel-trawling Duke of Queensberry and men such as Banastre Tarleton and George Hanger, two of the worst-behaved 'bucks and bloods'. Not surprisingly, the names of the Marquess of Graham, the Earl of Peterborough, Viscount Deerhurst and Charles Wyndham were also listed among the Prince's friends at events where 'not a woman of rank was to be seen'.

The Prince of Wales and his wayward troop drank, danced, fornicated and gambled with feverish compulsion. By the end of 1781 the heir to the throne had tasted and tired of Mary Robinson, Elizabeth Armistead and Grace Elliott. He had exchanged his court duties for hunting excursions with his 'insolent and arrogant' friend, Anthony St Leger and consumed 'pailfuls' of wine with the actor, John Philip Kemble. He and his coterie scattered their inheritances between the card tables of Brooks's Club and the race-courses at Newmarket and York. A passion for gambling levelled the fortunes of many of the Prince's 'fast set', who, like Lord Stavordale, might lose '£11,000 at a game of Hazard' or win it back 'in one hand'. The rich and reckless, whether sober or soaked in alcohol, threw money at any outrageous stunt: whether in a race 'a turkey would out strip a goose' or if Banastre Tarleton could run 'fifty yards with Lord Mountford on his back in less time than the Duke of Queensbury trots a hundred and ten on any horse'. 'I do not know what to make of such fools . . .' wrote Madame du Deffand to Horace Walpole, '. . . I should never have believed it, if I had not seen for myself that there could be such madness'. One of the Prince's closest confidants, Charles James Fox, she believed 'to live in a sort of intoxication'. The unshaven, unkempt Fox kept a typical schedule, in one twenty-four-hour period going 'to dinner at past eleven at night; thence to White's, where he drank until seven the next morning; thence to Almack's where he won £6,000; and between three and four in the afternoon . . . he set out for the races at Newmarket'. In the view of many, the future monarch was surrounded by corrupt characters: a tribe of untrustworthy, extravagant libertines and whores. Appropriately, it was among their ranks that Lady Worsley and George Bisset found a natural home.

This band of morally reprehensible but influential gentlemen, who included Lords Deerhurst, Graham and Peterborough, as well as Lords Maldon, Cavendish and Jersey, were among the lovers' loyal friends. In a show of gratitude for their support, Sir Richard Worsley's wife organised 'a ball to all her beaus' which, the *Morning Herald* announced, was given 'Immediately after the determination of a late well known crim. con. trial in Westminster Hall'. With 'the eyes of the whole world, as well as the *ton* fixed on their movements', Seymour was determined to cause a stir. Her victor's ball would be the first of a series of public exhibitions designed to court attention and exact further revenge on her husband. While Worsley haggled over the possession of her clothing, jewels and the details of their separation, Seymour returned fire with a continued campaign intended to grind salt into his wounded pride.

George Bisset's defence lawyers had taught Seymour a useful lesson: her most powerful tactic when doing battle with her husband was to blacken her own name. The court case had revealed Worsley's conceited sense of honour to be his Achilles' heel. By continuing to shame herself she would, by virtue of sharing his surname, humiliate him as well.

The newspapers and Grub Street were all too pleased to assist her. In the second week following the trial, the *Morning Herald* was shocking its readership once more with allegations that 'A certain Lady lately convicted of having sacrificed too freely at the altar of Venus, is said for the sake of dear variety now to contrast her devotions, and to this pious purpose offers plentiful libations at the shrine of the jolly god Bacchus!' Few sights were considered more disgraceful than that of an intoxicated highborn lady. Even among the women of the *demi-monde*, certain basic codes prevailed. As a rule, drunkenness was for gin-swilling streetwalkers, not the elegant mistresses of noblemen. In a fit of heady abandon, Seymour had stepped into deeper realms of disgrace. On the 21st of April came another, equally aggressive stunt designed to embarrass Sir Richard. Londoners opened their newspapers the next morning to read that 'a grand subscription masquerade ball was given at the Pantheon' which 'surpassed anything of that kind we remember to have seen'. Moving through the opulent rooms adorned with 'superb looking glasses . . . festoons of flowers and nine medallions painted by Biaggio Rebecca' was the Prince of Wales, his associates and approximately 1,500 other individuals. While the guests hid behind their veils and disguises, Lady Worsley entered the scene unmasked. Her bare face invited spectators to note that she gloatingly conducted her champion, 'Lord Deerhurst round the rooms almost the whole evening'.

As the months of 1782 passed, the brazenness of Lady Worsley's attacks on her husband increased. The moral support of her *demi-monde* circle, together with Sir Richard's defeat in court, seemed to bolster Seymour and Bisset's conviction that they had been unfairly persecuted for following their hearts' desires. Their belief that their elopement was justifiable, regardless of its illegitimacy in the eyes of the law, the church and society, continued to intensify. Lady Worsley became adept at playing to her public gallery by dangling promises in newspapers and pamphlets, pledging 'to acquaint . . . the inquisitive world' with 'her reasons' for instigating the separation, without ever fulfilling them. Long into the summer months, the lovers were still seizing opportunities to display themselves and rouse comment. The *Morning Post* reported on the 23rd of July that while sitting in the 'green boxes of the Haymarket Theatre . . . Her ladyship hung her white cloak over the boxes as an emblem of her innocence'. The writer continued that, 'the two turtles seemed not only happy in their own dear society but in sporting their figures to the infinite sport of the audience'. Whether the audience's sport came in the form of cheers or jeers, is undisclosed.

18

Variety

The crowd that gathered on that July evening had eagerly pushed their way through the doors of the Haymarket Theatre and spilled into the pit. The wine merchant had escorted his wife to her seat, beside the ironmonger and his children. Servants in livery elbowed each other at the back; the cabinet-maker exchanged coy glances with the milliner's apprentice, one of many women fanning themselves vigorously against the stifling heat. Linen wilted and rivulets of sweat washed away carefully applied powder. People smoothed the backs of their skirts and lifted the tails of their coats before settling on to the hard benches and seats. With the stage before them and the boxes hanging at either side, they were ideally situated to watch as the drama of the playhouse commenced.

Georgian London came to the theatre not only to watch the performances advertised on the evening's playbills, but to partake in the unscripted dramas around them. High within the candlelit semicircle of the house was a network of smaller stages. Nightly, the players treading the boards found themselves in competition with the actors of fashionable society who drew the attention of the audience with their own unpredictable plots. The draped and fringed interiors of the boxes hosted a full slate of entertainments – scuffles between peers, melodrama as the gaze of a wife met that of a mistress, political posturing between Whig and Tory supporters and even the occasional pyrotechnical display as a lady's stacked coiffure dipped into an open flame. On the night Lady Worsley and George Bisset cast Seymour's white cloak over the rim of their box, the audience was midway through a long-running serial of which this performance formed only one scene.

As the spectators called out to the lovers in their roost, Lady Worsley failed to show the slightest hint of embarrassment or remorse. Seymour wore her fallen status with delight, knowing that her carefree attitude would encourage Grub Street to produce further ammunition in her war against Worsley. Weekly, her character was pelted with printed insults. There was no crime against decency which she was not accused of committing. She was called 'an utter enemy to all *amorous monopoly*', a woman who 'laid her wares open to every fair trader' and who had become 'a horrid Picture of Infamy'. They marvelled at her unfeminine shamelessness in 'fully declaring her innermost sentiments without the least reserve' and 'openly plunging . . . into the Gulph of Carnal Variety without pourtraying even an inclination of Reluctance'. Over the course of several months, Seymour's baiting of the press had produced the desired outcome. In addition to the mocking caricatures gummed into the engraving shop windows, the printers of Grub Street had unleashed a tide of pamphlets, poems and purported memoirs on to the booksellers' shelves. Lady Worsley's 'notorious frailty', wrote the *Monthly Review*, had been 'a lucky thing for the catchpenny authors, versemen and prosemen' who feathered their nests with her misfortune.

While her husband bore the brunt of the caricaturists' ridicule, Seymour was the satirists' favourite target. Aside from the frequently reprinted trial transcripts and almost daily reports of her activities in the newspapers, by July there were at least seven works which claimed to detail her exploits. The first of these, *The Whim!!!* a mildly erotic poem which turned the events of the Maidstone bath into rhyming couplets, appeared in early March. Two weeks later, *Variety, or Which is the Man?* stole its thunder. Borrowing its title from the two popular plays being staged at the time of the criminal conversation trial, this inflammatory poem enraged moral sentiment with its speculation on Lady Worsley's lewd inner thoughts. The need to find 'that rich jewel, Content' led her to 'taste *carnal infamy*', the work claimed, before listing a series of experiences with an assortment of 'swains' who had failed to please her. She sighs,

> All diff'rent these poor garbage were,
> Some fat, some lean, some brown, some fair;

In short thro' every change I went,
But ne'er cou'd find to keep *Content*.

At last, after running through 'a variegated train' of lovers, Bisset had captured her 'incessant wand'ring eyes'. The filthy poem's unapologetic tone scandalised its readers, and as the author had hinted that these were the actual thoughts of Lady Worsley, the pages were destined to fly off the booksellers' shelves.

For the remaining weeks of March and most of April letters were handed into the offices of the *Morning Post* speculating on the work's authorship. 'It is astonishing to what number of authors the new poem *Variety* . . . is attributed,' wrote the *Morning Post*. 'Some declare it to be the production of Lord———; others say, who pretend to be in the secret, that it is written either by Mr Sheridan or Mr Tickell . . . but we can assure the public that this popular poem is not the production of either of these gentlemen.' On the 17th of April, the newspaper announced, 'After all the various conjectures concerning the real author of the poem *Variety* we can assure the public from indisputable authority that this popular poetic trifle is the production of a creature of Sir Richard Worsley's in order to expose his Lady in as ignominious a manner as possible', but this proved to be untrue. The baronet wrote to the editor himself to deny the claim and asked for a note of correction to be printed the following day, stating that 'the paragraph inserted in this paper yesterday asserting the above poem to be written by a creature of Sir Richard Worsley's is an impudent falsehood, and without the least foundation whatsoever'. This came only a week after another declaration had appeared, that 'The author of Variety . . . intends to shortly avow himself in the public papers in order to prevent all future controversies upon that subject.' He never did come forward.

Amid this confusion, Seymour chose to remain silent. The public were growing increasingly anxious to hear Lady Worsley's own voice, to have a justification for her debauched and unrepentant behaviour. They wanted to know her side of events, they desired an explanation for her elopement, a description of the horrors or all-consuming lust which drove her to abandon her husband. Instead, Seymour kept them waiting. In the last week of March, her decision to send 'one of her servants on Saturday morning to Mr Swift, on Charles St, St James with orders to purchase fifty copies of the new poem published by him entitled, *Variety or Which is the Man?*' baffled the public.

Was this an attempt to quash the work by removing an entire print run of fifty pamphlets from Mr Swift's shop? The *Morning Post* concluded to the contrary, commenting, 'the only reason which our correspondent can give for her singling out this poem from among many hasty productions that have made their appearance on the same subject is to distribute copies of it amongst her gallants that they may no longer be deceived with the flattering idea of their superiority over her affections but shew them the real man on whom she has fixed her attachment!' With neither a confirmation nor a denial that *Variety* represented Lady Worsley's true feelings, the curious continued to exchange their shillings for a peek between the covers. Like the Pye Donkin trial transcripts which were still spinning off the presses, *Variety*, 'due to uncommon demand', went through at least seven reprints in roughly six weeks. Two of London's more prominent booksellers, William Swift and Son and George Kearsley, could not replenish their stocks quickly enough and were prepared literally to fight in order to corner this lucrative trade in Worsley dross. At the height of the furore, as the printing presses were grinding out stanzas of *Variety* past midnight, the *Morning Post* reported that 'A challenge was lately sent by Mr Kearsley the bookseller to Mr Swift . . . to fight him near the Powder Mills, Hounslow Heath'. Gratefully, 'the dispute was amicably adjusted' without the need for bloodshed.

By April, *Variety*'s sensational subject matter had inspired not only a duel but an artist's imagination. Until now, Lady Worsley had avoided being the focus for caricaturists' ridicule, but James Gillray, the artist responsible for savaging her husband, was about to turn on her. Although lampoonists had taken every opportunity to fill their tablets with representations of her exposed breasts, naked hips and hiked-up skirts, no printmaker had dared to depict the rapacious whore of *Variety*'s verses with her conquests. Gillray's cartoon, *A Peep into Lady W!!!!y's Seraglio*, sprang from the *The Whim*'s introductory address, where the author reminds Seymour of 'a conversation with some officers' when she had 'expressed a wish . . . to form a *Male Seraglio*'. It was further whetted by the imagery from *Variety*'s couplets, in which she boasts of taking a 'strange motley crew' to her bed. From these points of inspiration the caricaturist created his licentious picture of Lady Worsley.

Along a staircase leading down to Seymour's bedchamber are nine assorted admirers, anxiously awaiting their turn. The 'Messalina of the Modern Age' can be seen in a cut-away, eagerly straddling her partially smothered partner. 'Give all thou canst and let me dream the rest!' she exclaims between kisses.

Her victim's troubled gaze suggests that the request has taxed him to his physical limits. Lady Worsley's insatiability had already laid waste to his predecessor, who is seen weakly pulling up his britches while limping out the back door. 'O dear,' he moans, 'I believe it's all over with me.' Where Seymour's libido is concerned, however, there is little cause for worry; the next of her stallions stands at the ready. With his ear against the door awaiting his cue, a fashionably dressed young man looks to his companion and comments, 'Hark! My turn's very near!' Smiling with anticipation his friend urges him, 'Then do pray be quick.' Behind this pair is an irritated figure in military dress, bearing an uncanny resemblance to Gillary's image of Sir Richard Worsley in his other lampoon, *Sir Richard Worse-than-Sly*. With hands on hips, he snarls over his shoulder at a bearded Jew with whom he argues. 'Tish!' exclaims the Yiddish speaker. 'My turn's to be served before you.' The Worsley character regards him impassively while grumbling, 'You lie, Sir. Damme.' Behind this feuding duo is an impatient man in country dress; with his walking stick tucked under his arm, he jostles the throng. 'Yoiks,' he calls out. 'Hark forward below there.' The next in the queue is more relaxed. A fat clergyman, half asleep on his feet is yawning broadly, resigned to a long wait. The thin fop who breathes down his neck is more agitated. Squinting into a pair of pince-nez spectacles, he surveys the long line and sighs, 'Bless me, when will my turn come?' He will not have to endure a wait as lengthy as the two rakish friends at the back end of the queue. 'Zounds my time will never come,' complains the last, grasping his head in frustration. His cheerful associate looks at him and laughs, 'Ha, ha, ha, the Devil take the hindmost, say I.' As the viewer pulls back from the drama, Gillray's commentary can be read on the architecture. Borrowing from the seventeenth-century playwright, Nicholas Rowe, he has framed the scene along the staircase with a quote from *The Fair Penitent*: 'One lover to another still succeeded. Another and another after that – And the last Fool is welcome as the former: Till having lov'd his hour out he gives place, And mingles with the herd that went before him.' Over Lady Worsley's bedchamber is placed a subtle, but stinging jest: a portrait of the chaste Lucretia, a Roman heroine so determined to preserve her virtue that she killed herself after a rape robbed her of it.

As shrewd men and women of business, London's booksellers and printmakers knew how to capture the public's waning attention. Affixing *A Peep into Lady W!!!!y's Seraglio*, described as 'an elegant frontispiece, designed and etched by an eminent artist', to the fifth and sixth editions of *Variety* was a foregone conclusion. Attaching a salacious picture to the lurid poem breathed further life into it. The publication's runaway success seemed unstoppable, until the 20th of April. On that morning the *Morning Post* ran a simple advertisement: 'Published today, *An Epistle from Lady Worsley to Sir Richard Worsley* printed by P. Wright'. The pamphlet was the one for which everyone had been waiting. Lady Worsley had spoken.

An Epistle from Lady Worsley to Sir Richard Worsley met the same frantic demand as its predecessors. By the end of the day, those who had sent their servants down to 'The Booksellers of Paternoster Row, Piccadilly, the Strand, the Fleet and the Royal Exchange' in the hope of buying a bound edition were 'to meet with disappointment'. The excited readers waiting for Lady Worsley's purported confessions were entirely unaware that this latest piece of Grub Street drivel had not been designed to answer their questions or even to titillate them. Rather, this production, composed by an anonymous hack, was the latest and biggest cannonball in Seymour's arsenal and she intended to fire it at her husband. Its strategic arrival on the booksellers' shelves was evidence of a continuing siege. Behind the public façade, pasted with engravings of Maidstone baths and cuckolds and decorated with slanderous verse, the legal battle of *Worsley* v. *Worsley* continued to rage.

For a variety of reasons, some of which are not entirely documented, Worsley's suit for Separation from Bed and Board faced a number of obstacles. Disagreements between the parties about the conditions of the separation continued long after the proceedings at Doctors' Commons had concluded in late February. In the early spring of 1782 Lady Worsley's most immediate concern had been her missing clothing. On the day after the trial, brimming with a victor's confidence, Seymour had 'appeared personally' alongside her solicitor Robert Dodwell at the Consistorial Episcopal Court in London to register her complaints in the form of a lawsuit. It was claimed that 'at the time of her separation' Lady Worsley 'took no other wearing apparel with her than what she wore at the time', and that in the intervening months she had 'received but very few cloaths and wearing apparel' from her husband. In spite of 'applications . . . repeatedly made to his agents to deliver the [clothing]' Worsley had 'consistently made a refusal' to give the items to her. No refutation of these accusations was forthcoming. As the baronet had gone into hiding following the trial's calamitous verdict, his solicitor, James Heseltine could only request time 'to verify . . . the truth of some matters'. Sir Richard was ordered to give an answer by the last day of the legal quarter.

Worsley's response to his wife's action was contemptuous. He made no effort to abide by the judge's request, choosing instead to ignore the edict and to address the issues at his leisure.

This was a game of wills and the baronet was stalling. His possession of Lady Worsley's clothing and jewels was one of his last levers of influence. The law had robbed him of justice, leaving him with little alternative but to mete out punishment in the way he saw fit. As his wife waited anxiously for her urgently required wardrobe, Worsley stubbornly sat on his hands. What he hadn't expected was his wife's outrage. In each of his attempts to trample Seymour's schemes and to contain her behaviour, he had failed, underestimating at every turn the ferocity he inspired in her. Lady Worsley's reaction to her husband's prevarication was swift. Prior to the trial, she had threatened to publicly denounce Sir Richard. Without an opportunity to defend her actions in court, she had no choice but to turn to the print media if she wanted to make her side of events known. Now, frustrated and furious, she was ready to fulfil that promise and 'fully declare her innermost sentiments without the least reserve'.

Like *The Maidstone Whim* and *Variety*, Lady Worsley's proclamation was written in verse by a hired scribe. A skilfully crafted work of insults and libertine philosophy, the *Epistle* is deeply vitriolic. 'Detested Man!' she barks at Worsley in the first line of her address, 'To Thee I write, no follies to confess'; instead, in this pronouncement it was her 'chief delight to own' that the baronet never satisfied her. Then, for the next sixteen pages, she elaborates on her complaints.

Foremost among these was what the lampoonists had already guessed: Sir Richard was impotent. That which 'from thine arms I never could receive' had driven her to seek comfort in the beds of his associates. After all, she claims, 'man was a creature made our wants to bless', and if 'husbands can't perform their dues' then 'surely they should excuse . . . The working passions of the tender Dame'. Then she twisted the knife; his good friend Bisset was quite capable of satisfying her,

> From him no teizing titillations came;
> He rais'd those passions which he well could tame

'Oh!' she cries, taunting him with the joys of her betrayal;

> ... had you seen me on his breast reclin'd
> Lips glu'd to lips, and limbs with limbs entwin'd
> With oft repeated acts of dalliance spent,
> My lust quite sated, and my heart content.

According to Seymour, Worsley was too effete, too foppish to please her, or any woman for that matter. She grouped him among the 'impotent Italian Beaux', a euphemistic reference to homosexual men. Failing to provide 'a more substantial food', such macaronis 'only serve to tantalize the Fair'. These are not real men, those 'Whose joy it is to flutter at a play' or who pass their time repeating 'the news or scandal of the day'. Lady Worsley's desire is for a man of physical and emotional substance, someone of 'intrinsic worth, not tinsel clothes'. Her husband, the antiquarian, the artistic patron, the enlightenment thinker, driven by rational thought rather than passionate feelings, bored her. 'Let other senses have an equal share,' she exclaimed with the enthusiasm of a Romantic, 'Nor think all pleasure center'd in the ear!'

Lady Worsley suggested that love played no role in the baronet's decision to wed her. Rather, it was the 'base chinking of *Ten Thousand Pound*' that had enticed him. As affection had always been absent from their marriage, their relationship was soon eroded. Referring to herself as 'the Wife whom Fortune made you wed', she eventually came to 'detest' his bed and 'loath' his name. On her part, she admits, it was her youthful capriciousness and 'inconstant charms' that brought her 'once a Virgin to thine arms'. However, marriage to Sir Richard held only disappointment. She felt like 'Some hapless *Fatima* . . . in some seraglio's dismal gloom', a 'solitary wretch' who, completely alone, 'tells to heav'n . . . her inward pains'. Removed 'from her country and her friends', but

> With pomp surrounded, impotently gay,
> In groans she spends the night, in tears the day:
> Compell'd alas! In horrid grandeur drest,
> To kiss the man her feelings must detest

The censorious world should show some pity, she declared, as such a fate 'might shock the hardest heart'.

She points her finger at Worsley for making her into what she became.

Although she possessed many 'charms' which lured men, these alone were not responsible for her or her husband's ruin:

> For wer't not THOU the *author* of thy shame?
> – what madness Worsley could possess thy brain,
> To help a Wife to an admiring swain?

A wife's 'desire' can not be blamed 'When Husbands are the cause' of their undoing, she continues. A woman is then free to 'Sneer at all discipline, and break their laws . . . And shew no dread of punishment, or G——d!' After all, as a married woman, a 'knowing, well-experience'd Dame', she has an entitlement to 'Enjoy the pleasure, and despise the shame'. And so, following 'nature's liberal plan', she admits to him that, ''tis true I fled, in hopes to find a pleasure equal to my lustful mind'.

The *Epistle* made clear to its readership that by the age of eighteen its heroine had found herself locked in a sexually dysfunctional and loveless marriage to a man with whom she was incompatible. Feeling isolated, emotionally unfulfilled, and finding her husband physically repulsive, her despondency soon grew into resentment, and eventually into hatred. This sentiment, which her separation hearings and disputes surrounding her belongings had been keeping fresh, throbs through the poem's stanzas. Cursing Worsley's vindictive decision to apply for a Separation from Bed and Board rather than a liberating divorce, she cries;

> And must I live; yet breathe this vital air;
> And must I then this name for ever bear?
> Yet, thanks to fate! The name remains alone,
> for all the duties of a wife are flown!

Although shackled to him in name only, and despite Worsley's 'decree' that she 'should be from such a Tyrant freed', 'this one deed' alone, she proclaims, is not enough to lessen the revulsion she feels towards him. 'I gratefully confess . . .

> If it was possible – I'd hate thee less;
> But fixt and firm as unrelenting fate
> Is my determin'd, everlasting hate

Their union has been truly crushed, their enmity as immovable as that of political opponents;

> Sooner shall Sackville be to Saville join'd;
> With Sandwich, Richmond, North with Fox combin'd;
> Than thou again should'st be ally'd to me,
> Or I again be ever [fucked] by thee.

With one strike of the pen, *An Epistle from Lady Worsley to Sir Richard Worsley* hit precisely the right note to raise a chorus of public outrage. The long-anticipated confession was everything that the followers of the Worsley scandal had been hoping. Depraved, yet elegantly written, it stunned society and generated a confused outpouring of condemnation, fascination and praise. Within three days of its publication, letters began streaming into the offices of the *Morning Post* and the *Morning Herald*. The work was 'certainly one of the most licentious and immoral productions that has been issued from the press for some time', wrote one indignant correspondent, who claimed that it was rare to find vice 'painted in such specious colours and morality and virtue so totally ridiculed'. Sensibilities had been so inflamed by this 'obscene trash' that no general consensus could be reached as to who was the most morally blameworthy: the author, the subjects or society for enabling the pamphlet to sell so successfully. After examining the *Epistle*, one *Morning Herald* reader decided that Lady Worsley came out of the situation all the worse, as her 'conduct is . . . rendered still more unpardonably vicious than the world has before supposed it'; further still, 'she leaves us at a loss to know which we are most to detest, the very extraordinary supineness of the husband or the libidinous and insatiable passions of the wife'. Another believed that the publication shamed the baronet more deeply. Even though 'The World has been led to imagine that Lady Worsley has been solely culpable', in her *Epistle*, where she 'endeavours to vindicate her own conduct', it is her husband who is painted 'in the most severe and detestable colour'. Scorn was also heaped on society at large by a moraliser who wrote to the *Herald* in order to vent his spleen on this 'instance of the licentiousness and depravity of the times'. 'The . . . eagerness with which the whole fashionable world purchase *An Epistle from Lady Worsley to Sir Richard Worsley*' was 'very shameful'. 'It abounds with severe satire, indelicate sentiments and corrupt morals', he comments, and certainly '. . . it would be much more commendable for persons of distinction instead of exerting themselves to promote its popularity to do all in their power to suppress it'.

Contrary to the wishes of the high-minded, the pamphlet continued to sell by the bundle. It was available to buy 'at every bookseller in London and all of the principal ones in every city and town in England'. By the first of May, it was reported that 'a capital bookseller at the west end of the town has orders to send 500 copies to a neighbouring kingdom', 'a number quite sufficient to corrupt the minds of all its inhabitants', commented the *Morning Herald*. In the spring of 1782, anyone possessing the faintest grasp of literacy, from the shop clerk to the gentleman of leisure, was burying their nose between the indecent pages of Lady Worsley's *Epistle*. According to one of the newspaper's more irate correspondents, where moral principles were concerned, the situation had truly spun out of control. Returning from an afternoon at the Royal Academy's summer exhibition he put pen to paper in a fit of righteous anger. At this polite location, the site of an annual show-case of taste and talent, he 'observed two young married ladies of fashion (whose names will be concealed) perusing this luscious morsel [the *Epistle*] in place of a catalogue of the pictures'; even more disturbingly, they 'were commenting in the loosest terms on one of its most obscene passages, a single line of which is quite sufficient to call a blush to the cheek of those who have the least pretensions to modesty'. Ruefully, he concludes that 'It is a shocking thing to think [at] what a shameful pitch libertinism is now arrived', when even 'ladies of the first fashion and distinction' are no longer 'ashamed' to be seen reading such filth and can 'go publicly into the booksellers' shops to purchase it'.

Frustratingly for moralists, the *Epistle* could not be so easily condemned. Although its sentiments were lewd, what made it especially dangerous was its recognised 'poetical merits'. Critics were forced to acknowledge that where literary style was concerned, *An Epistle from Lady Worsley to Sir Richard Worsley* was deemed to 'surpass all modern productions'. 'The lasciviousness of . . . [the] ideas might be almost pardoned,' wrote one of the *Post*'s aficionados, 'on account of the singular purity of the diction, and the unspeakable elegance of the versification'. Even the esteemed Dr Johnson was compelled to comment 'that it is without exception the best written poem that has made its appearance for these many years'.

Naturally, speculation as to the authorship was rife. As the verses contained such intimate information and the sentiments were so convincingly expressed, eyes turned immediately in the direction of Lady Worsley. However, as the publication was celebrated for its literary skill many remained sceptical. If this really was 'her own production she must evidently stand unrivalled as a poetical genius by any of the modern race of females', wrote the *Morning Post*. Another of the newspaper's correspondents continued that, although he could 'readily give her credit for the depravity of the sentiments and the indelicacy of the ideas', he had been 'well assured her ladyship does not possess talents that can for a moment justify the probability of its being her own production'. If Seymour herself was not capable of creating such a masterpiece then certainly the *Epistle* must have been a joint endeavour, the work of that terrifyingly immoral intellectual sisterhood, the New Female Coterie whom Lady Worsley mentions in her poem as meeting 'at midnight . . . in close divan', planning 'future schemes of happiness with man'. According to one of the *Morning Herald*'s 'correspondents of the ton', the publication bore all the witches' marks of the Coterie's pens. He 'affirmed' that he 'well knows the pamphlet . . . to be the joint production of Lady Grosvenor, Lady Worsley, Mrs Robinson and several others of the amorous corps – who are enumerated in the . . . epistle'; after all, 'such ideas could only flow from the imagination of a juncto of such characters in conjunction'. The league of *demi-mondaines* maintained their silence on the issue of the author's identity, though Lady Worsley eventually did step forward to put an end to the conjecture 'that she is the authoress'. 'Although the production is not mine,' she claimed, 'the sentiments it contains flow from my very soul.'*

In the months since the criminal conversation trial, Seymour had grown especially savvy in her ability to manipulate the press. Although they may not have realised it, the booksellers and printers along Fleet Street had been drafted into her crusade against Sir Richard. It served Lady Worsley's interest to make a spectacle of herself and it benefited the publishers to let her. Her scandals sold their pamphlets and their pamphlets were pure poison for her husband's reputation. Since the baronet had refused to free her with a divorce, she would drag their shared name through the dung. As she had anticipated, the *Epistle*, her latest tug at Worsley's chain, had brought about a reaction. Finding himself under renewed assault, the baronet abandoned gossipy London and took shelter in Epsom with Captain Leversuch and his family. Here, seven days after the publication of the verses, Worsley rode to Guildford in

---

*The author of the *Epistle* has never been identified but was most likely a Grub Street poet.

order to appear before a registrar. He decided to settle the matter of his wife's 'wearing apparel'.

Sir Richard swore via oath that he had recently given 'orders to Mary Sotheby and Lucetta Jones, two servants in my family to collect together the cloathes and wearing apparel of my wife . . . in order that they might be delivered to her'. These articles and 'other ornaments of her person' were then, on his orders, sent to Lady Worsley. He confirmed that this comprised everything, 'all the cloathes and wearing apparel' left in his custody, before pausing and adding, '. . . save and except the jewels and a quantity of fine and common laces, most of which had been worn by Lady Worsley while she cohabited with me'. These items 'of great expense' he announced defiantly, 'I . . . detain in my custody'. This would not be an absolute capitulation. Although he now stood in contempt of a court order, he was loath to allow her all that she demanded. The baronet would not permit £7,000 worth of gold and precious gems to simply slide through his fingers; some of it, he would argue, had been purchased with his money. What became of the two gowns of fine point lace is unknown, and the jewels were later sold by mutual consent rather than returned.

The ripples caused by the *Epistle* were felt in areas beyond Sir Richard and Lady Worsley's private lives. Its success had demonstrated to hungry publishers that there was profit still to be milked from the Worsleys' stories. In less than a fortnight after the *Epistle*'s sensational appearance, *The Memoirs of Sir Finical Whimsy and His Lady*, a work which disclosed the secret history of the couple's flawed marriage became available for public consumption. The pamphlet jostled for attention with *The Genuine Anecdotes and Amorous Adventures of Sir Richard Easy and Lady Wagtail* which arrived just over a week later. The race to publish these exposés was intense, as the author of this later pamphlet concedes that midway through his narrative he 'was almost induced to drop the pen upon seeing an advertisement in the papers of the publication of *The Memoirs of Sir Finical Whimsy*'. Rather than 'committing these pages . . . to the flames' he 'immediately communicated them to the printer'. Well into the second half of the year, a steady flow of witty rhymes and bawdy dialogue, such as that featured in *A Poetical Address from Mrs Newton to Lady W——*, *The Devil Divorced*, and *The Whore. A Poem Written by a Lady of Quality*, continued to dry on the racks of the printing shops. By the end of the summer the *Monthly Review* was writing with exasperation that 'surely the public are, by this time tired of Lady Worsley whatever may be the case with respect to her husband or her gallants'. They weren't.

Sir Richard, unlike his wife, had no wish to court publicity or flirt with the press. He wanted to remain invisible until the newspapers and Grub Street were distracted by another wealthy cuckold's misfortunes. Undoubtedly, the longevity of the scandal's appeal, which was continually fed by Lady Worsley's antics, surprised him. The appearance of the *Epistle* was for him the final straw. If Seymour had learned to utilise the press to smear his name, he might harness it in order to defend himself. Exactly two months after the publication of *An Epistle from Lady Worsley to Sir Richard Worsley* the baronet offered a response. *The Answer of Sir Richard Worsley to the Epistle of Lady Worsley*, a reply in verse, issued from his own pen.

As Sir Richard had not hired a poet to express his sentiments, the hurt and betrayal in his verses is more immediate. He, 'thy suppliant husband', pleads with her to be moved 'by compassion's tear, if not connubial love' to end her public persecution of him. It is the ceaseless defamation of his name which he finds unbearable, that 'the Grub Street Syrens . . . now strain their hackney'd throats with *Worsley's* name, and *Worsley's* crimes and *Worsley's* verse proclaim'. What must he do, the baronet begs, 'to save from Slander's tongue my injur'd name?' before displaying, in heartfelt words, his injuries;

> Too late I now complain – the fatal dart
> Grows to my side, and rankles in my heart.
> The whisper'd tale escapes from ear to ear,
> Lurks in a smile, and wounds me in a sneer.

Unable to endure her battery of words and humiliating stunts, Worsley concedes defeat. The actions he has taken, defensive or otherwise, seem only to rebound on him. 'Fruitless is my aim', he confesses, 'and vain the toil', as 'Back on myself the blunted darts recoil'. Lady Worsley's scheme to 'damn us both to never dying fame' by swelling 'our mutual shame' had been successful.

In addition to stirring the reader's sympathy for what he had suffered by his 'insatiate wife's' behaviour, Worsley used his *Answer* to denounce his betrayers. Sir Richard wanted the world to see that Seymour was not solely responsible for his disgrace. The blame could equally be laid at the feet of the so-called gentlemen who had breached the masculine honour code and colluded against him in court. As he had with Bisset, he regarded this treachery as a severe crime, as serious as the one committed by his wife. While acknowledging that Lady Worsley could have kept silent about the freedom he granted her and allowed him 'to have tamely borne, the destin'd horns, unknowing . . .' he would not have been made 'the leader of the cornute band', the king of the cuckolds, were it not for her conspirators. It was with their assistance that 'at a public bar', the Court of the King's Bench, his 'follies reign'd, the food of ev'ry ear'. Accordingly, Worsley's condemnation of this 'too victor'ous band', these 'young nobles' whose lives are ruled by 'am' rous joys and wanton loves', is sharp. 'You', he addresses them, 'who on record betray'd' me must remember that it is 'by noble deeds' that one will acquire 'a deathless name', not through acts of 'am'rous dalliance' with an insatiable Messalina whose sexual desires even 'your efforts never could remove' and who *you*, the renowned lovers, were ultimately incapable of satisfying. 'I rise above your breed,' the baronet boasted with angry arrogance, and 'More splendid honors deck my greater name'.

Throughout his *Answer* Worsley does not shy away from suggesting that his passions are not as 'fired' as that of his wife's. He refers to himself as a man 'of old', who looks to the cool, rational behaviour of the ancients and who admires 'the gorgeous temple of Diana', representative of chastity and restraint. The baronet offers no apologies for his sexual shortcomings and writes with surprising candidness about his bedroom failures;

> . . . I try'd the combat to sustain,
> Then first essay'd, but first essay'd in vain.
> Exhausted, spent, unequal to the fight,
> I wish'd the morn, and curst the ling'ring night.

His wife's appetite wore him out and although he was 'oft' entreated to pursue the race' he eventually came to 'shun . . . the loath'd embrace'. Worsley seems not to have cared what impact this admission might have on his masculine reputation. To his mind, Seymour's 'boundless rage of lust' was unnatural in a woman. In response to the *Epistle*'s attack on 'modern Beaux', with 'their looks, their air' and their 'pretty forms', he springs to their defence. He claims that she regards them as 'a doubtful sex', not 'men, nor women, yet so mix'd together' simply because they cannot staunch her lava flow of sexual desire. Worsley then makes a frank admission and addresses her directly; you have been urging 'me in print with vaunting terms' to explain why

> I, th'acknowledg'd guardian of thy fame,
> Should, like a pander, prostitute thy name,
> And at a public bath in open day,
> To the wild gaze of youth thy charms display?
> What madness, dost thou say, could fire my brain,
> To help a wife to an admiring swain?

And so he confesses that he had hoped to lighten his own burdens and 'calm thy mad wishes' through the assistance of other men, 'brought . . . jointly to my aid'. Only then, he believed might 'Their *pointed efforts* . . . have cool'd thy flame'.

Although Worsley concludes his missive with the same venomous sentiments expressed by his wife that he 'hates her person' as much as he 'dreads her heart', he intended to use the *Answer* not as a destructive weapon but a defensive one. Since February, the baronet had been subjected to a relentless tide of slander. His appeal to the public's sympathy was an attempt to stop the attack as well as to counter Lady Worsley's accusations. He did not wish to rekindle Grub Street's dwindling memories of his 'twelve penny verdict' or to once again cause society's critics to pass moral judgement against him. Instead, he wanted to issue a subtle but effective rebuttal.

The Answer of Sir Richard Worsley to the Epistle of Lady Worsley was printed once. It could be purchased at the shops of only three booksellers. In spite of having the Worsley name in its title, which would have guaranteed its sale at bookstalls across the British Isles, its availability was confined to the capital alone. Beyond an announcement of its publication on the 21st of June, the newspapers did not mention it. By bribing the *Morning Herald* and the *Morning Post* as well as the two most scandal-laden monthly journals, *Town and Country Magazine* and the *Rambler*, Sir Richard had taken the usual precautions to ensure that his verses would not be discussed, satirised or debated. It is likely that he knew his response would not bear too much scrutiny, that there would be only ridicule, not public sympathy for a man who could neither satisfy nor control his wife and who used his lack of virility as a defence for his actions. It is also probable that he feared his work would prompt others to come forward with additional tales of his sexual failings. At the time of publication, rumours were already in the air that Worsley had once pursued a number of fashionable courtesans, but that Sophia Baddeley, Elizabeth Armistead, Gertrude Mahon and Kitty Frederick had all jilted him for unspecific reasons. The author of *The Genuine Anecdotes and Amorous Adventures of Sir Richard Easy and Lady Wagtail* claimed that the baronet had been 'frustrated in the amorous pursuit' and that he was 'despised by the first rate *impures*'. Vanity, rather than lust had been his motive for courting them.

Fleet Street and Grub Street had become Sir Richard's persecutors and they dogged him to the point of despair. Their printed words and satires spread like poison into every corner of society, ensuring that knowledge of his misdeeds was distributed equally among men of politics, religion and law. It was with this last group that his greatest concern lay. Through the first half of May 1782, his suit for a Separation from Bed and Board was still pending at Doctors' Commons. On the 15th, Judge William Wynne announced his decision to approve the separation. As anticipated, Lady Worsley was awarded the continuance of her annual pin money, amounting to £400. Additionally, her widow's jointure 'of two thousand pounds per annum' and 'the use of a dwelling house for her life . . . at the rent of three hundred pounds per annum' were safeguarded. To the baronet's annoyance, this clause also contained a number of perks, such as her entitlement to £200 worth of 'household linen, china, furniture and plate' that she might select from 'his town dwelling house at his decease'. His wife would be well provided for in the event of his death. While these terms were not as severe as he had wished, to his mind they were not wholly unreasonable either. However, Judge Wynne's legal ruling contained something far more objectionable.

It is likely that a Separation from Bed and Board had appealed to Worsley's frugal instincts as well as his need for revenge. In contrast to a parliamentary divorce, husbands were rarely required to support their estranged wives with alimony payments. Provisions for pin money and a widow's jointure remained as enforceable clauses in the marriage contract, but Sir Richard could look forward to wiping his hands of any additional financial obligations to Seymour. When the baronet presented his case for separation, it appeared to him to be a straightforward situation where his adulterous wife was clearly in the wrong. Judge Wynne, a Londoner, who read the newspapers and passed the windows of the print shops, who dined in the company of gossips, had begun to think otherwise. Although he did not want to condone the behaviour of an adulteress, Wynne ruled that this was an unusual case requiring special consideration. Sir Richard's contribution to the destruction of his marriage meant that he should bear some responsibility for his wife's uncertain future. Therefore, in addition to the award of £400 annual pin money, he ordered that yearly alimony payments of a further £600 be made. This £1,000 in total was to be given to her in monthly sums, the first instalment of which, the judge proclaimed to Worsley's solicitor, 'was now due in fifteen days'.

The baronet was outraged. He ordered that Heseltine issue an immediate 'protest against the decree' which he 'found to be too much favouring Dame Seymour Dorothy Worsley' to his 'very.great detriment and prejudice'. The appeal against the ruling was then moved into the higher Court of Arches where on the 4th of June, Sir Richard's attorney appeared again to issue a complaint that 'Sir Richard Worsley . . . was very much injured and aggrieved by . . . the ruling'. The demand for alimony was an insult. Notwithstanding James Heseltine's fervent objections, the decision remained, with the minor concession that, rather than monthly, the instalments were to be paid on a quarterly basis.

All of his attempts at vindication had been crushed and Worsley was incensed. Incredibly, he had lost every skirmish to his wife; an enemy less well endowed and less justified in her cause. However, in this final struggle he refused to concede defeat. For the next six years, the baronet's attorneys would continue to dispute the finer details of the separation and attempt to overturn the award of £600 alimony.

For most of 1782, Sir Richard had bravely weathered a ferocious storm of legal battles and personal smears but after so much abuse, cracks had begun to appear in his fortitude. No longer able to bear the sneers and his wife's relentless taunting, unable to reside in London, unable to ride through Hampshire without exciting comment, the baronet realised that he must disappear. England must be made to forget him.

As Sir Richard retreated from the public glare, his wife surged forward. As the year progressed, Seymour's undignified behaviour began to veer even further off course. It was reported in the *Morning Herald* that Lady Worsley had recently 'been measured for boots at a well-known gentleman's boot maker'. Shortly thereafter she appeared in public, 'in buckskins, boots and long-heeled spurs'. However, it was not only her masculine dress that astonished but her sudden enthusiasm for dare-devil equestrianism. A 'correspondent' informed the readers of the *Herald* that 'every morning', dressed in tight breeches and straddling her horse, Seymour would ride 'sixteen miles within the hour . . . with all imaginable ease!' While riding in itself was considered a health-promoting pastime for both genders, extreme feats of sportsmanship were believed to be unsuitable for the female sex. Masculine competitiveness, in combination with too much physical motion, especially the jarring rhythm of excessive horse riding, was thought to damage the womb, which not only resulted in 'hysteria' but the masculinisation of women, possible infertility, and potentially miscarriage. Eager to observe this 'female jockey' tear across the fields, her legs akimbo, her bottom displayed and her thighs held taut in their sheaths of hide, the Prince of Wales arranged for a race on the Sussex Downs. 'The scene,' wrote the *Herald* on the 26th of September, 'was a train of dissipation and folly.' Everyone from the Prince of Wales and the Duke of Cumberland to 'the baron and the blackleg were in attendance'. On the rolling green hills, dotted with carriages and grazing horses, stood liveried valets and tailored men of the *ton* who had 'assembled to see this exhibition'. A prize of 50 guineas was raised in this match between Lady Worsley and 'Mr Villers', the Prince's master of the horse. Unfortunately 'after mounting her buckskins and half boots accordingly', much 'to the mortification of a great number of spectators' Seymour 'declared off at the moment they were expected to start'. The reasons for her withdrawal are not stated but she was to return later in the day to amuse her set of raucous acquaintances with further spectacles, this time as she raced in a two-wheeled phaeton, recklessly riding 'so long in equilibrio that the least touch in nature would have reverted her fate and brought her flat to the ground!' Even among the swaggering hell-raisers and *demi-mondaines*, these tricks were exceptional feats of audacity, not in the least because only two weeks earlier, Lady Worsley, without the slightest shame, had 'professed herself pregnant'. To the onlookers scattered amid the tall grass of the Downs, her sudden passion for dangerous gallops was perfectly explicable.

In spite of her attempts, her efforts to miscarry would fail. As the child inside her began to grow, the *Herald* and the *Post* found fewer adventures of Lady Worsley's to report. Although she continued to appear in Hyde Park dressed in men's riding gear and 'attended as usual by the Generalissimo Bisset', her changing condition would not permit her buckskin breeches to fit much beyond the month of October. In the absence of substantial gossip, silence caused the public to knit together a collection of invented possibilities for the two paramours: that the lovers had departed for the continent, that a reconciliation had been reached with Sir Richard, that they were living quietly in an attempt to atone for their sins. What the matrons over their tea and seedcake would not have predicted was the announcement that came at the end of January 1783. Midway through her pregnancy, George Bisset had left Lady Worsley. The great romantic interlude had ended.

19

Exile

Just before dawn, on the morning of the 12th of February 1785, Sir Richard Worsley rose from his bed at the Villa Negroni. From the courtyard below came the hurried sounds of his Italian household readying his specially built carriages for an excursion. The two light, low-wheeled calesses (carriages), upholstered in leather and sprung to take the jolts of Europe and Asia's pitted roads, were loaded with the equipment necessary for an epic journey. Mosquito netting, guns, candles, swords and copper cooking vessels, starched bedlinen and durable travel clothing, were strapped in next to boxes of maps and books on the history and antiquities of Greece, Egypt and Turkey. Eight horses were hitched to their vehicles. By 7 a.m., this lumbering train – which also ferried the baronet, his three servants and Willey Reveley, an English artist whom Worsley had hired 'to make drawings of architecture and the most interesting ruins' – set out across the hills of Rome bound for Greece.

This was to be the second and most significant leg of a journey that had begun nearly two years earlier. Since May 1783, the baronet had been following a network of rocky routes through some of the most desolate corners of continental Europe. The searing gaze of ridicule had finally driven him to abandon England. Worsley had realised that only prolonged absence and a complete withdrawal from society might resuscitate his injured character. Like many others in the wake of disgrace, he had slipped across the Channel, hoping that the passage of time would dull the memory of his misadventures. However, in light of his wife's persistent courting of scandal, the restoration of his reputation would be more difficult to achieve. The baronet needed to go to ground.

Neither France nor Italy, with their hotels and cafés bustling with English travellers, would have offered a respite from gossip. Instead, Sir Richard opted for a year-long sojourn amid the sunburnt hills of the Iberian Peninsula, a region beyond the itineraries of the casual tourist. Lisbon, the port city into which he arrived was little more than a network of buildings languishing in the rubble of the earthquake that had tumbled it twenty-eight years earlier. Few but the tubercular traveller in search of pure air, or the adventure seeker, could be found on the 'strange and disgusting' Portuguese streets, swarming with deformed beggars and feral animals. In terms of reputation, Spain fared little better. Its parched landscapes did not hold much interest for grand tourists, while its flea-ridden hostelries were considered 'worse than dog kennels'. This was not a location for the uninitiated, which suited Worsley perfectly. Between the spring of 1783 and the late winter of the following year, he snaked his way northward from Lisbon to Cadiz and Seville, through the olive groves of Andalusia to Granada, arriving in Madrid in time to pass the winter. After nearly twelve months of hiding in the shade and dust, he then felt ready to emerge in Paris.

By the autumn of 1784 Worsley had begun to set his scheme for a lengthy expedition through the Ottoman Empire into motion. In October he arrived at Rome. He did not intend to linger. Still wishing to avoid the snarl of British artists and grand tourists who strolled along the Via Condotti and gathered around the brazier at the Caffè Inglese, the baronet hired lodgings at the Villa Negroni on the outskirts of town and hid behind its walls. But for occasional visits to fellow collectors such as Sir William Hamilton and a handful of art dealers, Worsley avoided social interaction where possible. Even in the eighteen months since his departure from England there had been no shortage of sniggering spectators; those travellers eager to fill their letters home with tales of foreign sights and encounters with the 'Twelve Penny Cuckold'. It was precisely for this reason that Sir Richard had alighted on the idea of a Levantine journey.

Worsley hoped his absence from England would help the nation forget his dishonour, equally, he wished to rehabilitate himself in the eyes of his peers. His proposed tour of Greece, Egypt and Turkey, with a return journey through Russia and Eastern Europe, was to be not only a penance, but a self-imposed exile, a mortification of the character through the fire of the desert and the ice of the steppes. From this retreat the baronet intended to emerge both cleansed of past misdeeds and restored in the general esteem. To achieve this feat of rebirth, Sir Richard Worsley had to recast himself in an altogether worthier mould.

In the late eighteenth century there were few places so idealised and yet so frustratingly beyond reach as Athens. The mother culture which had given birth to the Roman Empire had in recent centuries received less attention from scholars than she was due. Travel to Greece, a region dominated by the Turks since the fifteenth century, was made especially unappealing by her frequent outbreaks of insurrection, war and plague. Consequently, the era's fascination with the classical was largely biased towards Rome. Like his contemporaries, Worsley had been reared from boyhood on an intellectual diet of Latin and Greek writing, but his interest in antiquity had been broadened by his father's influence. Sir Thomas had taken his young son up the steep Sicilian hillsides at Agrigento and Segesta and introduced him to the uniquely Doric forms shaped by the hands of ancient Greeks. This intriguing taste of an Hellenic past that predated even the revered foundations of Rome's Forum lingered in the baronet's imagination at a time when the scholarly circles of Europe were just beginning to consider the artistic contributions of Greece.

As few antiquarians had made pilgrimages to Athens or chanced a voyage through the outposts of Ottoman control to explore the Greek islands, the fertile banks of the Nile or the ruins beyond Constantinople, the precise influence of earlier civilisations on the sculpture and architecture of the Romans remained open to conjecture. It had only been in 1762, with the publication of James Stuart and Nicholas Revett's *Antiquities of Athens*, that a movement known as the Gusto Greco had begun to stir much interest among British patrons. At the time Sir Richard was contemplating his journey many remained sceptical of the merits of Greek design. In the years before 1801, when Lord Elgin took an assortment of friezes and metopes from the Parthenon and shipped these exotic treasures to London, examples of Hellenic artistry were sparse in the collections of English antiquarians. The antecedents of Roman greatness could not possibly be examined in the absence of compelling specimens. It was in amassing such a collection, in assembling a sort of museum of Greek art, that Worsley saw his future. He would bring to England what no one before him had: ancient Greece. In the process, he would immerse himself in the subject and emerge as an expert, Britain's most knowledgeable proponent of Greek antiquities. Of course, the purpose of this mission was entirely self-serving. It was a desperate attempt to salvage the Worsley name from infamy.

On the day the baronet embarked upon his prodigious voyage, the winter sky ballooned with grey and burst into a shower of snow. The two calesses bumped along the roads south of Rome, travelling through the villages of Campania towards Naples. After a stint at Paestum where he and Willey Reveley paused to study the Greek temples constructed on Italian soil, they pushed onward through the bandit-filled hills into Puglia before arriving at Otranto nearly six weeks later. Here the wheels of their vehicles were removed and the carriages packed into the hull of a ship bound first for Crete and then for Athens.

Charting a slow progress along the eastern Peloponnesian coast, Worsley's own three-masted sailing vessel, the polacca *Aurora* rounded the tip of Hydra on the 7th of May. By sunset of the following evening a spectacular vista rose from the water ahead of them. On the blustery deck Worsley pressed his prospective glass to his eye and watched the crest of the Parthenon take shape. This first sight of the exalted Temple of Athena filled him 'with an inexpressible joy'. Much to Sir Richard's frustration, adverse winds kept the ship beyond port until the 9th. When at last they weighed anchor, the baronet gave in to his excited impatience and came ashore. Refusing to wait for the assembly of his dismantled caless, Worsley, with Reveley at his heels, set off for Athens on foot, his enthusiasm propelling him along the five-mile route through a tangle of vineyards to the base of the Acropolis.

The structures on Athens's 'Sacred Rock', the collapsing shrines once dedicated to the worship of the goddess Athena, enthralled him. With his draughtsman at his side, the baronet devoted two weeks of intensive study to these ruins, poring over the Erechtheion with its unique 'porch of maidens' and the once majestic Propylaea, the gleaming gateway to the hilltop's temples. Long days were spent in the spring sunshine measuring, recording and drawing, investigating every worn pediment and cracked architrave. Of all these magnificent architectural creations, the Parthenon, its vivid metopes and friezes still *in situ*, gripped him with the greatest intensity. Worsley was mesmerised. No other experience during his voyages was to captivate him so entirely. This monument of human creation, Worsley eulogised in his travel diary, was 'beautiful beyond description'. He returned each day for contemplation, writing on the 23rd of June that he had 'passed the whole morning in the Acropolis admiring the beauties there'. 'I could not help observing,' he continued, 'that the oftener these objects are seen the more effect they have upon the mind.' Before his departure, he commented wistfully that 'the ruins of the city . . . had given me the greatest pleasure'. They had also given his empty life a sense of purpose.

However, Worsley was soon to find that neither the Greeks nor their Turkish overlords ascribed such emotional or pecuniary worth to the stones they possessed. Strolling through the narrow lanes of the small settlement of modern Athens was for an antiquarian like perusing the halls of a treasury. The current inhabitants of the town lived casually among the history of their celebrated ancestors, incorporating ancient masonry into their roofs and planting their laurel trees amid broken columns. Their outdoor spaces were scattered with marble remnants while headless deities were left half buried or abandoned to the mercy of the sun. Sir Richard was all too delighted to observe this and remarked, with an eye to acquisition, that 'there was hardly a house without some fragment of ancient sculpture over the door or in the courtyard'. During an excursion to Megara Worsley was able to purchase several discarded objects. In the courtyard of 'a prominent citizen' he noticed a three-foot statue of Asclepius, the god of medicine thrown carelessly on to its side. This piece as well as a 'small monument commemorating Cafision' and an intricately carved 'bas-relief' from the side of a sepulchre he obtained 'for a mere trifle'.

To Worsley and other connoisseurs like him, all of Greece seemed an untouched orchard whose mouldering bounty was desperate for harvest. Precious objects of great scholarly significance lay strewn across the islands like broken vases in a potter's yard. It therefore became the thinking gentleman's duty to reap the benefits of Greek and Ottoman ignorance and liberate as much from their grasp as possible. As Worsley's acquaintance J.B.S. Morritt wrote in the 1790s, Greece was 'a perfect gallery of marbles . . . some we steal, some we buy'. While there is no evidence to suggest that Sir Richard actively stole any of the pieces that came into his possession, he does neglect to record the prices he paid for many of the items he took away, as well as their specific provenances. Most of these objects could be possessed for a surprisingly meagre amount; Morritt learned that he could buy antique medals for 'under the price of silver' and 'the copper ones for halfpence', while the collector Charles Robert Cockerell paid £40 for fourteen excavated statues (which he had originally tried to steal) worth £4,500.

The ease with which Sir Richard acquired items increased his appetite for further finds. A successful tour through the Peloponnesian and Cycladic islands yielded a bumper crop of bas-reliefs, statuary, small cameo-like intaglios and engraved gemstones. However, the riches of the Hellenic age were not confined to the Greek territories. They lay scattered along a broad axis throughout the Mediterranean. In July 1785, Worsley decided to seek their remains in Egypt. Sailing from Rhodes, he landed at Alexandria on the 26th, after a nervous voyage through pirate-plagued waters. From this port he proceeded by water to Rosetto (Rashid), then a balmy paradise of 'luxuriant gardens', before sailing down the Nile to Cairo.

The unforgiving August sun was baking the clay walls of Old Cairo when he arrived. In its modern incarnation, the once exalted capital did not match his expectations, having 'lost a great deal of its ancient splendour and magnificence' under Turkish rule. Nevertheless, Worsley enjoyed moving through the colourful commotion of its foreign streets with their markets selling senna and saffron and workshops pounding out 'Turkish stirrups and all furniture for horses'. As authorities on Egyptian travel advised, both Sir Richard and Willey Reveley adopted Eastern dress and grew heavy Ottoman beards. Swathed in light robes and slippers, they slid into the eddying crowds of exotic faces, mingling among 'the moors, Arabs, Coptics, Greeks, Syrians, Armenians, some few Christians and Turks'. Worsley observed with curiosity the 'women covered from head to toe' and the stern-faced 'Janissaries patrolling the markets and gates to the city'. Wearing appropriate attire, which repelled 'the insults of the lower class of people', made a thorough investigation of Cairo's corners easier.

Although Worsley knew that without an official firman, or mandate from the Turkish government, the excavation or removal of antiquities was forbidden, he was prepared to try his luck without one. However, after visits to dealers and a trawl through the bazaars he had only managed to buy a handful of engraved gems: a head of Alexander, a small onyx figure of Minerva, a lion on cornelian, and a 'talisman of two crocodiles'. Much to his frustration he found the larger objects, those which he wanted most, virtually impossible to obtain. On a walk through the alleyways of Cairo, he noticed 'near a disused fountain . . . a most beautiful sarcophagus of grey porphyry with very beautiful hieroglyphic figures', which Worsley surmised had 'probably been taken out of the great pyramid'. After a few enquiries he learned that it had in fact 'been in this spot . . . above five hundred years'. His offer of money for the item refused and his plans of acquiring it thwarted, the baronet complained bitterly that although 'the Turks find no value to these wonderful and beautiful relicks of the ancients, they will not consent to have them removed . . .' For the baronet, this was an infuriating setback and one with which he was to meet continuously.

If the Ottoman officials in Egypt refused to accommodate his wishes, the population of Turkey positively obstructed them. In the autumn of that year, the *Aurora* made for Constantinople. Battling furious winds along the Anatolian coast she managed to reach her destination on the 14th of November. Worsley recorded upon his arrival that 'the English Ambassador had sent his servants with a boat for me', and as they rowed from his ship to the dockside at Pera he took in 'the striking appearance of Constantinople' as it lay between the sparkling Bosporus and the densely forested hills. The horizon, he wrote, was punctuated by 'an immense number of mosques with minarets' which 'added greatly to its beauty', while the narrow streets rolling down to the water's edge were enlivened by 'a large number of small houses built of wood and painted in imitation of brick buildings'. As a city, he concluded, it was 'perhaps the most beautiful and agreeable in the world'.

The baronet spent the winter at the residence of the English Ambassador, Sir Robert Ainslie, who entertained his guest with frequent visits across the Bosporus to the historic centre of Sultan Ahmet, and on several occasions saw him through the ornately tiled halls of Topkapi Palace for audiences with 'the Grand Signor'. Through Worsley's contacts at Constantinople he was able to obtain the royal firman necessary for furthering his acquisitive aims. In April of 1786, when the permeating cold of winter had begun to lift, Sir Richard set out on a collecting expedition which he was certain would bear fruit.

Casting into the Sea of Marmara, he sailed for the ancient ruins of Troy. His intention was to make a meticulous seven-week study of the area, where he would not only scour the remains of the once formidable city eulogised in the *Iliad* and the *Odyssey* but push deep into the rural heart of the region. At first Worsley was thrilled by the wealth of relics he encountered at outlying sites around the Dardanelles. 'I found several large pieces of the finest flushed white marble . . . a beautiful Ionic capital, several Doric pieces, many shafts of colums of granite,' he wrote excitedly after surveying the Tomb of Ajax at Rhoeteum. But the British vice-consul there soon dampened his enthusiasm. When the baronet displayed an interest in taking away 'a bas relief of several figures', the vice-consul recounted a story of when 'he had accompanied another English gentleman to that spot who had bid 400 Venetian sequins for this beautiful fragment' but who had 'met with a violent opposition from the inhabitants', who 'immediately began to beat the heads off the figures'. He explained that the area's villagers regarded these relics as talismans and would rather destroy their worth 'than be prevailed upon to part with them'.

Even with his firman, Worsley's designs were to meet with significant opposition. The impressive scale of the ruins at Troy only heightened his frustration. 'I hardly ever saw such noble or extensive ones,' he wrote. An hour was passed simply riding through 'a mass of antique columns and parts of buildings'. The remains, he concluded, 'could compare with the Colosseum at Rome for grandeur'. Left abandoned to the elements, their abundance and quality tempted him to distraction. To remove even a small piece of neglected marble would have required local manpower on which he could not have relied. Disheartened, he turned his back on Troy, commenting, 'It was much to my infinite regret that among such considerable remains I was not fortunate enough to find one bas relief or inscription.' His feelings intensified as they left the site through the adjoining village of Troiki, where along the road Worsley bristled to discover a pile of cannonballs 'made from antique stones, awaiting shipment to the capital'. 'The Turks,' he complained angrily, 'who are now the barbarous despots of the country' would only 'destroy or deface' the treasures in their care.

Where the baronet's hopes of expanding his collection were concerned, the situation was not to improve. Contrary to what he had believed, there were no hidden riches in the countryside. Worsley was horrified to learn that even antique medals and precious coins from the era of Alexander the Great, when found 'were immediately carried to the copper smith and melted down to be employed as kitchen utensils'. 'They place no value on them,' he bemoaned before declaring, '. . . what profound ignorance are the inhabitants of the delightful Mysia now reduced to!' To exacerbate matters, on his return journey to Constantinople he found his plans to visit the Palace of Balkisa, the alleged residence of Helen of Troy, foiled by the petty obstinacy of a local official who even prevented him from 'making copies of the inscriptions' he had discovered among several ancient buildings.

Disappointed and empty-handed, Sir Richard arrived back at the ambassadorial residence in May and immediately began making arrangements for his departure to Russia. However, before setting sail for Sebastopol the baronet was determined to make at least one purchase of significance.

In August of the previous year, Worsley had sat at a window belonging to a French merchant in Cairo, observing the waters of the river rush into the canal below. The inundation of the Nile was an annual event which drew hordes of spectators from across the city. In addition to Cairo's poorer inhabitants who came 'dancing and singing' and 'leading monkeys' to the festivities, could also be seen 'the wives and mistresses of many prominent Turks'. 'I had the opportunity of seeing several very fine women through the lattices of the opposite houses,' the baronet confided, after an innocent indulgence of his voyeuristic tendencies. He was enchanted by their mysterious figures, silk wrapped and bejewelled, as they fluttered like birds behind the wrought-iron cage-work. 'These women are slaves from Georgia, Circassia and Armenia,' he wrote with a stirring of arousal, 'and most of them are very fair and handsome.'

Slavery was a ubiquitous feature of daily life in the Ottoman-ruled territories. Slaves formed the majority of the labouring class, performing manual and menial tasks in and outside of the home, working in agriculture and industry. They comprised much of the army, guarded the mosques and the palaces, served as entertainers and bulked out the harems of wealthy men. Where in Britain, a tide of moral sentiment was gathering against the indignities of the trade in human lives, in Egypt and Turkey such notions would have been inconceivable. Slavery existed under the Ottomans in an almost classical context, as it would have in ancient Rome or Greece and Worsley, so consumed in his worship of antiquity, became increasingly fascinated with the state of subjugation that he witnessed. It appealed to something dark and unhealed within him: the desire to own and control a woman absolutely.

More than three years had elapsed since his betrayal by Lady Worsley. Thousands of miles of water, earth and sand had passed beneath his feet and still his months under a foreign sun had not managed to burn away the anguish. As the baronet's travel journals indicate, his heart continued to howl with pain. In the course of his voyages, Worsley not only maintained a log of his route, carefully recording details of each of the locations he visited, but also gave voice to some of his inner thoughts. At the back of his journal, Sir Richard wrote in bold ink at the top of a page 'Miscellaneous Remarks, observations, quotations and extracts from ancient and modern authors made in the course of my travels', and beneath it copied out lines of poetry and philosophy as they resonated with his mood. While some of these were ruminations on the rise and fall of empire, many more dwelt on the treachery of love. Perhaps the most revealing of these is the only modern excerpt to appear: the words of a Turkish folk song, 'translated at the beginning of the present century'. The lyrics, Worsley writes, 'were composed by a lover on meeting with a repulse from a lady he courted and wanted to make his fourth and favourite wife'. The vengeful, bloodthirsty verses relate the tale of a hard-hearted woman and the man whose pride she injured. Throughout the song, her rebuffed suitor threatens her with increasing vitriol:

> . . . She denied the proffered bliss,
> And durst refuse to wed
> But if she suffers not for this
> May I be lost when dead

Calling to the heavens to smite her, the author's curse becomes the song's refrain –

> O Mahomet, O prophet you who can,
> Hear and revenge an injured Mussul Man

– before ending with a crescendo of fury, undeniably reflective of Worsley's own impassioned resentment;

> But tho' she proudly dares rebel
> The time will come when I shall see,
> The poor inferior wretch in hell
> Not worthy once to look on me
> Then slight, conceited slave, if there you can,
> The proffered courtship of a Mussul Man.

Like the composer of the verses, the baronet was aching from an injury not just to his heart but to his dignity and sought to reassert his authority in another sphere in order to heal his wounds.

Instinct and curiosity had drawn Worsley to the Cairo slave market. His first encounter was with 'the Ethiopians' who 'bring the black slaves to sell'. 'I saw many of these wretched objects of compassion,' he wrote, 'who only seem anxious of getting masters.' When enquiring about their prices he was told 'that the women sell for more than the men', before being warned by the trader that 'Christians are permitted in Egypt but not in Turkey to purchase them.' 'They cost according to their goodness,' the Ethiopian continued, 'from three hundred piastres to a hundred', and then, guessing at the baronet's designs, cautioned him once more that these slaves 'were not permitted to leave Egypt'. However, the chained captives that Worsley surveyed were not the sort he had admired from his window. 'These unfortunate creatures,' as he compassionately calls them, 'come generally from Nigritia in the centre of Africa, but some come from the nearer countries of Nubia and Abyssinia . . .' He found their appearance striking: 'they are quite black and their heads are covered with a short black wool', but he concluded, 'they are not so handsome in countenance and figure as the Asiatic blacks'.

Although it was against Ottoman law for him to do so, the possibility of purchasing a female slave continued to tantalise Sir Richard while he remained within the domain of Turkish rule. His arrival at Constantinople presented him with further opportunities. The alluring Circassian slaves that he coveted, the renowned white-skinned jewels of the seraglio, prized for their exquisite features and accomplishments in singing and dancing, could be acquired at the city's Avret Bazaar, where women were traded every Friday. However, as Lady Mary Wortley Montagu, a visitor to Turkey earlier in the century observed, such treasures of the harem were a rarity in the marketplace. Rather than offering them for public sale, most owners 'who grew weary of them' might choose to 'either present them to a friend or give them their freedoms'. Consequently, when they did appear in the enclosed courtyard of the bazaar these precious commodities fetched a premium, often exceeding several thousand piastres. A man of not inconsiderable means, the baronet attended the slave market in anticipation of success. He bid on several Circassian girls but, according to the philosopher Jeremy Bentham who was also in Constantinople at the time, 'the price was too high'. Worsley had not anticipated that competition would be so fierce.

In spite of his disappointment, Sir Richard's determination to acquire a human prize persisted undaunted. In recent months, as if in anticipation of becoming a slave owner, Worsley's grip on his servants had tightened into a tyrannical stranglehold. He had become not only callous, but ruthless and violent. His aggressive temperament eventually drove Willey Reveley from

214

Maidstone Whim, by an anonymous cartoonist, shows Sir Richard smiling contentedly as he helps Bisset to a view of his wife.

A slightly more 'high-brow' interpretation of the bath house scene, *The Maidstone Bath or the Modern Susanna* draws on classical allegory, but not without a subtle reference to Sir Richard's impotence.

A Bath of the Moderns offers a more ribald version of events.

A variation on the theme: *Lady Worsley Dressing in the Bathing House*.

George James, 1st Marquess of Cholmondeley, painted by Pompeo Batoni as a young man while on his grand tour in Italy. Cholmondeley was legendary for his amorous conquests.

The son of a French aristocrat and a slave, Joseph Boulogne, Chevalier de Saint Georges was a gifted swordsman, musician and athlete. Lady Worsley became his mistress in the late 1780s.

The 7th Earl of Coventry, who was known as Viscount Deerhurst during his affair with Lady Worsley, is seen here with his son, the current Viscount Deerhurst. The 7th Earl had once been extremely handsome until a riding accident robbed him of his sight and his looks. In this picture of him as an older man, the green silk patch he wore over his eye is visible.

The Marquess of Graham, seen here on the left, was one of a handful of Lady Worsley's lovers who openly admitted to their affair. During the crim. con. proceedings it was revealed that he had 'conferred a venereal disease' on her.

A sketch of Lady Worsley by the artist John Russell around 1800, at the time she was living at Brompton House.

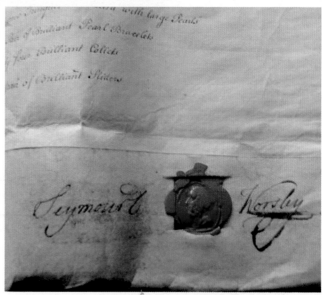

Lady Worsley's signature on her deeds of separation, 1788. She has written the name Worsley with a particularly heavy hand.

Brompton House as it looked in the mid-19th century. Seymour occupied the westernmost dwelling from the late 1790s until she and John Lewis Fleming moved to Paris around 1816.

This engraving of Sir Richard, circa 1802, was taken from a miniature and served as the frontispiece for later editions of the *Museum Worsleyanum*. At the time the image was made the baronet had become a recluse and was living at Sea Cottage.

An assortment of cameos and gems collected by Sir Richard.

his employment. On reaching Constantinople, the artist and his patron parted company. Reveley later complained to Bentham of his ill-treatment, saying that the baronet regarded him not as an educated gentleman but as a lowly drudge. Outraged, the artist reported that, 'His commands were given in the style of a pasha – in a word' and that 'his dependants were in the situation of slaves in the presence of a despot'. Worse still, Sir Richard had 'even menaced them with the rod and the scourge'. At the end of the eighteenth century, such unenlightened behaviour certainly would have raised censorious comment and even questions of legality among many of Worsley's contemporaries in Britain.

By the 29th of May, the day he boarded the Russian sloop *Danube* bound for the Crimea, an alteration in the baronet's character had become noticeable. The more sinister shades of his personality, 'the passions', that he had claimed to keep in check as a young man had been given much freer rein while he roamed the Mediterranean. Answerable to no one within English polite society, he had grown accustomed to inventing his own morality, one which was more suited to his notions of hierarchy, power and privilege. A sense of entitlement demanded that Worsley not depart the Ottoman Empire without a few spoils. After much perseverance and some bribery he had managed to obtain a handful of items for his collection, including 'a bas-relief from the floor of a cottage at Ephesus', which he purchased through a dealer in Constantinople. He had also made a few additions to his growing collection of intaglios and engraved gems. Among the most valued of these was 'an engraved sardonyx' on which appeared an epigraph written in Greek, *People say what they please, what then? I don't care'*. These objects, along with another of even greater significance, were secured below deck for a voyage to the Black Sea.

Sir Richard had come aboard the *Danube* following an afternoon lounging at the table of the Russian envoy. Full of dinner and conviviality, his spirits only began to dip 'on passing the first castles' along the Bosporus at which point 'the Turkish custom house officers came on board to visit the ship'. Worsley was not so concerned that they would confiscate the few antiquities in his possession for which he had been granted a firman, but he feared for his other property. As he explains in his journal, the customs officials were in search of smuggled slaves. Should any be found, Turkish law stipulated that the Sultan had the right to seize both the cargo and the ship transporting it. Sir Richard was anxious and later confessed in his diary that in spite of its unlawfulness, 'I had purchased [a slave] at Constantinople of a Turkish Aga who had been taken in Abyssinia, brought to Cairo, there sold and sent to Constantinople'. As the authorities paced the boards of the vessel, Worsley hoped they would not notice that 'the boy was concealed under the hatch way'. However, to his great relief, 'they did not pretend to make a regular search so he was not seen'.

While Worsley had been denied the pleasures (sexual and otherwise) of exercising his absolute authority over a beautiful female captive he found it impossible to give up his desire to experience total ownership of an individual. The Abyssinian boy whom he had taken into his service had been a second choice but a prudent one. Black footboys, attired in turbans and caftans, Moroccan slippers and satin sashes had been seen at the side of wealthy European masters and mistresses for the majority of the eighteenth century. As depicted in many of the period's portraits as well as in William Hogarth's engravings, *Marriage A-la-Mode* and *The Harlot's Progress*, a black page was a fashionable accessory. For this reason, Worsley's young addition to his entourage was unlikely to rouse comment. He could be easily trailed around the palaces of Russia and Eastern Europe and might even be shipped home to England unquestioned.

The dark, frightened face that peered from Worsley's carriage as he rode up the drive to the Ukrainian home of Samuel and Jeremy Bentham was that of the baronet's slave. *En route* through the newly annexed Russian territory of the Crimea to Moscow, Sir Richard had decided to visit Kritchev where Lieutenant-Colonel Samuel Bentham, under the command of Prince Potemkin was heading an extensive project to develop technology, trade and industry in the region. The baronet, who had met Jeremy Bentham only briefly while in Turkey, had invited himself to stay at the brothers' cavernous but ramshackle house. On the 7th of August he had appeared at the Benthams' door with little prior warning and two vehicles of servants and equipment. Once settled in, he stayed for a month. During that period, Jeremy Bentham, who had taken a dislike to the baronet on first acquaintance, became increasingly suspicious about the circumstances of the little child in Sir Richard's party.

As he had been when living with John Hesse, Worsley was an atrocious house guest. When not teasing the brothers with fabricated stories about the severity of Russian laws and the state of the British economy, the baronet occupied himself with the discipline of his footboy. Their home regularly shook with 'the lad's shrieks and agonies', a sound which 'often tormented' the philosopher. 'He treated the poor boy with barbarous cruelty,' Bentham recorded in his notebooks, 'nobody could be more wretched than he was in his master's presence'. The philosopher was especially unnerved by Worsley's vacillations; one minute distributing beatings and the next 'calling him his pet'. The worst display of this abuse occurred during an outing with Samuel Bentham to the site where a group of the Lieutenant-Colonel's soldiers 'were building some barges upon a new construction'. The party, which included the two brothers and an army general as well as Sir Richard and his page, set off for the banks of the Sozh River in a droshky, or open-topped carriage. Worsley was insistent that his servant should ride inside with them and 'made the boy sit at a little distance'. But much to Jeremy Bentham's horror, 'at any stage where they stopped' the baronet would drag the child into a place screened from view and thrash him. Those within earshot shrank as 'as they used to hear the boy crying out piteously, Signor Aga! Signor Aga!'

In his account of Worsley's stay with them, Bentham avoids describing 'the black Abyssinian boy' with whom 'Sir Richard travelled' as his servant. What he had observed of the baronet in Turkey – his attempt to purchase Circassian slaves and the vicious treatment of his household – probably led Bentham to conclude that the child who accompanied him was not a salaried member of his domestic staff.

On the 5th of September, Worsley and 'his pet' departed Kritchev for Moscow. Due to the state of Russia's deplorable roads, he had hoped to be in St Petersburg before the first snowfall. When the rivers had frozen solid and the thoroughfares iced into slick runways, the wheels of his calesses were removed once more and this time replaced with sled runners. After three years of travel and in spite of numerous frustrations, Sir Richard had managed to amass a sizeable collection of Greek antiquities, which included several busts and heads, funeral masks, bas-reliefs of 'the Games of the Circus', and of 'Hercules reposing', fragments of masonry depicting 'Pluto leaning on a couch', and 'a hero covered with the skin of a lion'. Among his haul were also several pieces 'found in the Acropolis': 'an interesting monument' representing 'a Syren in affliction for having been excelled by the Muses in singing' and a relief illustrating 'Jupiter and Minerva receiving the vows and supplications of an Athenian family' which Worsley judged 'to have formed part of the frieze of the cell of the Parthenon'. These 'with many other curious marbles' had been, throughout the period of three years, packed into straw-filled crates and 'transported to England'. His portable cabinet of engraved gems and intaglios would continue to travel with him wherever he ventured. Like a calling card, it guaranteed immediate recognition of his expertise. What became of the human item in Worsley's collection is unknown. Whether he fled or was abandoned in some foreign city by the baronet, who might have given his slave to a friend like one of his intaglios, may never be discovered.

In the first month of the new year, 1787, Sir Richard Worsley decided it was time to emerge from the obscurity into which he had thrown himself. Leaving behind the deep snow of Eastern Europe he journeyed south, back to Italy and into the renewing warmth of spring. His travels had cleansed him and he was determined to illustrate that he had shed all trace of his former foolishness. Not unlike the boy who had left on grand tour in 1769 and returned three years later as a gentleman, Sir Richard wished to demonstrate that he 'was greatly altered'. However, this time he would do more than 'profess to command his passions'. He would prove to the world that he had mastered them completely.

20

The Dupe of Duns

The Oxford Road at its junction with the Tottenham Court Road was a boisterous and bustling place. A continuum of horses and vehicles passed in and out of the mouth of the newly paved road. Strolling pedestrians and street vendors navigated their way between a treacherous river of hoofs and wheels and a bank of bowed shop windows. On hanging days, carts of the condemned followed by a baying, beer-soaked mob travelled down the long avenue to the foot of the gallows at Tyburn. Often 'frequented by persons of the lowest order', it was not the most salubrious corner of London.

On the north side of the Oxford Road, near to this busy convergence, was Newman Street and its modest assortment of houses and cottages. In the early 1780s it was a neighbourhood of the quietly comfortable middle class, the sort who regularly enjoyed large plates of roast beef and rarely worried about the expenses of heating their rooms. These were not grand people, but artisans and shopkeepers who had risen in their professions by balancing their ledgers carefully over the years. Newman Street, with the Middlesex Hospital at its far end and the construction of a parish workhouse in its early stages, was likely to be a location where a man of moderate means might install his mistress in lodgings. It was also home to a number of better-paid prostitutes who charged a guinea or two for a night's amusement, and at least one vaguely respectable brothel. It was here, among the perfumed whores of 'eminent cabinet makers' and the families of haberdashers and porcelain merchants, that Lady Worsley was living in January 1783.

A year of gambling, dining, drinking and dancing in the train of the Prince of Wales had ravaged Seymour and Bisset's finances. After a prolonged period of victory celebrations and public gloating, reality and the creditors had caught up with them. On the 23rd of January, the *Morning Herald* declared that Captain Bisset had 'seceded from her ladyship's invincible charms and retired to the continent for the better arrangement of his health and his finances'. Beyond this titbit of gossip, little else is known about the circumstances which drove apart the once passionately devoted couple. It is possible that pressure to renounce the embarrassing alliance had come from Bisset's religious family, in particular from George's brother William, who was at the time seeking a living in the church. In debt and with his reputation dishonoured, Bisset's decision to leave Lady Worsley signalled a definitive end to his flirtation with 'the fast set' and a life of excess. His intention was also to turn his back on the Isle of Wight, where his shame was likely to be remembered. That year, he let out Knighton to Captain Leversuch, a neighbour to whom Sir Richard was not likely to object. There is no evidence that he returned to his estate until 1789, two years after his marriage to Harriot Mordaunt, the half-sister of the Earl of Peterborough. According to John Wilkes, a fellow island inhabitant, Sir Richard and George Bisset skilfully avoided one another thereafter. Eventually, Mr and Mrs Bisset and their two daughters abandoned Knighton, which was pulled down in the 1820s.

After his short spell of infamy, Maurice George Bisset seemed content to withdraw into the quiet rural life from which he had come. He sat as a Justice of the Peace in Hampshire and is remarked upon as being a generous neighbour. John Wilkes was the frequent recipient of his hospitality as well as baskets of fruit from his orchards at Knighton. In 1816, towards the end of his life, he became the unexpected heir of his distant cousin's estate of Lessendrum in Aberdeenshire, and it was there that he chose to pass his final days. By the time of his death in 1822, Bisset had reformed himself to such an extent that his friends and family were more likely to remember him for 'the many virtues that adorned his endearing character' than the many vices that had coloured a brief period of his past.

The sad truth of Seymour and Bisset's love affair was that its inevitable end had been inscribed on the legal documents handed to Lady Worsley at the Royal Hotel. The writ served to her had not been the liberating parliamentary divorce for which she had hoped. Regardless of the outcome of the criminal conversation trial, Seymour would remain shackled to Sir Richard and unable to remarry until his death, if she was fortunate enough to outlive him. Despite affirmations of undying love, her relationship with Bisset was destined to become untenable. Knighton demanded a legitimate heir and Bisset would require a wife of unquestionable character to provide one. Unable to free herself or to gain access to the fortune entailed on her, Lady Worsley could offer nothing more substantial than the fleeting pleasures of the bedroom.

Perhaps it was in part this realisation that had led Seymour to attempt a miscarriage earlier in September. However, the baby inside her had been determined to grow. By the time Bisset had left her, Lady Worsley was at least four months pregnant with his second child. When Seymour had chosen to elope with her lover she had taken an enormous gamble that her drastic actions would increase rather than diminish her happiness. Fourteen months later, it was questionable whether she had made any gains at all. Deeply in debt, estranged from her family, having suffered the bereavement of losing her daughter and prohibited from seeing her son, she was now alone as well. More than anything, Bisset's departure would have impressed upon her the dismal actuality of her circumstances. While Lady Worsley had chosen with defiant pride to wear the epithet of 'whore' as she had hung from her lover's arm, the true meaning of the term only revealed itself to her in his absence. Without him, Seymour faced a future where her financial need, not her heart, determined whom she would be embracing.

It is unlikely that love compelled her to accept the advances of the West Indian plantation owner, Isaac Byers when he approached her at the beginning of 1783. Like many wealthy 'planters', Byers had come to London in the hope of establishing himself among the elite and cutting a dash in society. As historian Eric Williams explains, the West Indians' 'fondest wish was to acquire an estate, blend in with the aristocracy and remove marks of their origin'. Noted for their 'lavish expenditures' and 'vulgarity', they dressed with extravagance, lived dissolutely and frequently 'were made the butt of ridicule'. Isaac Byers may not have been among the most affluent of this class but he was equally committed to penetrating the circles of the fashionable. Lady Worsley, now bereft of a lover but with a collection of influential noblemen among her 'friends', was an attractive mistress for a man of social aspirations. Her pregnant state held advantages for him as well; a womb could only contain one man's bastard at a time. Byers could enjoy several months of Lady Worsley's renowned sexual appetite without suffering the burdensome financial consequences of fathering an illegitimate child. In need of a male protector to pay her expenses and to keep her in lodgings, Seymour eventually acquiesced. Unfortunately, Byers's resources did not extend to leasing a town house in the stylish district of St James's or Mayfair. Instead, he took a dwelling on Newman Street, where, as the *Morning Herald* reported, 'he at present cohabits with her ladyship *en famille*, at a snug house taken for that purpose'.

At the end of a profligate year of spending and now confronted with legal bills, gambling debts and assorted expenses, Lady Worsley's immediate priority became the securing of financial solvency. With Byers she could at least find some steadiness. A woman of Seymour's social rank would have possessed no practical knowledge of economy. Understanding the worth of money in real terms, what it might buy and how far a farthing might be stretched, served no useful purpose to 'ladies of quality' who rarely even had occasion to handle coins. Transactions were usually dealt with through servants, bankers and solicitors and most goods were secured on shop credit. For the duration of her life as a wealthy gentlewoman, Lady Worsley was accustomed to being indulged, to having her material desires gratified with little consideration for expense. Removed entirely from the process of commerce and deprived of any real understanding of value, Seymour found it virtually impossible to regulate her expenditure.

Although it was traditional for lovers to cover the costs of their mistress's lodgings and present her with gifts such as jewellery and fine clothing, Lady Worsley found it necessary to make purchases of her own as well. As she had fled from her husband's care Seymour no longer had a home of her own. Dependent on the indulgent kindness of her lovers, she might suddenly find herself without accommodation if they tired of her and refused to pay her rent. She faced an itinerant life spent between hired addresses with no guarantee of security or comfort. She also had no legal entitlement to any of the items she had left behind and therefore found herself in the unusual position of having to establish and equip a separate household. A list of debts compiled by her solicitors reveals that a significant amount of money was owed to linen drapers, coal merchants, grocers, upholsterers, wine merchants, purveyors of kitchen ware and china, as well as Longman and Broderip, a maker of pianos. But necessities were not the only items she bought. In an effort to maintain appearances she also invested over £242 15s. and 12d.

on her own carriage, made purchases from jewellers, spent over £32 on stockings, £13 13s. and 6d. on Italian lessons, and made several gifts to gentleman friends from the Pall Mall haberdasher, Butler & Crook.

Despite Sir Richard's attempt to publicly 'cry down his wife's credit with tradesmen' in November 1781, shopkeepers who had been keeping abreast of developments via the newspapers were still willing to extend credit to Lady Worsley in her own name. Although she had absconded from her husband, women in Seymour's circumstances were usually entitled to payment of their pin money, and as it was widely known that she was an heiress, this sum was likely to be a healthy one. Indeed it was. The yearly payments of £400 that she was guaranteed could easily have supported any of her neighbours on Newman Street in smug bourgeois luxury. It was enough to fill a home with necessary furnishings and to lay a dignified table of silver and china. But it is likely that after May 1782, on the notification that the Court of Doctors' Commons would be forcing Sir Richard to pay her a further £600 per annum in alimony, shopkeepers were willing to extend her credit even further. The amount of £1,000 per annum would have maintained Lady Worsley in a grand style, to the extent that it could potentially grant her a degree of independence from male support if she was prepared to curtail her thoughtless expenditure. Had Worsley not made an attempt to appeal this ruling and settled the matter before embarking on his Mediterranean travels, Seymour might have been in a less troubled position. However, by the end of 1783, the appeal had still not been finalised and the additional sum of £600 had not arrived in the hands of Lady Worsley's bankers. Sir Richard, somewhere among the olive groves of Iberia could not be compelled to put it there.

Denied the money she had been promised, Lady Worsley's financial footing began to slip. By late 1783, her creditors came calling. Benjamin Turtle, the Duke Street butcher who had been supplying Lady Worsley's kitchen with meat, underwriting her lavish dinners of beef, suet puddings and oxtail soup, was lumbered with an unpaid bill of £88, an enormous amount for a man who might support his entire family on £300 a year. After numerous requests for payment yielded nothing, Turtle attempted to use Lady Worsley for the amount outstanding. Here he and doubtless other shopkeepers were foiled by a legal anomaly. In spite of the overwhelming sum owed, Seymour had managed to keep herself out of the Fleet prison by pleading 'coverture', a law which made a married woman's husband responsible for her debts. As their case for separation had not yet been settled nor the deeds finalising it signed, Sir Richard remained liable for his wife's bills. Unfortunately though, while the baronet remained on the continent, beyond the reach of English law, he was under no obligation to pay them.

Frustrated by the courts, the aggrieved merchants soon took matters into their own hands. Lady Worsley began receiving visits from the bailiffs. The debt collector, or bully or dun, was one of the Georgian era's most menacing figures. These men, hired by creditors to extract money by any means possible were often little better than extortionists. Bailiffs could haul defaulters to their privately operated gaols (known as sponging houses) or simply frighten them into making payments. Even when residing outside the walls of a dun's sponging house a debtor was not safe from his demands. Those stalked by a bailiff were frequently assaulted in public, pulled from their carriages and menaced in the street. Indebtedness granted bullies free rein to humiliate and coerce for their own advantage. As the *Gentleman's Magazine* reported, in addition to exacting the sums owed, 'It has been common for bailiffs when they have arrested a person for debt to drag him to some public house and order liquors of their own accord for which they oblige him to pay.' A similar campaign of terror was launched against Lady Worsley. Because she could not be prosecuted for her debts in court, an alternative means of securing repayment had to be found. According to the *Rambler*, 'The Modern Messalina' . . . was 'now . . . the dupe of duns and the prey of bullies'. However, moralists had little sympathy for her plight. Now that she was no longer the triumphant vanquisher who paraded herself about town, the voices of Fleet Street, which had goaded her on a year earlier, turned ruthlessly against her. For one who had so brazenly flouted the conventions of decency, this punishment was 'a just reward for bringing prostitution before the public eye so often clad in the allurements of dress and equipage'.

As bailiffs pounded at her door, Seymour gave birth to Bisset's child in May 1783. The fate of the infant, whether it was born screaming or feeble, whether it died immediately or was sent away to a country wet-nurse never to be retrieved, is unknown. Like their daughter Jane, this child too has disappeared without a trace. But Bisset's baby was not the last she would bear. With little hope of having her separation finalised and of receiving her outstanding alimony, Lady Worsley fled abroad in an anxious attempt to evade her creditors. Byers accompanied her to Holland and to the Belgian resort of Spa before abandoning her for more illustrious prospects. To fashionable gentlemen, mistresses were exchangeable commodities, expensive ornaments with whom one eventually grew bored, before being distracted by another more alluring object. For Byers, this new distraction was Gertrude Mahon, the hotly pursued 'Bird of Paradise.' Following Seymour's jilting, the newspapers found it difficult to trace her whereabouts until May 1785 when she appeared unexpectedly in London, heavily pregnant and alone. The *Rambler* reported that she had 'returned from the continent for the purpose of lying-in', possibly enticed back to England on the false belief that the case for her separation had been progressed.

The news of Lady Worsley's arrival in the capital immediately sprung her debt collectors out of the shadows. She had hardly been in town for six weeks before a programme of harassment recommenced. Although Seymour had instructed her creditors to appeal in writing to her husband's stewards and bankers for the money owing, she was an easier target. Once more as she reclined in her lodgings, resting her round, tired frame in preparation for the birth, the bailiffs gathered at her door. Desperate for respite and on the advice of her lawyers, she eventually agreed to make a small settlement. With sneering *double entendre* the *Rambler* reported that Lady Worsley had 'called a meeting of her creditors and means to make compound payment as far as her little all will go'. As the press sniggered at her misfortunes and the bullies circled, Seymour took to her bed and gave birth for the fourth time. This child was a girl.

On the occasion that his daughter was born, the infant's father was notably absent. Neither prying hacks nor meddling gossips had been able to discover his identity. As Lady Worsley had conceived the child while in France, it is possible that her unnamed lover was still there. She was especially eager to return as soon after the birth as possible. Her fragile newborn was only weeks old when Seymour and her lady's maid packed their belongings in preparation for an emotional journey across the Channel. Not yet twenty-eight, Lady Worsley had gained considerable experience of parenthood and the emotional agonies it brought. When children could be so easily removed from their mother's arms by the strictures of the law or by death, it was folly to love a baby. Seymour had neither a home of her own nor a stable income, nor could she expect a lover to support another man's child. When her own survival depended on the generosity of men it benefited her to remove any obstacles to attracting their interest. Before the child that she had named

Charlotte Dorothy Worsley had even been born, Seymour must have recognised that to keep her would have been virtually impossible.

In July, Lady Worsley departed England with her daughter. Once in France, she travelled northward through the velvety forests of the Ardennes towards Spa. It was near here that she handed over her infant to the protection of a local family called Cochard. This practice of quietly depositing a baby 'in a distant province . . . with a respectable family who would never connect it to its mother', was, as historian Evelyn Farr explains, a common solution to the problem of illegitimacy among the fashionable in eighteenth-century France. Who precisely the Cochards were, if they had a connection to the child's father or if they were simply hired to raise Charlotte from infancy, will remain a mystery. However, as her carriage turned toward Paris Lady Worsley certainly held one thought in her mind: whether she would ever again see her daughter.

The sumptuous *hôtels particuliers* and clipped gardens of the French capital offered a retreat like no other for the *demi-mondaines* of England. Distance from London placed Paris safely beyond public scrutiny and nearly out of Fleet Street's range. For those whose reputation had been soiled by scandal, a sojourn across the Channel in the fresh, permissive atmosphere of Paris, promised to breeze them clean. Here, among the French elite, a sexual code of conduct prevailed which contrasted sharply with the accepted moral practices of the British. Unlike their English counterparts, French high society revelled in its extramarital *affaires du coeur* and sexual desire was rarely tempered with shame. Between the English tea table and the French salon, attitudes to such matters could not have been more divergent. As British readers searched for vicarious titillation in the reprinted transcripts of *Worsley v. Bisset*, which appeared in March 1782, the French *beau monde* were eagerly cutting the pages of a new novel, *Les Liaisons Dangereuses* in search of depictions of themselves.

The British preoccupation with 'virtue' and the maintenance of a chaste character, especially among gentlewomen, was not an interest shared by their counterparts in France. By contrast with the circumspect, restrained behaviour expected of 'ladies of quality', their continental sisters were granted a great deal more sexual licence. The conventions that governed French marriage contributed largely to this situation. Even by the late eighteenth century aristocratic unions were predominantly arranged and mercenary. Young couples who knelt at the altar might have had no more than passing acquaintance before uttering their eternal vows. In Britain the elite were now allowing love to dictate their choice of spouse, but their French neighbours had come to divorce the feelings of the heart from the duties of matrimony. By way of compensation, the *haute noblesse* created an entire mode of life based around the pursuit of romantic and sexual gratification outside marriage. After the obligations of her wedding night were performed, a young woman might look forward to the most exciting years of her life.

To any moralising English observer a French married woman's reputation would have seemed virtually indestructible. To accuse a wife of reckless flirtation or displays of immodesty in such a liberal climate would have been considered absurd. Gouverneur Morris, the American plenipotentiary to France was at first quite shocked by the open behaviour of aristocratic ladies. While the practice of entertaining company as one's hair was dressed or face was painted was customary in the eighteenth century, Morris felt that his French acquaintances took this to an extreme. On one occasion, while attending such a toilette he was taken completely by surprise when his married friend stripped off in front of him and 'began washing her armpits with Hungary water'. He later wrote that among French women, he believed, 'the public performance of the toilette' to be 'merely a game played out of coquetry'. Morris was amazed at how active wives could be in encouraging sexual advances, wryly noting that in Paris, 'nuptial bands do not straighten their conduct'.

The elaborate game of pursuit and seduction known as *galanterie* was played with equal enthusiasm by both sexes. It included an implicit agreement that a husband should blithely ignore his wife's love affairs, her flirtations and male friendships while she tamely tolerated his mistresses. Beyond these ground rules, men and women were permitted to roam through the bedrooms of whomever they pleased, often engaging in short but passionate trysts. Perhaps surprisingly, this was an arrangement which suited female sensibilities as well as male. Evelyn Farr explains that, in a competitive environment where a woman's allure came to be measured by the number of hearts she had captured, 'the only reputation worth preserving was that of a desirable woman'. French society ladies would hardly have batted an eye at Seymour's list of indiscretions, nor entirely understood what had precipitated such a scandal in the first place. According to one of the most fashionable *femmes galantes*, Madame de La Tour du Pin, women were not only proud of their catalogue of conquests but were 'remarkable for the boldness with which they flaunted their amours'. Quite converse to its definition in Britain, a lady's 'good reputation' in France was defined by her skill at amorous intrigue, while the figure of the virtuous wife was 'ridiculed and dismissed'. This complete reversal of the rules made Paris the destination of choice for those maligned English ladies seeking absolution from the sins they had committed at home.

Fortunately, for the many who flocked there, in recent years the French *beau monde* had developed a liking for the English. In the late 1780s, partially sparked by a burgeoning political interest in the tenets of liberty, high society had become fascinated with England and its traditions. The influence of this Anglomania was felt in everything from garden design to furniture, and from the cut of a man's coat to his choice of horse. First among the Anglomaniacs was King Louis XVI's cousin, Louis Philippe, the Duke of Orleans, one of the richest and most fashionable men in France. The philandering, hedonistic Duke had taken Britain to his bosom, literally as well as figuratively. Orleans had not only acquired a taste for the elegant, simply styled tailoring favoured by English gentlemen, but a liking for their mistresses as well. By the time Grace Dalrymple Elliott succeeded to his bed in 1786, the Duke had already wooed Mary Robinson in vain. Orleans's penchant for notorious English women had the *Rambler* exclaiming that 'La Quadrille de Beauties Angloises' (Lady Craven, Lady Worsley, Grace Dalrymple Elliott and Mary Robinson) had conquered the French *haut ton*. They were not the only English imports to do so. The Duke's passions were distributed equally between the bedroom and the stable. His preoccupation with horse racing took him and his entourage frequently across the Channel to Newmarket and on raucous visits to a kindred spirit: the Prince of Wales. At home, English jockeys on English steeds entertained him with exhibitions of their equestrianism in races *à l'angloise*. With such an audience, Lady Worsley, known for her daring feats on horseback, was given numerous opportunities to display her skills, although her risky stunts on one occasion resulted in her being thrown while riding in the Bois de Boulogne.

It was through the Duke of Orleans's circle of racing enthusiasts that Seymour was introduced to the composer and swordsman, Joseph Boulogne, better known as the Chevalier de Saint-Georges. Like the English *demimondaines* who had been pulled into the Duke's orbit, Saint-Georges had great novelty value. The son of an eminent Guadeloupean plantation owner and his mistress, an African slave, the Chevalier had been brought to France at a young age and provided with an extensive and rigorous education. He excelled in both academic pursuits and the martial arts. At a time when an even mix of physical prowess and courtly manners defined the essence of a gentleman, Saint-Georges with his remarkable strength and impeccable charm came to embody that ideal. The Chevalier made his name as a champion with the stiletto. The fencing master, Henry Angelo who staged Saint-Georges's famous duel with the cross-dressing swordsman Chevalier d'Eon in 1787, claimed effusively that 'No man ever united so much suppleness with so much strength'. He later commented that the Chevalier seemed to possess almost super-human abilities, triumphing in 'all the bodily exercises in which he engaged'. This included dancing, at which 'he was the model of perfection', and horsemanship: he was known to ride 'the most difficult mounts bareback and make them docile'. If these physical talents were not enough, Saint-Georges was also recognised as an accomplished violinist, conductor and composer. Referred to as 'Le Mozart noir', he made his début playing with the Concert des Amateurs at the age of thirty in 1769 before becoming the orchestra's director and later the founder of the prestigious Concert de la Loge Olympique, for whom Haydn composed his Paris Symphonies. To the *beau monde* who were perpetually in search of the latest distraction, Saint-Georges with his dark skin and striking physique became an object of fascination. Admirers were drawn to him, wrote the author Alfred Marquiset, like 'a rooster who receives the adulation of a swarm of beauties'. His popularity made him an ideal addition to the Duke of Orleans's coterie, among whom he acquired a reputation as 'a very valorous champion in love'.

It was as the mistress of the handsome Chevalier Saint-Georges that Lady Worsley made her return to England in 1788. While the swordsman cut a dashing figure, this liaison, like her relationship with Isaac Byers, may have been based more on necessity than romantic inclination. Although she received pin money, the demands of fashionable living in Paris were extreme, requiring constant additions to her wardrobe and a fluid stream of cash to replenish all that had been drained away at the card tables. Only the year before, the *World* had proclaimed 'Lady Worsley to be living in poverty'. Since Sir Richard's departure for the continent in 1783 she had been eagerly awaiting some advancement in the resolution of their suit for separation. In the spring of 1788, after five years of fleeing from bailiffs and fending off creditors, she received word that it had come.

While Worsley had led his friends and fellow collectors in Rome to believe that his intended journey to London in April was for the purpose of publishing the intellectual fruits of his travels, his underlying motive was to settle the outstanding matter of his separation. After much legal manoeuvring, by 1788 the baronet's attorneys had succeeded in overturning the ruling which awarded his wife a further £600 in alimony. Once satisfied with the terms, Sir Richard was willing to sign. He had not, however, anticipated the complex snarl of bills and legal demands that also awaited him. In his absence, Worsley's attorneys, bankers and his steward, Richard Clarke had been besieged by the claims of his wife's creditors, all of which had to be discharged before the separation could be finalised. Lady Worsley's debts were considerable and clearing them would require drastic measures.

In June, the deeds for their separation were at last drawn up. This was to be an absolute parting where it was 'declared and mutually agreed' that both sides would live 'in all things . . . separate and apart . . . as if unmarried'. After their signatures had dried, only their shared name would remain between them. The document outlined in plain terms that Seymour would 'be freed and discharged from the power, command and restraint of Sir Richard Worsley' while he would 'make payable to Dame Seymour Dorothy Worsley . . . the several annual sums of £100, £100 and £200 for her separate use'. Although the sum of £400 was less than she had anticipated, the law required Sir Richard to ensure he had the funds to pay it promptly each year. In order to effect this and also to cover the expenses his wife had accumulated in his name, the baronet would be forced to sell the Stratford Place town house along with its entire contents of 'household goods, linen, china, furniture and plate'. Worsley's attorneys, fearing that the liquidising of this asset alone would not yield a sufficient amount to entirely reimburse creditors and defray the baronet's legal costs, also suggested that he sell the portion of his wife's jewellery still in his possession.

While Worsley had been purchasing marble fragments in the Mediterranean his legal representatives had been maintaining a tally of Seymour's debts. In June 1788 these amounted to at least £3,445 5s. 2d., a total (roughly equivalent to £4.3 million) which had been amassed between London and Paris. In the French capital she had accured 'small bills' of £130 and had managed to persuade a Monsieur Le Clere and a Monsieur de Selve to loan her £350 and £200 respectively. Although a list of names and a tabulation had been formulated of the sums outstanding, Worsley's attorneys were not convinced that this represented the entire amount for which Seymour had made him liable. To settle these costs, the lawyers required Lady Worsley's complete honesty and a promise that 'she will aid and assist them to the utmost of her power in getting in the bills of her creditors and expediting the payment thereof'. In truth, it is likely that Seymour had lost count of what she owed and her debts far exceeded the sum she had disclosed. For the next several years, as her correspondence with Sir Richard's bankers suggests, she would find herself periodically reminded of expenditures she had long since forgotten.

Although the law required him to do so, £3,445 5s. 2d. was not a figure that Sir Richard was willing to discharge passively. For such an exorbitant outlay, the baronet felt entitled to demand something in exchange. As the deeds for separation were being drafted he expressed a particular concern that he 'should be secure from any future debts Lady Worsley may contract'. Furthermore, he demanded to know if there were any measures which might be taken to 'to prevent her from harassing him in future?' Although Sir Richard was assured that he would no longer be held liable for Seymour's financial troubles, there did not exist a legal means of removing her menace entirely. Lady Worsley would remain free to resume her malevolent campaign of persecution against him whenever she chose. It was within her power to reveal further tales of the baronet's exploits, to shamelessly publicise private details of their marriage, to perpetuate rumours and to fell the character he was striving to reconstruct. As the law could not offer him a safeguard against such attacks, he devised one of his own.

Included in the final paragraph of the Worsleys' deeds for separation is an exceptionally unorthodox stipulation. It was a proposal deemed so outrageous that when examining the draft of the document, Sir Richard's attorney felt compelled to scribble in the margin, 'I can by no means as a British subject approve of this clause'. It suggested that 'Seymour Dorothy Worsley . . . in the space of six months . . . absent herself and withdraw herself from the Kingdom of Great Britain for the space of four years commencing from the time of her departure . . .'. The contract held that if she were to return before this period had elapsed, her husband would be entitled to withhold payment of her pin money. Without this lifeline of resources, Seymour would be truly destitute. This imposed exile was, as his lawyer observed, 'very far from legal'. Notwithstanding objections from the couple's solicitors, Lady Worsley, perhaps out of desperation to finalise the separation and liberate herself from her husband's manipulations, agreed to the conditions. The form that her signature takes on the deeds speaks clearly of her relief at this long-yearned-for resolution. Whether out of anger or exultation, Seymour gripped the pen and violently scrawled on the parchment the name she had come to loathe, Worsley. With each pass of her hand she drew an emphatic underscore beneath it, causing the lines to bleed into an indistinct blur of ink. It was as if she wished to cancel it out altogether. Later, Seymour would look back on that day, the 14th of June 1788, which promised her release to a happier, more carefree existence. At the time, relinquishing her right to remain in Britain or to retreat to its safe havens doubtless seemed an inconsequential price to pay for the guarantee of financial security. She could not have imagined how wrong she would be.

It was with eagerness that she departed for France at the onset of winter and returned to her friends in Paris. But the attractions that drew her there, the possibility of a life pursued without shame, the 'whirlpool of dissipation, pleasure and indulgence' described by the comte de Tilly, were at their twilight when her carriage re-entered the capital. In less than a year, the freedom in which she delighted, along with the walls of the Bastille, were to come tumbling down.

21

Museum Worsleyanum

Over the years, Sir Richard Worsley had grown accustomed to inspiring fascination. The searching eyes and the quizzical expressions, the smirks and gasps
were reactions he often received when in company. But after 1786 the expressions of amusement were more often born of delight than ridicule. With his
box of ancient gems and a portfolio bulging with Willey Reveley's sketches
of foreign lands, Worsley had acquired the power of entertainment. Like a
magician, he would slide open the drawers of his cabinet and raise translu-
cent cameos to the light, illuminating the figures of dancing fauns and
goddesses in chariots. Intaglios featuring the heads of Mark Antony and
Caesar graven into precious stones were passed among his audiences.
Ceremoniously, his valet would lay his collection of drawings on a table.
Egyptian landscapes, the exotic streets of Constantinople and views of the
Acropolis were unfolded in front of his spectators. Each scene and artefact
prompted the spinning of a traveller's tale and with relish Worsley recounted
his heroic odyssey: the skilful avoidance of Barbary pirates, the dances of
slave girls, the discovery of treasures. At a time when a rare few were fortunate enough to glimpse the pyramids of Giza or the friezes of the Parthenon,
the baronet's voyages were regarded as journeys of awesome proportions. His
stories and souvenirs would have seemed as wondrous as those brought back
from a trip to the moon. For the baronet, these displays were opportunities
not just to showcase his possessions but to present his reinvented persona
to the world. Whatever people may have heard before they met him, his

dazzling box of relics and adventurous tales stirred admiration for his bravery, knowledge and wealth.

It had not taken Sir Richard long to realise that when equipped with his cabinet of curiosities, he had the ability to disarm potential critics and charm his way into the good will of strangers. While in Constantinople he had encountered Lady Craven, an associate of his wife's and also a friend of Horace Walpole, a fellow collector who in the past had been less than complimentary in his opinions of the baronet. Worsley wooed her with his stories before reaching into his box of treasures and cordially 'entreating [her] to accept of some Egyptian pebbles as knife handles'. Eager to cultivate Walpole's esteem, he then presented her with 'a coloured drawing of the Castle of Otranto' which it was suggested that she 'as a friend of Mr Walpole's might have the pleasure of giving to him'. The generosity of these gestures achieved a favourable result. The flattered Lady Craven not only arranged Sir Richard's passage to Russia on the frigate she had sailed aboard but delivered the drawing to Walpole, who received the baronet's 'very valuable gift' with 'delight'.

Worsley's greatest success had been with the royal courts of Russia and Eastern Europe. By the time he arrived in Russia, Sir Richard had become accomplished at beguiling company with his movable feast of curios. His reputation secured him invitations to present his collection and to examine those of other enthusiasts. In Moscow, the baronet was offered a rare glimpse of the private museum of a 'Mr Dinedoff', the exceedingly wealthy owner of several Siberian ore mines who had amassed 'a very extensive collection' of 'a few good antiques and some good pictures' as well as 'many curious petrifications and a fine collection of chrystals'. Worsley was less impressed by Dinedoff's 'courtyard paved with iron', decorated with 'several iron statues and busts in a bad style'. The collections at the recently constructed Hermitage Palace as well as 'the apartments of the Kremlin' with their 'great amount of gold and silver plate of different sizes and shapes' were also made available for his inspection. More significantly, Worsley's renown bought him an audience with Catherine the Great, a devoted patroness of the arts. In St Petersburg he was summoned to the Hermitage, where he 'went at 12 o'clock to Prince Potemkin's apartments in the palace'. '. . . The Empress came and stayed two hours to see my drawings,' he recorded in his diary. Sir Richard's stories and images of sand-swept antiquity made a marked impression on Her Imperial Highness, who later described Worsley's pictures to the French

Ambassador as well as to Baron von Grimm, her art dealer. In Warsaw, Sir Richard met with a similar reception from Stanisław August Poniatowski, the King of Poland, at whose enlightened court he was invited to dine with a circle of nobles, 'artists and men of science'. The monarch was captivated by the baronet's *objets d'art* and for the short period that Sir Richard resided in Poland drew him into his confidence; escorting him to the salon of the mistress he had recently married and introducing him to other members of the royal family, to whom Worsley also displayed his treasures. Even after his return to Rome, word of the baronet's drawings and antiquities circulated throughout the capital's community of scholars, both resident and visiting. Among them was the German philosopher Goethe, who commented that Worsley's 'striking reproductions' of the Acropolis had 'left an indelible impression' on him.

But while the accolades of foreign heads of state and continental collectors were appreciated, it was the approval of his countrymen that Worsley truly desired. The unique objects he had amassed had been intended for their eyes, for the admiration of his learned peers of the Royal Society and the Society of Antiquaries, for men of state and influence. As Worsley had not simply purchased his collection from art dealers but personally dug it from the ground or bartered for it on foreign soil, he felt that it merited a grand fanfare. He did not believe that the conventional route of announcing his findings by publishing in the Royal Society's journal would trumpet his achievements sufficiently. Instead, the baronet decided that his collection deserved its own book.

Although Worsley falsely protested that the idea of publication came to him after 'listening to the earnest solicitations of some literary friends', he had returned to Rome from his travels in 1787 with the intention of immediately beginning work on a text. For what would be an extensive task of gathering and assimilating materials, the baronet enlisted the help of Ennio Quirino Visconti, a noted antiquarian and the President of Rome's Capitoline Museum. Sir Richard's ambitions demanded that the volume, which was to be entitled the *Museum Worsleyanum*, would be written in both English and Italian. The decision, he claimed, was not due to his obvious desire to make his reputation as a collector known as widely as possible, but inspired by his 'warm attachment' to Visconti. Additionally, he commented with a hint of intellectual superiority, he had acquired 'an early partiality for the Italian language', which he felt was 'best adapted for the explanation of monuments of art'.

Sir Richard intended his *Museum Worsleyanum* to be a work of tremendous proportions, in its scholarly impact and its physical form. Every detail was designed to impress its readership and testify to its creator's exquisite taste. He spent part of 1790 and the early half of 1791 searching for 'the very best paper to be had . . . on which to print my Museum' and examining the copper plates to be used in the printing process. By the time the first volume was published in 1798, he had spent a formidable £2,887 4s. for the publication and binding of 150 copies. This sum doubled with the production of a second volume in 1802. It was later estimated that the entire expense of the project, including the cost of Sir Richard's travels, amounted to upwards of £27,000. Not a penny had been spent with profit in mind. The *Museum Worsleyanum* expressly was not to be sold. Instead, this academic text, designed exclusively for the erudite gentleman, was to be awarded to select recipients whose esteem the baronet wanted to cultivate. He would not allow it to fall into the 'inappropriate' hands of booksellers, who would compromise its elevated subject matter by ascribing a price to it. Worsley went to extremes to ensure his volumes remained beyond the reach of commerce. In 1804, when hearing that a copy he had given to a friend was about to be auctioned at Christie's, he hastily reclaimed his gift.

In 1798, after eleven years in preparation, copies of the *Museum Worsleyanum* were generously dispatched to at least twenty-seven gentlemen as well as to the Royal Society and the Society of Antiquaries. Among those to receive these grandiose gifts were his friends and brother collectors, Sir William Hamilton, Charles Townley, Richard Payne Knight, and Thomas Astle, as well as the President of the Royal Society, Sir Joseph Banks, the Prime Minster, William Pitt, the leader of the opposition, Charles James Fox, the naval hero, Lord Nelson and the Duke of York. The parcel that arrived at their doors would have been enormous. Due to its weight and size – 16 x 22 inches – the unfortunate servant who took the delivery would have found it difficult to carry. When its wrapping was removed, the *Museum Worsleyanum* gleamed in its supple blue leather binding and gold embossed lettering. Its size meant that it would not sit easily on library shelves beside other tomes of dull brown: it required its own large space or to be exhibited decoratively on a book stand, where as a focal point it would command admiration. The *Museum Worsleyanum* was more than a lavish bribe from a disgraced baronet, it was also a blaring advertisement for the new and improved Sir Richard Worsley.

The publication of the *Museum Worsleyanum* represented the culmination of his ambitions and his final determined attempt to restore his name. The words of his introduction, puffed with pomposity resound from the page like those of a master of ceremonies. 'Impelled by the love of the Fine Arts and anxious to view the celebrated remains of sculpture when it was carried to the highest perfection by the most elegant nation in the universe, the Greeks,' he announces, 'I determined to visit Athens . . .' After several effusive paragraphs commending Visconti and Reveley for their contributions and boasting of the support he received from his distinguished associates, 'with whom I lived in the closest of friendship', he at last provides the reader with the meat of his book. As might be expected of 'Sir Finical Whimsy', the ordering of his objects is meticulous and scientific. The baronet divided his work 'into six classes or chapters containing one hundred and fifty one copper plates including a title page', the text for which alternated between Italian and its English translation. The first three classes were composed of Greek and some Egyptian reliefs, busts, full statues, heads and fragments. The next three were dedicated to his collection of engraved gems (the intaglios and cameos) and his collection of drawings 'taken on the spot'. Each item was illustrated with detailed accuracy, which Worsley felt would make the work especially useful not only to the connoisseur but to the artist who wanted to learn from 'specimens of ancient sculpture at the most flourishing period of its existence'.

In the mind of its maker, the *Museum Worsleyanum* represented a colossal accomplishment. In the true spirit of enlightenment, Sir Richard, as a member of the gentry had embraced his ordained role as a patron of the arts. He had utilised his wealth to liberate the highest examples of human craftsmanship from their neglected positions in the Mediterranean and delivered them to Britain in the name of scholarship. He intended the *Museum Worsleyanum* and the unique collection it described to be his legacy. Accordingly, the baronet felt entitled to brag about his achievements. On the publication of his *magnum opus*, Worsley wrote to Sir William Hamilton, a man whose life had been devoted to the production of his own exquisite books, that 'without vanity' he believed the *Museum Worsleyanum* 'to be the finest printed book I have yet seen'. As the years advanced, such insensitive expressions, even towards a man who regularly addressed Sir Richard as 'my dear cousin', became expected from the increasingly anti-social baronet.

Worsley had spent roughly fifteen years engaged in a penance. This epic undertaking to assemble an unrivalled collection of antiquities had absorbed his thoughts, his heart and much of his wealth, but whether these Herculean labours achieved their ultimate aim is questionable. Sir Richard's extensive travels on the continent may have been responsible for the government's decision to award him the diplomatic position of British Minister-Resident to Venice in 1793. Although the baronet had been campaigning for Robert Ainslie's position in Constantinople, William Pitt would have seen Worsley's intimate knowledge of Italy as an asset at a time when Europe was about to tilt headlong into war. This posting, and two re-elections for the rotten borough seats of Newport and Newton between 1790 and 1793, went some way towards soothing his injured dignity, but failed to restore it entirely.

In his ambassadorial role, Sir Richard was able to assume what he considered his rightful place in the hierarchy of worthies. He could live with all the self-importance and splendour of a foreign dignitary. Centrally placed at the Palazzo Querini with a view across the Grand Canal, Worsley became the master of a fiefdom of British subjects. Any English man or woman of rank whose boat crossed the harbour to the Republic was greeted by him. Through his hands passed all of King George's concerns with respect to British interests in La Serenissima. Matters of war and highly confidential correspondence came directly from Westminster to his desk. The baronet's assiduous application to tasks meant that he was tireless in their execution, from his regular reports to the Secretary of State, William Wyndham Grenville, about the activities of the French to the watch he kept on British subjects sojourning in Venice.

His situation in Venice also ensured that he was perfectly placed to make additional acquisitions. To his plushly adorned residence he had carried his cabinet of engraved gems and the exotic drawings which had captivated Catherine the Great and the King of Poland. To these objects he added further pieces: dramatic canvases painted by baroque and Renaissance masters, sweet-faced Madonnas and Venuses and pastoral visions of Arcadia. Ornate, gilt frames held masterpieces by Titian, Veronese and Caravaggio. Marble sculptures and busts, fragments of friezes and masonry filled the corners and lined the corridors. The Minister-Resident's apartments were a casket of treasures, a visit to which promised a dizzying spectacle for any British traveller fortunate enough to be admitted. The surroundings also served as a stage for the performances that Sir Richard continued to mount.

John Morritt, the heir to Rokeby Park, and his friend Robert Stockdale, a Fellow of Pembroke College were just the sort of travellers that Worsley enjoyed entertaining with his tales and artefacts. In May 1796, they were *en route* for England after a lengthy expedition through Greece and Turkey. Like Sir Richard, Morritt had been caught in the flurry of enthusiasm for Greek antiquities, and he was eager to examine the baronet's treasures. He was not disappointed. As they were 'Greecian travellers' Worsley made a show of hospitality, paying them 'great attention' and giving them 'free ingress and regress to his cabinet, which is very well worth seeing, and particularly rich in cameos and antique stones', Morritt surmised. Worsley then hosted a dinner for his guests where wine warmed their memories of the Acropolis and the sight of the sparkling Bosporus. After the dishes were cleared, the baronet allowed them to inspect the larger objects in his collection, which Morritt found to be 'very fine in the way of sculpture and painting'. At last, Sir Richard opened his portfolio of Reveley's images and, as the young man wrote, 'gave us a gallop on our own hobby-horse through from the plains of Greece and Asia'. But in spite of the fulsome welcome, the exceptional contents of his cabinet, the artistic expertise of the drawings, the show-manship and the knowledge displayed by his host, Morritt spent most of the evening sitting rather uncomfortably. None of the baronet's remarkable objects could distract him from the greatest spectacle in the Palazzo. As Morritt observed Worsley immersed in recollections or expounding on Greek history, he 'could not help now and then thinking of the *peeping* scene'. The more intently he watched Britain's Minister-Resident to Venice, the less able he was to shake the twelve-penny cuckold from his mind; that fat figure with his dumb smile, bearing the weight of his betrayer on his shoulders. The young man later admitted to being 'rather surprised at him, as, from his conversation and ideas, he by no means seems as if he had been such an ass'. The strength of this impression even undermined that of the glittering *Museum Worsleyanum*. All of the relics of antiquity would fail to obscure it entirely.

22

Repentance

In September 1792, the French Revolution which had begun with the fall of the Bastille and a whoop of political idealism three years earlier had taken a terrifying turn into bloodshed and chaos. Declaring an end to the monarchy, revolutionaries stormed the Tuileries Palace on the 10th of August and massacred over 600 guards, courtiers and servants. Paris was cast into turmoil. Gangs of violent, often drunken thugs wearing the 'bonnet rouge' patrolled the streets with sharp weapons and shouts, accosting enemies of the revolution. 'Every person who had the appearance of a gentleman, whether stranger or not, was run through the body with a pike,' wrote a correspondent for the *The Times* on the 10th of September, 'He was of course an *Aristocrate* . . . A ring, a watch chain, a handsome pair of buckles, a new coat, or a good pair of boots in a word, every thing which marked the appearance of a gentleman, and which the mob fancied, was sure to cost the owner his life.' According to *The Times*, limbs and heads were strewn throughout the public squares and causeways, while 'carcases lie scattered in hundreds, diffusing pestilence all around'. After such carnage, the sight of death was so common that bodies were simply 'passed by and trod on without any particular notice'.

Following the assault on the Tuileries, it had become virtually impossible to secure the papers necessary to leave the city. The international diplomatic corps, including the British Ambassador, Lord Gower, had been ordered to return to the safety of their home countries. They were some of the last to depart. Behind them the gates of Paris were shut and an assortment of their unprotected nationals were sealed into a violent labyrinth. Within it was trapped Lady Worsley.

Long before the summer of 1792, many of Seymour's noble friends were able to read the portents of impending danger; they could see that the *ancien régime* and its comfortable privileges were on the brink of extinction. As early as 1790, Seymour had observed the traffic of French nobles and those sympathetic to the monarchy move northward from Paris, seeking refuge in Brussels, Lille, Calais and Britain. Even the King and his family had mounted an escape attempt to Varennes which ended in their capture. In the face of these developments, Lady Worsley had become increasingly concerned for her own security and in March 1792 took up temporary residence in Lille among a community of royalists. At that time, only weeks before the conflict in France would escalate into a war with Austria, she wrote an urgent letter to Sir Richard's banker, Mr Drewe. In it she not only 'complained of want of money' but 'hinted an intention of coming to England'. As she had waived her right to return to her homeland Mr Drewe was forced to remind her of the consequences of this course of action. Corresponding with William Clarke he assured Worsley's steward that 'the letter I have written to her today will induce her to drop that idea'. With eight months left to elapse on the period of her exile, Seymour could do little more than hope that the situation around her would not deteriorate further.

Initially, the life she had returned to in Paris at the end of 1788 had promised a fresh start. Although her relationship with the Chevalier Saint-Georges ended the following year, Lady Worsley soon attached herself to another skilled duellist. However, unlike Saint-Georges, Dick England fought with pistols. He was a 'black-leg', a fast-living, boot-wearing disciple of the turf and card table, and it is likely that Seymour had got to know him through her association with the Prince of Wales long before he had arrived in Paris. The circumstances that brought him there were nearly as sensational as Seymour's. In June 1784, England had challenged a brewer named William Peter Lee Rowlls to a duel over an unpaid gambling debt. Pistols were drawn in the garden of an inn near Ascot and rather than shooting over his opponent's shoulder (a gesture necessary to restore honour while preserving a man's life) England aimed at Rowlls's torso and fired. The brewer died instantly and England, in fear of the law, fled to France. This imbroglio did little to improve the gambler's reputation. Even among the knavish fraternity of blacklegs and prior to this incident, he was, according to *The Particulars of the Late Dick*

England by an Old Crony, 'considered by some to be beneath contempt'. With a 'Herculean form and an athletic constitution', as well as a 'natural ferocity, hardness of heart and a selfish passion', the Irish-born England could be both a dangerous adversary and an ideal protector for an unattached woman in revolutionary Paris. He also had an expert knowledge of the gaming hall.

It may have been Lady Worsley's connection with the Duke of Orleans that enabled her and Dick England to be among the first to establish a Faro table at the Palais Royal. By the time he inherited his family property in 1785, the Duke was a slave to horse racing and card games, two habits which managed to deplete even his overflowing coffers. Unwilling to curtail his pleasures he instead came up with a scheme which utilised his home to fund his extravagant lifestyle. Determined to make his Palais Royal 'the capital of Paris', Orleans employed the architect Victor Louis to convert the ground floor into a ring of 180 exclusive shops, while adapting the top two floors into rented lodgings. The building's capacious cellars were transformed into spaces for restaurants, cafés and social clubs, locations which later became hives of political intrigue during the revolution. The most elegant rooms within the palace, those tucked into the first floor *piano nobile*, became the preserve of gamesters.

Surprisingly, this had never been part of the Duke's original design. Outside the mirrored salons of the aristocracy (into which the law could not extend its long arm) gambling had been banned. But as Orleans let his shop fronts and lavish apartments to a variety of individuals, circumspect and otherwise, they assumed that his name guaranteed security for whatever enterprises they launched. The lantern-lit arcades soon became populated by brothels offering girls as expensive as the fine merchandise peddled by the Palais Royal's shop-keepers. Eager to make a handsome return, many of the madams subsequently sublet their best rooms on the first floor to gambling salons. In August 1790, when the actors Michael Kelly and Jack Johnstone 'met with the well-known Richard England' there was only a modest collection of gaming tables within the precincts of the palace. England's *salle*, which 'was kept in conjunction with the celebrated Lady Worsley', Kelly remarked was among the most fashionable of these and 'was frequented by the *beau monde* of Paris'. Lady Worsley's presence would have been vital to the operation. While Dick England acted as the card table's banker, Seymour passed her evenings circulating among her guests, lending a genteel air to the scene. Ultimately, her role as a 'hostess with savoir-faire', as described by Jean Paul Marat in his contemporary periodical, *L'Ami du peuple*, was to ensure that players were manipulated to the banker's advantage. A gentle word of encouragement might keep a loser at the table one game longer, while striking up a conversation at a decisive interval might distract another player's judgement. The most successful hostesses were able to cloak their manoeuvres discreetly in charm and could earn as much as 96 *livres* in a day (equivalent to roughly £500 today). However, as Seymour's pleading letters to her husband's bank suggest, it is unlikely that their gambling venture was as lucrative as they would have wished.

By 1791, the Palais Royal's first floor was supporting the weight of over a hundred tables where games of chance could be played. Lady Worsley and Dick England's concern was cast adrift among a sea of others. Gambling now competed with an array of equally attractive entertainments both inside and outdoors. The 'steerers' or touts employed to direct passing trade to the gaming tables upstairs were frequently defeated by the shouts from the sideshow booths where Prussian giantesses and 500-pound men awaited spectators. The cross-section of Parisian society which poured through the entryways and into the enclosed garden could enjoy activities ranging from spontaneous political debates to theatrical performances while prostitutes, pick-pockets and police informers circulated freely among them. Critics such as the marquis de Bombelles lambasted the 'habitual indecency' of the 'nasty place' where 'the most indefensible debauchery' transpired in darkened rooms. The liberality of the Palais Royal, the progressive ideology preached in its cafés, the dissoluteness of its gaming tables, and the presence of *filles de joye* within its colonnades, horrified many in the court. The increasingly anti-monarchical Duke intended this. Along with the populist alterations he made to his ancestral home, the Duke of Orleans sealed his reputation as a champion of the people by re-branding himself Philippe Égalité, a name given to him by the radical Paris Commune. Unfortunately, in the end neither this title nor the democratic façade of the Palais Royal could shield his neck from the guillotine.

When Philippe Égalité was arrested in April 1793 along with the other members of the ruling house of Bourbon, a shadow of suspicion was thrown across his associates as well. The Duke's extended circle of free-thinking hedonists, horse-loving Anglomaniacs, and well-dressed members of the *beau monde*, whether nobility, bourgeoisie or servants, whether French, English or Irish, were all regarded as potential enemies of the republic. In May the Chevalier Saint-Georges was denounced. At the end of 1793 Dick

England was imprisoned, as was Lady Worsley's friend, Grace Dalrymple Elliott. By September that year British subjects not already in one of fifty places of detention in Paris were by order of the Jacobin government 'seized as hostages for Toulon'.

After December 1792 Lady Worsley's correspondence with Sir Richard's banker, the only trail by which it is possible to trace her movements, comes to an inexplicable end. Given the restrictions placed on travel, the scantiness of her financial resources, the individuals with whom she was affiliated and her status as an enemy national, it is highly probable that she, like most of her confidants, was imprisoned during the Reign of Terror. Grace Dalrymple Elliott, who left an intriguing though embellished account of her experiences during the revolution, frequently mentions a friend whose true identity has always been subject to question. Mrs Meyler, or Naylor, was an English woman of genteel birth and compromised circumstances who moved within the circle of the Parisian *haut ton*. What precisely her matrimonial status was seems to be unclear. According to one of Mrs Elliott's biographers Horace Bleakley, she was either a widow or a woman whose husband had some association with Italy. Whatever her marital position, her lifestyle at the onset of the Terror was not a comfortable one. Elliott describes her as living 'very retired' and keeping 'but one maid . . . in a part of Paris very private' (or unfashionably down-at-heel). This 'English Lady' was in fact living 'up four stairs', in a garret on 'the Rue de l'Encre behind the old Opera house', an area known for its dancing girls and prostitutes. As a supporter of the royalist cause and without assets to protect or a political agenda to pursue there was no logical reason why this friend should have chosen to remain in Paris at a time when her safety was in jeopardy, unless compelled by external factors to do so. At some point between 1793 and 1794, 'Mrs Meyler' was confined at the Carmes Prison along with Grace Elliott and other fashionable women of the court such as the duchesse D'Aiguillon, the marquise de Custine, and Josephine Beauharnais, the future wife of Napoleon Bonaparte. After their release, Elliot and her friend remained intimate. The editor of Grace Elliott's journal mentions that she later 'resided at Brompton' with 'Mrs Meyler', from 1801 until 1814, a period that coincides with rate book records stating that Mrs Elliott was living at Brompton House with Lady Worsley. Elliott's account had passed through two sets of meddling hands before it was published in the Victorian era. As a result it is littered with errors and deliberate deceptions to distract readers from the fact that its heroine had been a courtesan. Given the circumstances, it is likely that identities were confused and notorious names changed.

If Lady Worsley was imprisoned, the length of her detention is unknown. The death of Robespierre which brought the Reign of Terror's machinery to a halt at the end of July 1794 threw wide the doors of many of Paris's prisons. Grace Elliott and the mysterious Mrs Meyler were released from the Carmes in August, but they as well as many other British nationals who had been incarcerated found it difficult to secure a return passage to their homeland in the midst of war. It can therefore be assumed with some certainty that Seymour would not have been in England when, in the following year, her son Robert died unexpectedly.

In the years since her elopement, it is unlikely that Lady Worsley had so much as glimpsed her son. As a separated woman, the law stripped her of access to her children. The repercussions of this cruel measure, when combined with the bitterness of her daughter Jane's death and her parting with the infant Charlotte, must have grieved her incessantly. Although communication between mother and child was forbidden, Lady Worsley received occasional reports of Robert from her husband's steward. In December 1791 he wrote to inform Seymour of her son's academic progress, news which delighted her. 'I am very happy to hear that my Dearest Worsley is so well and that his master is so contented with him,' she enthused before her memories were flooded with anguish. 'Pray give my love to him,' she continued, 'I hope he will not forget a mother that dotes upon him. A time may come that I shall be able to prove to him how much I love him, but I will say no more on a subject that causes me much pain.' Sadly, the day that she had longed for was never to arrive.

If any party was made to bear the sharp end of the Worsleys' misadventure, it was their son Robert Edwin. The short life of their sole legitimate heir was a desolate and tragic one. Correspondence and family documents contain so little mention of him that it is as if his name, inextricable from that of his parents, also carried their shame. The few references that do survive sketch out a childhood led without a mother and only a shadow for a father. When Seymour last held her son in 1781, Robert was five years old. Over the years and with Sir Richard's encouragement, the early recollections he retained of his mother were eventually outgrown. Raised by nursery maids, servants and tutors, he had little contact with his father who had disappeared abroad when his son was not quite seven and returned to him a stranger when Robert was twelve. Within a year, Worsley had enrolled Robert at the school he had attended as a boy, Winchester College, where he remained until 1793. That June, only months before the baronet again left England for Venice, he purchased his son an Ensign's commission in the King's Royal Rifle Corps.

Like his father, Robert's blossoming talents inclined towards the intellectual. In 1792, he was awarded a school prize for a poem entitled 'The Execution and Death of Lady Jane Grey' and when John Wilkes encountered him across a dinner table in December 1788 the old politician found Robert 'a very handsome and promising youth'. Wilkes also noted that, as expected of Sir Richard's boy, 'he is reading Virgil and Ovid'. Undoubtedly, the baronet hoped to send his son on the grand tour, but the bloodshed on the continent prevented him and many other wealthy parents from doing so. A period of military training was seen as a fitting alternative. At the time he joined his regiment, the King's Royal Rifle Corps was stationed on the Isle of Wight and seemingly beyond harm.

The cause of Robert Edwin Worsley's death on the 10th of April 1795 is undisclosed. He is noted only as having died in Gloucestershire, quite probably while on exercise as 'a Lieutenant in Prince William of Gloucester's Regiment'. Given his father's posting in Venice and his estrangement from his mother, Robert would have been committed to the family vault with little ceremony. The news of the loss of Appuldurcombe's only heir must have come as a debilitating blow to both Sir Richard and Lady Worsley. One can only imagine how the baronet, a man whose entire philosophy turned on the notion of an inherited family legacy and who had devoted so much effort to cleansing the Worsley name, contended with this.

Evidence suggests that Seymour was not able to return to Britain until at least a year and a half after her son's death, in early 1797. The adversity she had suffered in France, compounded by her recent bereavement, had drained her fortitude as much as it had her finances. With little of the flamboyant spirit and carefree demeanour that had so astonished society, Lady Worsley slipped quietly back to England. Shortly after establishing herself at a discreet and inexpensive address, she became seriously ill. 'I did not think some time since that I should have ever been alive,' Seymour wrote of those despairing days when 'an inflammation upon the lungs' and 'the expense of a long illness' drove her to reach for her pen. Since the public disgrace of the criminal conversation trial, all communication between Lady

Worsley and her mother and sister had, for propriety's sake, ceased. Her sister, Lady Harrington had been abroad with her husband on his postings to Jamaica and in Ireland and was therefore spared the full force of Seymour's embarrassment as it rebounded on to the family. Her mother and her stepfather had been placed directly in the path of the storm. Until this time, how much they knew of her suffering in France or the extent of her impoverishment is questionable.

Her family offered reconciliation tentatively at first. After two months of Seymour's illness, Lady Harrington and her mother, the recently titled Baroness Harewood, crept to her bedside. 'You will now be glad to hear that I am restored to the love and regard of all my family,' she wrote triumphantly to her husband's steward: 'they have all been to see me and . . . they are all goodness to me.' Their reunion was soothing medicine. 'Think what happiness I must feel at an event that I have so long wished for,' she exclaimed.

Although the support of her sister and mother helped Lady Worsley to recover from the worst of her affliction, her empty purse continued to cause her distress. Seymour claimed that her doctor had directed her 'to go immediately to the sea' in order to recover her 'lost health', but in May 1797 she could not afford the trip. 'I am quite ruined,' she wrote to William Clarke, 'and now without a guinea'. She required an advance of £50 on her quarterly allowance which would allow her to travel to Weymouth and breathe the fresh air thought to cure respiratory illnesses. 'If you can not make it convenient,' she implored him, 'I must remain here until my quarter is due . . . nothing but my bad health could induce me to ask so great a favour of you.' Due either to her husband's intervention or Clarke's obstinacy, only half of the funds were granted.

However, salvation did arrive from an unexpected source. In the early summer, Lord and Lady Harrington escorted Seymour to the sea, first to Weymouth and then Brighton. As both the Earl and Countess held positions in the royal household and sat at the very centre of respectable social circles, their appearance in public with Lady Worsley was a conspicuously grand gesture of forgiveness. Once the road to *rapprochement* had been officially opened, others were swift to come down it. Soon her 'dearest mother' was also seen unashamedly accompanying Seymour on her Brighton promenades. She had 'come 280 miles to see me', Seymour wrote, 'and you may imagine how happy this new proof of my mother's love and affection must make me'. Even relations on her husband's side were prepared to offer forgiveness: 'All my family are very good to me,' she said; in particular she mentions Lord Cork, who 'paid me a visit at Bristol' and even her mother-in-law, Lady Betty Worsley who was 'very good in enquiring kindly after me of my mother'. These events and the magnanimity displayed by her family made her reflect on her situation. 'I really think one of the greatest blessings is being beloved by ones nearest and dearest,' she wrote.

Unfortunately, although her relatives were willing to embrace her, they were in no position to alleviate her poverty and debts. 'If I were not so poor I should indeed be comfortable,' Seymour complained to William Clarke and later, on hearing that Sir Richard would be returning to England, she suggested that 'if he does come . . . it would be very desirable for us both to come to some arrangements'. Lady Worsley would never be satisfied with the size of her allowance while the bulk of her assets remained beyond her grasp and entirely at the disposal of her vindictive husband. Now that the rift with her family was healed, what Seymour desired most was the reinstatement of her fortune, which was possible only if she managed to outlive Sir Richard.

With the assistance of the Earl of Harrington, one of the trustees of her and her sister's property at Brompton, Seymour was able to take up residence in the house that was rightfully hers but which the law prevented her from owning. Although the Brompton estate had been inherited by her father, the Fleming family had never used the dated seventeenth-century manor house, its outlying buildings or its land. Behind the estate's walls lay over 95 acres of fields, gardens and nurseries filled with 'several kinds of fruit trees and evergreen shrubs', as well as an impressive array of rose bushes. In 1784, the trustees of Brompton Park House had renovated the building and divided it into a row of three separate dwellings. These new homes, along with Hale House, a smaller residence near the estate's perimeter, were then let out to an assortment of tenants. With its location off the main road, and lying just outside the village of Brompton, the collection of houses became a favoured retreat for those wishing to escape the public eye. When Lady Worsley established herself in the westernmost of these, her neighbours were Henry Richard Fox, 3rd Lord Holland, and his mistress, Elizabeth Vassall Webster, who was then embroiled in a divorce. The easternmost house was occupied first by Seymour's banker, Thomas Hammersley and later by his business partner, Charles Greenwood. As friends of the Prince of Wales and the Duke of York, both men had a reputation for fast living, Greenwood in particular; he died in the arms of the Duke of Clarence after an over-stimulating game of cards. They were eventually joined by Grace Elliott when she rented the middle house.

Lady Worsley owed much to the Earl and Countess of Harrington and her mother. But Seymour was on a short lead and recognised this. With the zeal of the recently reformed, she boasted of her altered character and of the regard that others now had for her, commenting to William Clarke that she had 'entirely given up' unreliable associations and 'when at Brompton . . . am very often with my mother and sister and many ladies of their acquaintance'. In fact, Lady Worsley, having settled into a nest of rakes and *demi-mondaines*, was by no means prepared to reform entirely. But with maturity she had acquired a sense of discretion, a virtue she had lived without for so long.

Her persistent financial troubles as well as her desire for excitement made Seymour continue to court and accept the advances of men who would subsidise her lifestyle. On two separate occasions her name became entangled with those who lived on the Brompton estate. In the summer of 1797, while claiming to have rehabilitated her character, she was engaging in a liaison with her 'near neighbour', Colonel George Porter, a fortune-hunting Whig politician devoted to the Prince of Wales and the pursuit of divorced ladies. He later married the notorious Lady Grosvenor, in 1802. His bride was at least eleven years his senior. Another of Brompton's tenants with a similar taste for experienced older women was the man who lived in Hale House, Jean Louis Hummell.

Like Dick England, and the Chevalier Saint-Georges before him, Jean Louis Hummell would not have been considered fitting company by Seymour's 'mother and sister and many ladies of their acquaintance'. Hummell had been born Jean Louis Couchet (or Cuchet) in Geneva in 1779. As children, he and his sister Eugenia had been taken to London by their mother Françoise Couchet and their stepfather, Charles Hummell. The family eventually settled in Covent Garden where Charles Hummell traded as a 'stocking manufacturer', but aspired to make a living as a composer. A fondness for music was something he shared with his stepson. As a boy Jean Louis developed a powerful singing voice, and living within earshot of the capital's two principal theatres enabled his guardian to push him under the appropriate noses. From as early as 1794, 'Master Hummell', who had not quite reached the age of fourteen, was appearing on stage at the Theatre Royal in performances of Handel and Corelli's choral works. The name Hummell would certainly have worked to his advantage in the musical world. Although Jean Louis bore no relation to Johann Nepomuk Hummel, a musical child prodigy of almost identical age who lived in London during the early 1790s, there was much scope for a favourable confusion of identities. Charles Hummell used his stepson's successes to further his own career and by 1799 the duo was composing music together. None of their works, which include a number of popular songs and sonatas as well as military music, are especially memorable, though Jean Louis did cultivate a name among the English musical establishment of his day.

Jean Louis Hummell must have been an alluringly romantic figure. A frequent performer at private musical parties, he could be found standing by the side of a fortepiano, his voice warbling the lyrics to 'My True Love's on the Sea', one of his melodies. It is likely that Lady Worsley met him in such circumstances, just after the start of the new century. With a family background in trade, earning a living as a singer and minor composer, Hummell would not have been wealthy. Seymour, in her mid-forties, was old enough to be his mother. Neither was in any way appropriate for the other but mutual attraction drew them together. In Jean Louis, she may have imagined something of the son she had lost. In Lady Worsley, with an ageing husband and an heir in his grave, he would have seen the distant possibility of £70,000.

23

A Deep Retirement

On the 23rd of May 1797, Britain's Minister-Resident to Venice disembarked from a sloop of war in the Hungarian-ruled port of Fiume on the border of Dalmatia. Amid a disarray of trunks and boxes stuffed with personal items and documents, Sir Richard sat down to write an account of the events that had sent him fleeing from Italy. Long before his first letters arrived in London, England had learned of the Venetian Republic's fall to Napoleon's forces. As the French entered on the 12th of May, the city erupted into riot. General Bonaparte had pointed his cannons at the Republic's celebrated domes and bell towers and demanded ransom. Wishing to avoid a siege, the Great Council of Venice capitulated within twenty-four hours. The *grande dame* that had been La Serenissima, the proud city-state of 1,070 years, was then ravished; stripped of her territories, her gold, and her art.

Worsley had been at the ambassadorial Palazzo as the French troops sailed through the canals and mustered in the Piazza San Marco. From his windows he had seen the masts of their gunboats as they glided into the lagoon. This sight left him little 'room to doubt as to what manner in which they would treat the capital'. Sir Richard's sense of alarm began to swell as the crowds of Venetian citizens pushed their way across the bridges and splashed through the water in a terrified exodus. Throughout the night of the 12th, their shouts could be heard outside his residence. His apartments glowed with lamplight into the early morning as the Minister's household staff stripped his lodgings of their treasures and frantically packed them for transportation. In his three and half years in Venice, Sir Richard had transformed his Palazzo into an extravagant showroom of masterworks. Not only had he lined his corridors with a second collection of marbles, but by 1797 his rooms were adorned with fifty-eight paintings by Italy's most pre-eminent artists, living and dead. The great prizes that filled his home were as precious to him as children. Upon the arrival of Napoleon's forces, he paced through his apartments accounting for each of them, scribbling a hurried inventory of careful descriptions and precise values to the last Venetian sequin. From their hangings the servants pulled his proud triplet: three Titians featuring images of St Jerome, the Prodigal Son 'and a small head of cupid'. A Veronese and a Raphael nestled beside them. Quickly they loosened from the walls *The Continence of Scipio* by Caravaggio, scenes by Correggio, Sebastiano del Piombo, Carracci, Salavator Rosa, Guercino, Canaletto, Albani, Guido Reni, and 'a small picture representing Redentore Giovanna,' by Leonardo da Vinci. Then, believing his 'person to be in some danger and my effects in still greater' he said, he 'immediately hired two very large sailing boats' in preparation for his flight. It was only 'with much difficulty' that Worsley obtained an exit visa from the French chargé d'affaires, who had been asked by the recently divested Doge to discharge the diplomatic corps from the city unharmed. On the day that the fleet carrying Napoleon's reinforcements arrived into port, the British Minister cast off from the lagoon and watched from his ship as Venice diminished into the horizon.

In his letter to William Clarke, Worsley recounted the frightening experience, claiming that 'it would be scarcely possible for me to describe to you the dangers which I have run and the difficulties I encountered in getting away'. Once put to sea in the Adriatic, Sir Richard and his cargo were no safer than they had been in Venice. Seventy miles into their journey they narrowly escaped discovery by 'a French 40 gun frigate with several armed vessels', and were saved only by a thick fog which had 'sprung up immediately as if directed by the hand of providence'. While the French patrolled the coasts of Italy, Worsley's small convoy remained vulnerable and so at the first opportunity Sir Richard transferred himself onto 'a sloop of 14 guns' and parted with his cherished objects. Instructions were given that his ark of valuables was to idle in port at Fiume until political events allowed their safe passage to England. When the baronet fretted in his letter to Clarke about having 'saved many things' while 'leaving many others behind', his thoughts were as much at sea with his floating collection as they were in Venice among his abandoned household possessions.

Sir Richard's arrival in Fiume marked the beginning of an even greater overland trek homeward across a continent besieged by war. Though 'little recovered from the fatigue of my voyage', he wrote, Worsley prepared to 'proceed through Croatia and Hungary to Dresden' where he would 'await His Majesty's leave to return to England'. 'May it please God that I escape the Dangers of so long a journey,' he added.

Worsley eventually crossed the North Sea from the German port of Cuxhaven and landed on English shores in mid-September. Although in his absence the corporation of voters on the Isle of Wight had secured his re-election to Parliament for the seat of Newtown, Sir Richard had little appetite for public life. On his return he purchased a town residence in Grosvenor Square for the sake of convention, but rarely used it. Instead, he preferred to retreat almost entirely to the isolation of a cottage on the fringes of his estate. According to the correspondence of John Wilkes, work had begun in 1791 on the conversion of a small building 'on the brink of the Ocean in the Parish St Lawrence'. By the following year, a 'neat and elegant building' with a slated roof and sashed windows had been completed. The house, designed with the new fashion for informality in mind, featured two spacious reception rooms on the ground floor. Its large windows and doors opened directly on to 10 acres of picturesque gardens which tumbled down to a rugged coastline. While Sea Cottage attracted curiosity, it was the property's grounds that piqued the most interest.

Although Sir Richard had grown into an introvert over the years, he gave open expression to his personality and interests on the land surrounding his home. Like the travels of many late eighteenth-century gentlemen, Worsley's experiences on the continent influenced the shape his property assumed. Exotic foreign vistas and the untamed elements of nature were combined and transplanted into his grounds. Inspired by the vineyards of the Mediterranean, Worsley was convinced that his parcel of land, situated on the temperate Undercliff of the Isle of Wight, was capable of supporting wine-producing grapes. In 1792, 'three acres containing seven hundred plants' were laid out 'on a terrace of seven stages' and tended to by 'a French Vigneron', whom the baronet had brought over from Brittany. The experiment failed to yield the desired results, but it did contribute to the overall sense of what one observer described as 'the picturesque and romantic scenery'.

Amid the landscape of 'bold fragments, jutting rocks, irregular lawns, a crystal rivulet, and natural groups of fine elms' Worsley had installed several manmade features. A grotto was created over the property's well where 'a pillaried stream burst from its spring' and ran 'through the verdant lawns' before terminating 'in a cascade to the beach'. An 'Elegant Grecian Temple' to Neptune, an orangerie 'in the design of a Temple dedicated to Virgil', and 'a pavilion . . . fitted up as a banqueting room' decorated the view from his windows. However, none of these garden follies reveal more about the baronet's state of mind than what he erected on the property's periphery. After his return from Venice, Worsley gave instructions for 'a battery of several pieces of cannon' to be constructed 'for protection against invasion'. As he began to sever more of his ties with the world beyond Sea Cottage, it is likely that Sir Richard was as concerned about invaders from his own country as he was about those from France.

As Worsley had learned much to his bitterness, any action or creation associated with his name was certain to provoke fascination. According to *Bon Ton* magazine in 1794, 'everyone would be glad to take a *peep*' at Sir Richard Worsley's 'residence at the Undercliff', especially as 'the whole domain seems laid out for the residence of some fairy prince'. In the eighteenth century it would have been difficult for Sir Richard to have achieved a greater degree of isolation than on the sparsely populated Isle of Wight. Even behind the walls of Appuldurcombe, where Worsley had professed to 'live in the deepest retirement' and 'scarcely pass the park gates', he had begun to feel exposed. Sea Cottage, balanced virtually on the edge of England, was as far as he could withdraw from the leers and jibes which he now recognised would pursue him to his grave. As the writer M.P. Wyndham discovered, Sir Richard was unlike most country house owners in that he had no desire to open his secluded retreat to censorious busybodies. After making his way to this sequestered part of the island, Wyndham commented that he was 'surprised . . . to see a painted board at the entrance, with the following words, *The Sea Cottage Is Not Shew'd*'. 'It is remarkable,' he continued, 'that there should be much the same forbiddance to the house at Appuldurcombe, and even to the road through the park; for though a ticket of admittance for a particular day, is, occasionally granted by Sir Richard's steward at Newport, yet the application for it has been known to be refused.'

In spite of his disastrous relations with members of the opposite sex and the legal entanglements they brought, Sir Richard was never interested in leading a chaste life of solitude. By prohibiting access to his residences Worsley was in part protecting his domestic arrangements from prying spectators. He was determined to conduct any further amorous relationships in complete secrecy. Furthermore, since the ecclesiastical establishment still regarded the Worsleys as married, any romantic affair that either party pursued was tantamount to an act of adultery, although conventional opinion was kinder to estranged husbands who kept mistresses than it was to estranged wives who took lovers. Consequently, insight into the baronet's thoughts, desires or conquests following the trial and separation have remained shrouded in mystery, but for two poorly disguised instances.

Perhaps adding credibility to the rumours of Sir Richard's early associations with a number of fashionable courtesans is a document that attests to his affair with one such woman in Paris. In May 1784, *en route* from Spain to Rome, Worsley passed several months in France in the company of a lady calling herself Clara Margaretta Sophia de Auguste de Ceve de Villeneuve Solar, the Countess d'Amey. In reality, the Countess d'Amey's claim to noble birth was complete fabrication; she was commonly known as 'Madame Palmerini'. Sir Richard had been fully aware of her identity when she became his mistress and subsequently attempted to defraud him of 75,000 *livres*. Their four-month liaison ended at the baronet's solicitors in 1787, after the Countess d'Amey had travelled to London in an unsuccessful bid to obtain her money.

Worsley's next relationship was concealed only slightly better. In December 1796, Lady Berwick wrote from Venice glowingly of the British Minister-Resident to her friend, Lady Bruce. She had believed that the 'very civil' gentleman who paid them visits and sent them 'all the newspapers' would have made a suitable husband for her eldest daughter, had she not learned that he kept 'a bad woman'. 'I am afraid,' she wrote with gravity, that 'she is *one very bad woman*'. The person to whom Lady Berwick referred was a self-professed widow by the name of Mrs Sarah Smith. Sarah Smith's background and history are unknown, but she is thought to have entered Worsley's life on his return from Italy in 1788. On legal documents she is cited as Sir Richard's housekeeper, an eighteenth-century euphemism frequently employed to veil a relationship when a couple of unequal social status were cohabiting. Having travelled with her lover from England to Venice and braved the perilous journey by sea and land back to the Isle of Wight, Mrs Smith was undeniably a most dedicated mistress. It is hard to imagine that anything but a genuine love held the two together.

Although his relationship with Sarah Smith managed to withstand the adversities of the 1790s, Worsley's finances did not fare so well. The protracted dispute surrounding his separation, and the expenses necessary to underwrite his travels and fondness for collecting, had by 1792 become a drain on the profitability of his estate. His situation was worsened still more by his hasty removal from Venice and loss of a position that had paid him a living of £600 per annum. He returned home in 1797 to a pile of bills, many of which had been outstanding since his departure four years earlier. Re-establishing himself in England involved further costs and resulted in the mortgage of several of his properties as well as a request for a £10,000 bank loan. The worst in a series of pecuniary calamities was to befall him in 1801.

By then four years had passed since Worsley had abandoned his collection of masterpieces in Fiume. As one of Napoleon's objectives in his conquest of Italy had been the appropriation of the country's celebrated works of art, Sir Richard's vessel, its creaking hull loaded with booty, must have been an appealing spoil of war. After February 1801, when the defeat of Austria ceded further territories in Europe to the French, concealing the ship and its cargo would have proved even more difficult. In March, Worsley had ordered that the *Robert Pattison*, the hulk carrying his possessions, attempt to run the French blockade of the Mediterranean and sail for England. Six months later he received a letter. The vessel, which 'had been brought into port at Malaga by a French Privateer', had been emptied of its contents. 'The pictures were bought up by the orders of Lucian Bonaparte on very moderate terms,' wrote his correspondent, an agent of the British government. '. . . All that remains at present are the antiquities which it is in my power to purchase'; the 'original drawings of the Museum Worsleyanum and the other engravings' he commented, 'may also be had for a price'. In Venice, Sir Richard had purchased a number of historic manuscripts which, the agent mentioned with regret, 'were all seized by the French Commissary' and, with the other items, 'forwarded to Paris'. Edward Bedingfield, the fateful letter's author had requested that Worsley advise him on the size of ransom he wished to pay to have the remnants of his collection returned.

The baronet had valued his collection of fifty-eight Italian paintings at £14,000, a sum that is difficult to translate into modern worth when today one work by Titian alone might command as much as £7.48 million. For a short while, Sir Richard had been one of the few connoisseurs to have profited by the upheaval of the war, and now it was the turn of others to gain through his misfortune. With a certain smugness he had crowed too loudly and too soon about the acquisitions he had made at the expense of those caught up in the conflict. Many of the smaller objects he had added to his expanding cabinet of curiosities (which fortunately had accompanied him overland from Fiume to England) he had boasted of purchasing for a fraction of their actual worth. In 1794 he had acquired 'a remarkable fine opal set around with diamonds' from the collection of 'a famous banker at Paris' who 'sent it to Italy to be disposed of'. Worsley had bought it for '278 sequins, but it has been valued by several jewellers at 1,000'. A cameo of 'Alexander the Great, beautifully engraved' had come from the closet of 'the late Duke of Orleans', a 'beautiful head of cupid' and 'a vase with two pigeons' had been sold by the Prince of Santa Croce, and 'a head of Cybele on a large onyx' came 'from the Prince of Comte' whose 'Valet de Chambre sold it at Milan'. A significant number of the baronet's treasures had once lined the corridors and salons of Europe's noble families, many of whom were in need of emergency funds and preferred to sell their holdings rather than 'have them fall into the hands of the French'.

In spite of the precarious state of his finances, Sir Richard agreed to the demands of the French and paid the bounty placed on his antiquities, drawings and engravings. However, the loss of his paintings was a defeat that far superseded the agonies of an additional and unnecessary expenditure. The emotional value ascribed to this vanished assembly of art by an heirless landowner determined to create a positive legacy for his damaged name was immeasurable. Bedingfield had conveyed what undoubtedly were the sentiments of many when he wrote at the end of his letter, 'I feel sincerely for the loss you have sustained ... it is a painful circumstance that you as a literary man should also be involved in the fatal consequences of the present war'.

This latest calamity finally induced Sir Richard Worsley to abandon what remained of his sense of restraint. The once prudent, methodically minded Finical Whimsy, who had balanced the King's accounts with scientific precision, had been pushed to the brink. After 1801, the baronet dispensed entirely with caution. His lifelong interest in art suddenly boiled over into mania. Worsley's bid to immortalise his memory by affixing it to antique sculpture and old master paintings reached new heights of desperation. These objects, the embodiment of the highest taste and scholarship, would represent him in centuries to come, where no living legacy could. In the last four years of his life, the baronet seemed determine to run through every penny his estate could yield in order to preserve his own memory for posterity.

Like a character from one of the era's Gothic novels, Sir Richard sank deeper into the isolation of Sea Cottage. The dark temperament that Jeremy Bentham had identified as 'haughty, selfish and mean' had over time evolved into one which was also angry, embittered and withdrawn. Rarely straying beyond the boundaries of his property, Worsley recoiled from social contact but for occasional visits from those who shared his artistic interests. By making it known that his sole concern was the expansion of his collection, the baronet laid himself open to the schemes of conniving art dealers.

Worsley's chief agent on the art market was the London-based William Dermer, who bombarded him with frequent propositions. He was also regularly approached by those with a sideline in the sale of paintings, such as the artist Benjamin West and fellow connoisseur, Charles Birch. Weakened by avarice and obsession, Sir Richard found it difficult to refuse their constant solicitations, especially when couched in grovelling flattery. 'When I consider the admirers of the elegant arts in this country and how few there are who feel the higher excellencies of the great schools of painting – I know of no one I can address on that subject who feels those excellencies in a higher degree than yourself,' wrote Benjamin West in a bid to sell Worsley a painting by Alessandro Paduano which had been 'acquired on moderate terms . . . when the troubles commenced in Paris'. On occasion, when hesitation got the better of the baronet, dealers joined forces in a double assault. William Dermer, eager to sell 'an exceptional work by Claude', employed Charles Birch to write with an 'impartial' connoisseur's opinion. His thoughts were that 'Mr Dermer's Claude is decidedly the most enchanting and capital performance in this kingdom' and that naturally, 'so high a character as yourself for discernment and encouragement of art' should own it. In spite of the transparency of their intentions, on this and many other occasions Sir Richard accepted their approaches without much scepticism, and let himself be swept away in the current of their designs.

By 1803, Worsley seems to have purchased nearly every work offered to him by Dermer. The Claude was joined by a Velázquez, a 'frost piece' by the Dutch painter Cuyp, three paintings by Andrea del Sarto, a Greuze 'from the late King's collection in Paris' and an Annibale Carracci, also brought from across the Channel. The very act of acquiring these paintings became a dance of futility. No sooner would Worsley agree to buy them than his bankers, solicitors or stewards would remind him of his financial shortfall. The art he had bought six months or a year earlier would then be sold back to Dermer at a loss. Towards the end of his life it is unlikely that Sir Richard so much as glimpsed a number of his pieces, a large selection of which were stored at his house in Grosvenor Square, a home he no longer visited. Others were delivered by cart to Appuldurcombe where they lay stacked in the uninhabited rooms. After his return from Venice, the ancestral dwelling of which he was once so proud, and so eager to embellish with fashionable Chippendale furniture and neo-classical décor, held nothing for him but the poison of memories. With its owner unwilling to live within its walls, Appuldurcombe grew into a cold mausoleum of antiquities and silent painted faces.

Sir Richard was unwell for most of the summer before he died. Yet even as he lay on his deathbed he allowed Dermer (obviously distressed at the prospect of losing such a good client) to continue to tempt him with objects. His letters were filled with promises of a picture which could 'vie with the famous Mary in the Orleans collection' and two more Carraccis 'brought into England by Mr Day'. 'I trust and believe that your collection will go down to posterity unrivalled both as to its founder and the beauty and perfection of the respective pictures,' he reassured him. But all of Dermer's obsequiousness and even a special batch of his own 'ginger extract remedy' failed to sustain the baronet's flagging health. In 1805, on the 5th of August Worsley suffered an apoplexy (or a stroke) and expired. Mrs Smith had been with him throughout. Fifty-four was not an inconsiderable age at which to die in the early nineteenth century, but his life would hardly have been regarded as a long one. A miniature portrait made of him in his final years shows a man with an expression not unlike that of the self-assured young baronet in Reynolds's image of 1775. The eyes of this older Sir Richard Worsley with his jowly jaw line and puffy face are as defiant as they had been in his youth, but the gaze is different. Whilst the young baronet regarded his viewer with a hint of disdain, the old baronet looks out from his frame with suspicion, as if wary that anyone should want to observe him for any length of time.

Ultimately, the legacy that Sir Richard Worsley left fell far short of the one he had envisioned. At his death his estate was more than £6,679 in debt. With so few assets which he could legally claim, the baronet had not bothered registering an official will. Instead he had written out directions to his steward to reward Sarah Smith with an annuity of £250 per annum so she could continue her life in comfort. The estate of Appuldurcombe – the land, the house, its contents and its unpaid bills – was passed to his niece, Henrietta Anna Maria Charlotte Bridgeman Simpson, the daughter of his sister, Henrietta. Sir Richard had left his affairs in such extreme disarray that it would be another twenty years before the estate was released from an entanglement of legal red tape. By then, his niece had died and what remained of any inheritance had passed to her husband, the 1st Earl of Yarborough.

More unfortunate still was the fate of Sir Richard's collection of Greek marbles, the objects on which he had pinned his hopes of achieving immortality. Two years after his death, a shed on the corner of Park Lane and Piccadilly opened its doors to the public. Its content, a breathtaking assortment of metopes and friezes extracted from the Parthenon, belonged to another infamous cuckold, Lord Elgin. The impact of these pieces on the early nineteenth-century British psyche was profound. Lord Elgin's marbles were so celebrated in literature, art, architecture and design that they overshadowed the significance of any other assortment of antiquities. The headless torsos, broken feet and masonry absorbing the chill on the Isle of Wight were soon forgotten. After the 1st Earl of Yarborough's death 'a large part of the museum of objets d'art' at Appuldurcombe was sold in 1859. Although some of the finer pieces were kept by the Earl's descendants, the remnants along with a clutch of Worsley's paintings had been completely dispersed by 1863.

Indefatigable in his efforts to be remembered, one of Sir Richard's last wishes was that a suitable monument be erected to him inside All Saints church at Godshill. Henrietta Bridgeman Simpson executed this desire in the shape of an imposing Grecian, claw-footed sarcophagus. Its austere and sombre appearance had been intended to reflect the gravity of the man it represented, but its tub shape soon gave rise to sniggers among the congregation. By 1904 this distraction had become a nuisance and 'the pretentious monument' was dragged to the back of the church and a pipe organ was placed in front of it. But hiding the stone structure could not obscure the memory of the man. They knew his story too well. In honour of it, they dubbed his memorial 'Worsley's bath'.

24

Mr Hummell and Lady Fleming

Although Seymour Worsley claimed to have reformed her character, society would have seen nothing commendable in the event which took place on the 12th of September 1805. Her husband's coffin had not been in the family vault for a month when his widow and her twenty-six-year-old lover exchanged their wedding vows in Farnham, Surrey. Few would have believed that love had compelled Jean Louis Hummell down the aisle to greet his recently endowed forty-seven-year-old bride. However, the sincerity of his attachment and the scorn of others was of little concern to Lady Worsley. During her life she had learned that love could assume a variety of forms, spawned by passion or necessity.

Seymour would not have entered into this, her second marriage, naïvely. The charming Swiss musician may have loved her but it was undoubtedly an affection that had been fastened firmly in place by the possibility of an inheritance. Having never been considered a beauty in her youth, her appearance, as seen in a sketch by the artist John Russell, had failed to blossom in middle age. Double-chinned and slightly wild-eyed, her face was worn with tiredness. She was too old to provide her husband with an heir. In lieu of this, she could give him the blessings of wealth. Lady Worsley had not been coy about the situation. Their wedding plans were set in motion so quickly after Sir Richard's death that the possibility of remarriage had evidently been discussed beforehand.

As soon as Seymour received word that her ailing husband had breathed his last, arrangements were made to ensure her and Hummell's future happiness. Eager to be rid of her past, her first act was to shed 'that detested name of Worsley' and on the 3rd of September, by royal licence, she resumed her maiden name of Fleming. The road was then cleared for her beloved one day to accept ownership of her estate. In homage to his wife and the family whose riches he would enjoy, Hummell also embraced the surname of Fleming and agreed to exchange the French-sounding Jean Louis for the Anglophonic John Lewis. More importantly, to avoid any legal obstacles which might have barred him from owning English land, John Lewis Fleming applied to become a national of Great Britain.

After decades of want and frustration, the assets that had been bequeathed to the young Seymour Dorothy Fleming at last fell back into her possession on the 29th of August. Remarkably, the newspapers and gossip-mongers who had perpetuated the myth of her financial worth thirty years ago were able to recollect the rumoured value of her holdings. Once more the printed page boasted 'of a jointure worth 70,000 1.' due to Lady Worsley, while society's ceaseless chatter increased this sum exponentially. The diarist Joseph Farrington claimed that she was due £90,000 in addition to half of Sir Richard's estate. In truth, the amount, although substantial, had always been less than most individuals believed.

In spite of lengthy legal disputes, Lady Worsley's fortune remained intact, protected from the turmoil by the clauses of her marriage contract. Her widow's jointure, which Sir Richard had attempted to reclaim, guaranteed her a further annual allowance of £2,000, as well as 'the use of a dwelling house for her life' to the value of £300 in rent per year. The agreement had also granted her £200 worth of goods from her husband's town house. In order to ensure that Lady Worsley would not benefit from his prized art collection, the baronet made certain that the entire collection at his Grosvenor Square house was sold or moved before his death. Nevertheless, Seymour was free to claim any of his 'household linen, china, furniture and plate'. More significantly, her £20,000 share of the lands purchased on her behalf on the Isle of Wight (which had been subsumed into the Appuldurcombe estate) was returned to her ownership. Her half of the Brompton estate was also restored to her. Technically unable to hold land in her own name, Lady Worsley was free to nominate a male trustee of her choice to safeguard her interests. Without hesitation she inscribed on her deeds the new name of John Lewis Fleming in place of that of Sir Richard

Worsley. For the first time in her life, Seymour would be able to exercise some control over the wealth she had inherited. She had weathered nearly twenty-four years on the slim hope of this event. Now that it had arrived, there were others equally eager to share in her bounty.

In 1807, a 'gentleman' by the name of Charles Hammond and his new bride, Charlotte rented a house in a part of Kensington known as Little Chelsea, between what is now the modern Fulham Road and the edge of the Brompton estate. The Hammonds' appearance at the foot of Seymour's property was no coincidence. Rather it was a strategic advance towards breaching the wall that separated their lives.

The infant girl that Seymour had brought to northern France and deposited in the care of the Cochard family in 1785 had grown into a woman. What the intervening years of her daughter's life had held or indeed what precisely she knew about her real mother beyond her name and noble status may never be known. What is certain is that at some point before her twenty-first birthday, Charlotte Dorothea Cochard had returned to England in search of an inheritance and a husband. Undoubtedly, mention of her pedigree aroused much interest among potential suitors. The possibility that Charlotte might be the legitimate heiress to the combined Worsley – Fleming fortune was enough to whet Charles Hammond's appetite for a legal battle as well as a marriage. In the year that the recently wedded Mrs Hammond reached her majority, Lady Fleming's attorney received an unexpected letter.

The Hammonds' claims were so outlandish that it would have been immediately apparent to Seymour's trustees and her solicitor that the couple had gleaned all of their information from the latest newspaper announcements. Probably at the encouragement of an unscrupulous attorney, Charles Hammond put forward the assertion that his wife was not only the daughter of Lady Seymour Dorothy Worsley but also 'the only child of the late Sir Richard Worsley living at his death to be entitled to all the benefits secured to an only daughter by the settlement made on the marriage of Sir Richard Worsley and Seymour Dorothy Fleming'. Completely unaware of the details of the Worsleys' separation, or, that at the time of Charlotte's conception the couple had been estranged for nearly five years, Hammond demanded that 'a proper conveyance be executed' to release Sir Richard and Lady Fleming's estates into his wife's possession. Despite the absurdity of the suit, both parties' solicitors would be obligated once again to begin the unpleasant business of rummaging through Seymour's dirty laundry. Understandably, the prospect of this 'occasioned great uneasiness to all parties concerned'.

Whether prompted by the dread of another legal action or by the emotions of motherhood, in early 1808 Lady Fleming called a halt to the proceedings and extended her hand to her daughter. No letters or diaries record their meeting or the details of the reconciliation; whether there were tears and pledges of forgiveness or simply remorse and stoic silence. For a woman who had believed all her children lost to her, this reunion in the later part of her life must have been an overwhelming experience. Fortunately, it yielded happiness for both. As stated in their legal agreement, Seymour was elated at having found Charlotte. In consequence 'of the love and affection which Dame Seymour Dorothy Fleming has and bears towards her daughter', a settlement of £1,000 was granted to Mrs Hammond. Additionally, Seymour directed that 'a sum of three thousand pounds was to be made to any issue' of the Hammonds' marriage. It was a comfortable, if not generous sum and one which would secure the couple and later their two children, Charles and Seymour Louisa, a family home in Lewisham. Sadly, as social convention would have rendered intimacy between them inappropriate, it is unlikely that the Hammonds passed much time in the company of Lady Fleming and her husband after their initial meeting.

More than a quarter of a century had elapsed since the details of her misdeeds had appeared in print, yet few beyond her highborn relations and the louche members of fashionable society would have regarded Seymour Dorothy Fleming as a suitable companion. Even in an era when wealth could purchase respect, the restoration of her fortune was not in itself enough to rinse away the residue of her sins. Neither was her remarriage. Her choice of second husband had only fanned the dying embers of a scandalous reputation. But unlike Sir Richard Worsley, Seymour had no interest in cultivating good opinion on a wide scale.

The morally minded middle classes, who had relished tales of her titillating adventures and avariciously consumed the transcripts of *Worsley* v. *Bisset*, were the least likely to forgive her transgressions. Although they had delighted in her shocking story, in the new century their religiously grounded principles were responsible for blotting it out. As a letter from Sarah Burney, the sister of the celebrated author Fanny Burney reveals, nowhere was this more the case than in provincial circles. The unmarried Miss Burney, who was at Lymington in September 1812, found herself at a gathering alongside 'an elderly woman married to a very young man'. She was among a number of friends invited to the cottage of a Monsieur de Chapelle. 'It all seemed perfectly natural,' Sarah Burney had thought at the time. 'After hearing the young man perform with great admiration and looking at his nasty old wife with great contempt for marrying such a boy', Miss Burney 'came home in the carriage of this ill assorted pair, thanked them for their civility, went to bed and thought no more about them'. In less than twenty-four hours, word of her association with Monsieur de Chapelle's disreputable guest flew into the far corners of Hampshire and Sarah suddenly found herself the recipient of letters which admonished her for 'keeping bad company'. A friend of her father's 'wrote folio pages of self-justification' on the subject, warning her that 'Lady Fleming, as she now calls herself' had 'once discreditably been known as Lady Worsley and that her former fame got her blazoned here', a fact unknown by her French hosts who were too busy 'shewing her the most civility'.

With her tarnished past, it is likely that Lady Fleming felt more at ease in the tolerant society across the Channel. After the declaration of an armistice in 1814, many British nationals, including a number of Seymour's Whig associates, returned to Paris with eagerness. Lady Fleming and her husband were certainly among their numbers by 1816. They settled in a villa at Passy, a suburb 'only a half mile distant from the capital' situated on 'a lofty hill over looking the river, the city and a great expanse of gardens'. More tranquil than merry, the restful environment suited Seymour, whose health had begun to weaken.

It was at her home in Passy that Lady Fleming died of an undisclosed illness on the 9th of September 1818. She was nearly sixty-one and just shy of her thirteenth wedding anniversary. According to her wishes, John Lewis had her body committed to a modest white tomb at Père Lachaise cemetery, onto which the words 'Yes Thou Shalt Be Obeyed' were inscribed.

For a woman who had defined her life through flagrant acts of disobedience, this seems an ironic epithet. John Lewis may have been the only person to truly understand its coded meaning. Indeed, her second husband appears to have been the only individual who truly understood her. No other man had demonstrated such fidelity to her, while she lived or after her death. Among all the paramours who floated in and out of her life, Fleming remained at her side the longest. While he may have been lured by her inheritance, his respect and affection for her seemed genuine.

At her death, he was reborn as a wealthy, single land-owning gentleman. In honour of his departed wife, he adorned himself in the fine silk mourning clothes that her money had purchased for him. Not wishing to seem inappropriately enthusiastic at the prospect of remarriage, he waited a year and a half before wedding the twenty-four-year-old Ernestine Jeanne-Marie d'Houdetot, the daughter of César Louis Marie François d'Ange Houdetot, the Comte d'Houdetot, a celebrated French Marshal of the Camp. His second wife bore him a child to continue his name. The little girl, Césarine Fleming would become the next heiress of the Brompton estate.

By the end of his life in 1836 the Baron Fleming, as he had come to be known, had achieved a great deal. The Swiss stepson of a stocking manufacturer ended his days as a member of the French lesser nobility. He did so with the generous assistance of one of the eighteenth century's most notorious women. The respectable world from which she had been thrown would always regard Seymour Dorothy Fleming's name as a stain, one to be hidden or scrubbed out. John Lewis might have done just that and rid himself of the association when he laid her to rest. But this was not his wish. Rather than fleeing from her, he hoped that posterity would remember them together. He may have been the only person to do so. His final request was 'to be buried along side' his 'dearly beloved first wife, Lady Seymour Fleming', a woman of whom he had never been ashamed.

Acknowledgements

At the end of this long journey many people deserve gratitude and recognition for their assistance.

First, the unflagging patience, expert advice and kind support offered to me by three wise women: my agent Claire Paterson, my editor Jenny Uglow and my publisher Alison Samuel at Chatto have carried me though this writing experience. I am also grateful to Parisa Ebrahimi for her assistance. Similar sentiments and a debt of gratitude should be expressed to Tina Bennett at Janklow in New York and my editor at St Martin's, Charlie Spicer, who believed in this story from the start.

Over the past three years I have pestered a good deal of people in a number of archives. Richard Smout, Christine Broom and the team at the Isle of Wight Record Office have helped me tremendously, as have Lisa Snook at the Worcester Record Office, Deborah McVea at the Bentham Project, Hazel Cook at the Kensington Central Library and the indefatigable Alison Kenney at the City of Westminster Archives. The staff at the Lincolnshire Archives, the Lambeth Palace Archives and the British Library's Rare Books & Music Reading Room also deserve my sincere thanks.

Many others have offered their expertise. I have Stephen Brumwell to thank for providing me with information about the militias and the British military during the War of American Independence. R.S. Taylor Stoermer's advice about the last days of Lord North's government was also invaluable, as was Simon Chaplin's correct identification of Lady Worsley's physician.

I'm also grateful for the input of Wendy Moore, Christopher Jessel at Farrer & Co., Ivor Coward at the British Consulate in Venice, Father John Ryder at All Saints Godshill, Vic Barrett at Sea Cottage, Lord Teynham at Pylewell, and Jill Toovey for her assistance with the Croome Court papers, now at the Record Office in Worcester.

Where the creation of this book is concerned there are three exceptional people who may be named as its godparents. In March 2006, I invited a trio of strangers into my home for lunch. Over a lasagne and several bottles of wine the Worsley Society was born. Ann O'Conor has been overwhelmingly generous with her time, support and the Worsley books in her collection. Richard Grenville Clark's insights and the work in his unpublished MA dissertation helped to form my initial thoughts on the Worsley case. Last and certainly not least, the brilliant Karen Lynch has been instrumental in assisting me to form a picture of Lady Worsley. A personal interest in the subject matter meant that she had already blazed a trail to many of the sources long before I began my research. These three people have demonstrated to me that research needn't be a closed, jealous pursuit but collaborative, co-operative and fulfilling. Their friendship and expertise has sustained me in this endeavour.

Finally, I could not possibly have completed this work without the love and assistance of my family and especially my patient, supportive husband to whom this book is dedicated.

A Note on Eighteenth-Century Values and their Modern Conversions

Because issues of financial worth play such a large role in this book I felt it was important to try to convey an idea of eighteenth-century values by converting sums into approximate modern equivalents.

I have used two approximate measures which I have applied to eighteenth-century values according to their type: land or product/labour. I have relied on the work of the economic historian Gregory Clark at the University of California at Davis for my figures for Britain's GDP in the 1770s (see his paper, 'The Secret History of the Industrial Revolution', 2001).

The first approach is a 'proportion based comparison'. This looks at the estimate of gross domestic product in the 1770s and establishes the fraction of domestic product represented by £1,000 in the decade beginning in 1770. Having established the fraction of GDP represented by £1,000 in 1770, the 2006 GDP figure can be divided by that fraction in order to identify the current level of economic output required in 2006 to allow an individual in the present decade to be as relatively well off today as a person having £1,000 disposable income in 1770.

The second approach is an 'expenditure based approach'. This identifies a commodity common to the 1770s and the present. In this case, I've taken the cost of labour. According to Clark, the average daily male wage in the 1770 was approximately 17.5 pence, meaning that £1 (240 pence) purchased the labour of approximately 14 men. The average annual wage in the UK in 2006 was £23,700 (Office of National Statistics). Allowing for the shorter working week, this results in an average daily wage of £91. The cost of the labour of 14 people for one day equals £1,274 at current prices. If amounts are multiplied by a factor of 1274 we arrive at figures which permit a contemporary value to be placed on the eighteenth-century figures.

BIBLIOGRAPHY

As the sources in this book have not been foot-noted, I have arranged the bibliography to assist those who might want to research specific aspects of the Worsleys' lives or their criminal conversation trial and separation. The bibliography is broken into several categories and sub-headings and also includes a list of general material consulted.

SIR RICHARD WORSLEY

ARCHIVAL AND UNPUBLISHED MATERIAL

British Library: Correspondence to or from Sir Richard Worsley
Add. MSS: 27915 (f. 13), 30873 (f. 146), 30874 (f. 62), 34886 (f. 400), 37935c, 37060 (f. 72, f. 77), 41192 (f. 18), 46501 (f. 79, 114), 46825 (ff. 64–83b), 51315 (f. 66), 61867 (f. 178)
Hoare's Bank Archives: Banking Records of Sir Richard Worsley: Volumes 1774–1805
Lincolnshire Archives: Worsley Papers:
1 Worsley 14–17, 23, 24, 27, 31, 38, 39, 42, 44, 53;
1 Worsley 55/7, 55/8, 55/11–14, 16–42, 55/44, 55/46–8;
1 Worsley 56, 59, 61

Isle of Wight Record Office:
Swainston Papers (Barrington Family): SW/812, SW/794a–b, SW/794d–e

Worsley Family Papers: JER/WA/3/9/56, JER/WA/33/25, 33/36, 33/44–9, 33/52, JER/WA/35/23–4, 35/25a&b, 35/28, 35/26–9, 37/22–31, 38/1, 38/3, 38/6–8, 39/4–6, JER/WA/AppV/12

Public Record Office, Kew
PCC Wills: Sir Richard Worsley, Sir Thomas Worsley
Foreign Office Papers: Correspondence as Minister-Resident in Venice FO/81/9–14 (1793–1805)
Probate Inventory: Prob 31/1002/374
Court of Chancery: C/12/612/34 Worsley v. Worsley, C/12/618/40 Worsley v. Lady Worsley, C/12/149/6 Countess d'Amey v. Worsley, C12/643/20 Poor of the Isle of Wight v. Worsley

Shropshire Archives: Attingham Collection: Letters from Lady Bruce to Lady Berwick, 112/23/3/22/1–11

CONTEMPORARY PUBLICATIONS

Almon, John (ed.), *The Correspondence of the Late John Wilkes* (1805)
Anon., *An Epistle from Lady W——y to Sir R——d W——y* (1782)
Anon., *The Abbey of Kilkhampton or Monumental Records for the Year 1780* (1780)
Anon., *The Abbey of Kilkhampton, an improved edition* (1788)
Anon. (Sir Richard Worsley), *The Answer of S——r R——d W——y, Bt. to the Epistle of L——y W——y* (1782)
Anon., *The Genuine Anecdotes and Amorous Adventures of Sir Richard Easy and Lady Wagtail* (1782)
Anon., *The Memoirs of Sir Finical Whimsy and His Lady* (1782)
Anon., *The Whim!!!, or the Maid-Stone Bath, a Kentish Poetic* (1782)
Anon., *Variety, or Which is the Man?* (1782)
Craven, Lady Elizabeth, *A Journey through the Crimea to Constantinople* (1789)
Marshall, *Catalogue of Five Hundred Celebrated Authors of Great Britain, Now Living* (1788)
Savage, James *The Librarian* (1808)
Wilkes, John (ed.) *A Collection of All the Hand-bills, Squibs, Songs, Essays, etc. Published during the late Contested Election for the County of Hants. between the Right Honourable Sir Richard Worsley, Bart. and Jervoise Clarke Jervoise* (Winchester, 1780)

Worsley, Sir Richard, *A Catalogue Raisonné of the Principal Paintings, Sculpture, Drawings etc. at Appuldurcombe House* (1804)

Worsley, Sir Richard, *Museum Worsleyanum; or, A Collection of Antique Basso Relievos, Bustos, Statues, and Gems; with Views of Places in the Levant taken on the Spot in the Years 1785–6–7*, Vol. 1 (1798)

Worsley, Sir Richard, *Museum Worsleyanum; or, A Collection of Antique Basso Relievos, Bustos, Statues, and Gems; with Views of Places in the Levant taken on the Spot in the Years 1785–6–7*, Vol. 2 (1824)

CONTEMPORARY NEWSPAPERS AND JOURNALS

Anon., 'The Cuckold's Reel or; a Dialogue between the Matrimonial Advocate, the Atlas Cornuto, and Admiral Easy', *Rambler's Magazine*, March 1783, p. 105

Anon., *The Britannic Magazine; or Entertaining Repository of Heroic Adventures, 1794–1807*, vol. 12, p. 96

Anon., *Monthly Register*, July 1803, p. 150

Anon., 'Obituary of Sir Richard Worsley', *Gentleman's Magazine*, vol. ixxv, pt. ii (1805), pp. 781–2, 874–5

Juvenis, 'On the Marriage of Sir Richard Worsley, Bart of Appuldurcombe in the Isle of Wight to Miss D.S. Fleming, of Harewood in the County of York', *Hampshire Chronicle*, 9 October 1775, p. 4

GENERAL MENTIONS AND GOSSIP 1775–1805

The Annual Register
Bon Ton Magazine
European Magazine
Gazetteer and New Daily Advertiser
Hampshire Chronicle
Leeds Intelligencer
Leeds Mercury
London Chronicle
London Gazette
Monthly Review
Morning Chronicle
Morning Herald
Morning Post

Public Advertiser
Rambler's Magazine
St James' Chronicle
Sussex Weekly Advertiser
Whitehall Evening Post
World

PUBLISHED SOURCES

Boucher, James E., 'The Worsleys of the Isle of Wight', *Letters Archaeological and Historical* (1896)

Bowring, John (ed.) *The Works of Jeremy Bentham*, vol. 10 (New York, 1962)

Boynton, Lindsay, *Appuldurcombe House* (1990)

Boynton, Lindsay, 'Sir Richard Worsley and the Greek Revival', in *Ancient History in a Modern University*, ed. T.W. Hillard et al., vol. 1 (Cambridge, 1998)

Boynton, Lindsay, 'Sir Richard Worsley and the Firm of Chippendale', *Burlington Magazine*, vol. 110, no. 783 (June 1968)

Christie, Ian R., *The Correspondence of Jeremy Bentham, 1781–88*, 5 vols (1971)

Cross, Anthony, *By the Banks of the Neva: Chapters from the Lives and Careers of the British in Eighteenth Century Russia* (Cambridge, 1997)

Ingamells, John, *A Dictionary of British and Irish Travellers in Italy, 1710–1800* (1997)

Lewis, W.S., *Horace Walpole's Correspondence* (New Haven, Conn., 1937–80)

Mannings, David, *Sir Joshua Reynolds*, 2 vols (2000)

Morritt, J. B.S., *A Grand Tour: Letters and Journeys, 1794–6*, ed. G.E. Marandin (1985)

Prothero, Rowland E. (ed.) *The Private Letters of Edward Gibbon*, 2 vols (1897)

Radice, Betty (ed.) *Memoirs of My Life by Edward Gibbon* (1984)

Royal Commission on Historical Manuscripts, *Report on Family and Estate Papers of The Worsleys* (1895)

Smith, A.H., *A Catalogue of Antiquities in the Collection of the Earl of Yarborough at Brocklesby Park* (1897)

Worsley, Henry Arthur Mant, *Family, Baronets of Appuldurcombe, 13th–19th centuries*, no. 84/9 (1984)

Worsley, Henry Arthur Mant, *The Pedigree of the Family of Worsley Completed to date and in Continuation of that Appearing in 'Berry's Hampshire Genealogies'* (1895)

Worsley, Sir Richard, *The History of the Isle of Wight*, ed. R.M. Robbins (1975)

LADY SEYMOUR DOROTHY WORSLEY (NÉE FLEMING)

ARCHIVAL AND UNPUBLISHED MATERIAL

Isle of Wight Record Office: Worsley Family Papers: JER/WA/35/23–24, 35/25a&b, 35/28

Hammond Papers: HG/2/110 a&b, 2/107, 2/8–9, 2/69–71, 2/86, 2/76

Kensington Central Library, Local Studies Archive: Brompton Estate Papers: MSS 2694, 2695, 2696, 2698, 2701, 2702, 2733, 2738, 2739, 2753, 2767, 2774, 2779, 2782 (10), 2790 (5), 2818, 2819, 2830, 2834, 2840

Nottinghamshire Archives: Foljambe Family Papers: 157/DD/FJ/11/1/3/427–8, 157/DD/FJ/11/1/4/33–4, 157/DD/FJ/11/1/4/43–4

Public Record Office, Kew

PCC Wills: Lady Seymour Dorothy Fleming, Sir John Fleming, John Lewis Fleming

Sheffield Archives: Spencer Stanhope Muniments Sp/St 60635/4

Grenville Clark, Richard, 'Contrasting Notions of Female Propriety in Late Eighteenth Century England, c. 1780–1800', unpublished MA dissertation, University of Greenwich, 1987

Harewood House, *Maids and Mistresses* (exhibition guidebook, 2004)

Lynch, Karen, *Some Lascelles Ladies* (essay accompanying the exhibition 'Maids and Mistresses' at Harewood House, 2004)

CONTEMPORARY PUBLICATIONS

Anon., *A Fifteen Days' Tour to Paris* (1789)

Anon., *A Poetical Address from Mrs Newton to Lady W——y* (1782)

Anon., *An Epistle from Lady W——y to Sir R——d W——y* (1782)

Anon., *The Abbey of Kilkhampton or Monumental Records for the Year 1780* (1780)

Anon., *The Abbey of Kilkhampton, an Improved Edition* (1788)

Anon. [Sir Richard Worsley], *The Answer of S——r R——d W——y. Bt. to the Epistle of L——y W——y* (1782)

Anon., *The Devil Divorced or the Diabo Whore* (1782)

Anon., *The Genuine Anecdotes and Amorous Adventures of Sir Richard Easy and Lady Wagtail* (1782)

Anon., *The Life of Dick En——l——d, alias Captain En——l——d of Turf Memory* (1792)

Anon., *The Memoirs of Sir Finical Whimsy and His Lady* (1782)

Anon., *Variety, or Which is the Man?* (1782)

Anon., *The Whim!!!, or the Maidstone Bath, a Kentish Poetic* (1782)

Anon., *The Whore. A Poem Written by a Lady of Quality* (1782)

Hartley, J., *History of the Westminster Election, Containing Every Material Occurrence from its Commencement on the 1st of April to the Final Close* (1784)

Pindar, Peter, *The Lousiad* (1785)

CONTEMPORARY NEWSPAPERS AND JOURNALS

Anon., 'Anecdote of Mrs N——t——n and Lady W——s——y', *Rambler's Magazine*, May 1783, pp. 60–2, 101–2

Anon., 'Obituary of Sir Richard Worsley', *Gentleman's Magazine*, vol. ixxv, pt. ii (1805), pp. 781–2, 874–5

Anon., 'The Court of Scandal or The New Female Coterie', *Rambler's Magazine*, June 1783, pp. 270–1

Anon., 'The Most Fashionable Votaries of Venus', *Rambler's Magazine*, April 1783

Anon. 'Spa Intelligence', *Rambler's Magazine*, August 1785, p. 359

Robertson, Thomas, 'Cytherian Discussions', *Rambler's Magazine*, July 1783, pp. 248–50

(from January 1782 to December 1784 regular updates of Lady Worsley's activities can be found in:)

Morning Herald

Morning Post

Rambler's Magazine (from 1783)

Newspapers and Journals: General Mentions

Annual Register

Gazetteer and New Daily Advertiser

Hampshire Chronicle

European Magazine

Leeds Intelligencer

Leeds Mercury

London Chronicle

London Gazette

Monthly Review

Morning Chronicle

Public Advertiser
St James' Chronicle
Sussex Weekly Advertiser
Town and Country Magazine
Whitehall Evening Post
World

PUBLISHED SOURCES

Bleackley, Horace 'Lady Worsley', *Notes and Queries*, 11 S. I (1 January 1910), pp. 14–15

Cave, Kathryn (ed.) *The Diary of Joseph Farringdon*, vol. 8 (New Haven, 1982),

Chitty, Joseph et al., *A Practical Treatise on the Law of Contracts Not Under Seal* (1855)

Clark, Lorna J. (ed.) *The Letters of Sarah Harriet Burney* (Athens, Georgia, 1997)

Elliott, Grace Dalrymple, *Journal of My Life During the French Revolution*, ed. Richard Bentley

Greening, Henry, *Chitty's Treatise on Pleading and Parties to Action* (1876), Appendix to vol. 1, p. 473, *Turtle* v. *Worsley*

Historical Manuscripts Commission, *Carlisle Manuscripts* (1897), Appendix pt. v. p. 536

King, A. Hyatt (ed.), *The Reminiscences of Michael Kelly* (New York, 1968)

Lewis, W.S., *Horace Walpole's Correspondence* (New Haven, Conn., 1937–80), vol. 25, pp. 228, 245–6

Mannings, David, *Sir Joshua Reynolds*, 2 vols (2000)

Penny, N. (ed.) *Reynolds* (1986)

Rizzo, Betty (ed.) *The Early Journals and Letters of Fanny Burney, 1780–1781*, vol. 4 (Montreal, 2003)

Ruvigny, Melville H., *The Nobilities of Europe* (2000)

CRIMINAL CONVERSATION TRIAL AND 'DIVORCE' PROCEEDINGS
ARCHIVAL AND UNPUBLISHED MATERIAL

Cumbria Record Office, Barrow-in-Furness: Hart Jackson & Sons, Solicitors
BD HJ Precedent Book 6/Page 321–48 (Worsley Deeds of Separation)

Isle of Wight Record Office: Worsley Family Papers: JER/WA/38/1–2, 38/4–5

Lambeth Palace Archives: Court of Arches
10302 Worsley v. Worsley (Suit for Divorce)
Supporting Materials and Counter Suits Aa 77/15, 18, 37, Aa 78/2–3, D 2324,
    E 45/17, G 129/68 G 152/14–15, J22/8

CONTEMPORARY PUBLICATIONS

Anon., *A New Collection of Trials for Adultery or, General History of Modern
    Gallantry and Divorces* (1802)
Anon., *The Cuckold's Chronicle* (1793)
Anon., *Trials for Adultery: or the History of Divorces Being Select Trials at Doctor's
    Commons, for Adultery, Fornication, Cruelty, Impotence, etc., 1779–1781*, 7
    vols (1781)
Pye Donkin, Robert, *The Trial with the Whole of the Evidence between the Right
    Hon. Sir Richard Worsley, Bart, and George Maurice Bissett, Esq. Defendant
    for Criminal Conversation with the Plaintiff's Wife* (1782), editions: 1–2, 4–5,
    8

CONTEMPORARY NEWSPAPERS AND JOURNALS

Anon., 'The Trial between Sir Richard Worsley and Captain Bisset', *European
    Magazine*, i 154 (February 1782), pp. 17–18
'Crim. Con. Intelligence', *Hampshire Chronicle*, 25 February 1782, p. 3
Monthly Review (March–August 1782)
Morning Herald (15, 22, 27, 28 February, 2 March 1782)
Morning Post (22 February 1782)
World (22 February 1782)

PUBLISHED SOURCES

Fitzpatrick, John C. (ed.) *The Writings of George Washington from the Original
    Manuscript Sources, 1745–1799* (Washington, DC, 1931)
Lloyd, Sarah, 'Amour in the Shrubbery: Reading the Details of English Adultery
    Trial Publications of the 1780s', *Eighteenth Century Studies*, no. 39 (2006)
McCreery, Cindy, 'Breaking All the Rules: The Worsley Affair in Late
    Eighteenth Century Britain', in *Orthodoxy and Heresy in Eighteenth Century
    Society*, ed. R. Hewitt and P. Rogers (2002)

Staves, Susan, 'Money for Honor: Damages for Criminal Conversation', *Studies in Eighteenth Century Culture*, ed. Harry C. Payne, vol. 11 (London, 1982)

Wagner, P. 'The Pornographer in the Courtroom: Trial Reports about Cases of Sexual Crimes and Delinquencies as a Genre of Eighteenth Century Erotica', in *Sexuality in Eighteenth Century Britain*, ed. P. Bouce (1982)

Wood, J.L., 'A Picture of the Times: the Crim Con Suit over Lady Worsley', *Factotum* no. 25 (February 1988), pp. 7–8

GENERAL

ARCHIVAL MATERIAL

British Library

General Catalogue of Engraved Portraits, compiled by Sir William Musgrave: Add. MSS 25393–5 Musgrave Descriptions: Add. MS 5727

Correspondence to or from Lady Jane Fleming: Add. MSS 38309 (f. 1, f. 7), 38217 (f. 122) The Print Collection of Judith Baker of Elemore Hall in Co. Durham

Chatsworth Archives
Papers of the 5th Duke of Devonshire: Chatsworth 214 (14 July 1778)

Derbyshire Record Office
Stanhope family of Elvaston, Earls of Harrington: D518M/T442–5, D518M/F32, F35

House of Lords Archive
HL/PO/PB/1/1807/47G3s/n44 (Naturalisation of John Lewis Fleming)

Isle of Wight Record Office
Worsley Family Papers: JER/WA/33/25, 33/36, 33/44–9, 33/52, 35/26–9, 37/22–31, 38/1, 38/3, 38/6–8, 39/4–6, JER/WA/AppV/12
Bisset Family Papers: AC/90/50/44, 50/9, 50/12, 50/53, 50/39, 50/44
Oglander Family Papers: OG/DD/7–16, OG/RR/3, SW/1550.
Uncatalogued Papers in Jerome Clarke Collection (1782–92): Unknown to Unknown, 30 January 1782, James Worsley to William Clarke, 6 July 1784

Lancashire Record Office
Journal of Sir William Farrington on Continental Tour: Farrington MSS, DDF/14

Leeds Record Office
Harewood Estate Papers: HAR/ACC/492, HAR/CORR/5, Stewards Letter Book, WYAS HAR/ Estate Correspondence/ Misc. 18 & 19c, WYL250/3/188, 3/247–8, 3/250, 3/263, 3/213, 3/203, 3/264, 3/491, 3/510, 3/14, 3/397, 3/270–285

Library of the Royal Institute of British Architects
Manuscript Travel Diary: Journey through Italy, Greece, Egypt, etc. by Willey Reveley

Lincolnshire Archives
Worsley Papers: 1 Worsley 13, 1 Worsley 49, 1 Worsley 55/5–6, 1 Worsley 60

University of Nottingham, Manuscripts and Special Collections
Papers of the 3rd Duke of Portland: (Regarding the Worsleys of Pylewell): PWF 2293, 2295, 2296, 10642

Public Record Office, Kew
PCC Wills: Maurice George Bisset, Sir John Fleming, Lady Seymour Dorothy Fleming, William Hargrave, John Frederick Adam Hesse, Edwin Lascelles, Sir Richard Worsley, Sir Thomas Worsley
Home Office: HO 44/ 46/ff. 29–35 (Naturalisation of Jean Louis Cuchet, alias Hummell)

Westminster City Archives
Anglican Parish Registers:
Burials Records for the churches of
    St James, St Margaret & St John, St Martin-in-the-Fields, St Anne, St Marylebone, St George Hanover Square
Baptism Records for the churches of
St Marylebone, St George Hanover Square

Worcestershire Record Office
Family Papers of the Coventrys of Croome Court:

Uncatalogued Correspondence from George William Coventry, Lord Deerhurst in folder F.81: Deerhurst to Lady Coventry (no date) 1778/9, 25 July 1779, 5 Sept. 1779, 9 Jan. 1780, 28 Feb. 1780

Letter Regarding the Divorce of Lady Maria Baynton, 29 Dec. 1781

CONTEMPORARY PUBLICATIONS

Aikin, Arthur, *Brayley's and Britton's Beauties of England and Wales* (1805)

Alfieri, Vittorio, *Memoirs of the Life and Writings of Vittorio Alfieri*, 2 vols (1810)

Andrews, J., *Remarks on the French and English Ladies in a Series of Letters Interspersed with Various Anecdotes, etc.* (1783)

Anon., *A Congratulatory Epistle from a Reformed Rake to John Fielding Esq., Upon the New Scheme of Reclaiming Prostitutes* (1758)

Anon., *A List of the Officers of the Militia of England and Wales for the Year 1778* (1778)

Anon., *Coxheath Camp, A Novel in a Series of Letters by A Lady* (1779)

Anon., *Memoirs of Mrs Sophia Baddeley* (1787)

Anon., *Nocturnal Revels: Sketches and Portraits of the Most Celebrated Demi-reps and Courtesans of the Period*, 2 vols (1779)

Anon., 'Tete a Tete; The Stable-yard Messalina and the Hostile Sailor; Memoirs of Lord Barrington and Lady Harrington', *Town and Country Magazine*, 1771

Anon., *The Complete English Peerage: or a Genealogical and Historical Account of the Peers and Peeresses of the Realm to the Year 1775* (1775)

Anon., *The Life and Amours of Lady Ann F——I——y [Foley]* (1782)

Anon., *The Military Register or Complete List of the British Army* (1779)

Anon., *The New Complete Guide to All Persons Who Have Any Trade or Concern in the City of London and Parts Adjacent* (1783)

Anon., 'The Particulars of the Late Dick England by an Old Crony', *Sporting Magazine*, 1813

Anon., *The Torpedo, A Poem to the Electric Eel* (1777)

Anon., *The Trial of His R——H——the D——of C—— [Cumberland] July 5th 1770 for Criminal Conversation with Lady Harriet G——r [Grosvenor]* (1770)

Anon., *The Trial of Lady A. Foley; for Adultery with Charles Henry Earl of Peterborough* (1785)

Anon., *The Westminster Election* (1784)

Anon., *Ways & Means* (1782)

Calvert, Frederick, Baron Baltimore, *A Tour to the East in the Years 1763 and 1764 With Remarks on the City of Constantinople and the Turks* (1767)

Capper, Col. James, *Observations on the Passage to India through Egypt and across the Great Desert* (1783)

Chapone, H., *A Letter to a Newly Married Lady* (1777)

Cooke, William Bernard, *A New Picture of the Isle of Wight* (1808)

Coxe, William, *Travels to Poland, Russia, Sweden and Denmark,* (1784)

Devonshire, Duchess of, *The Sylph* (1779)

Dick, William, *Bell's Complete and Correct List of the Army, including the Militia* (1782)

Espinasse, Isaac, *A Digest of the Law of Actions and Trials at Nisi Prius,* 2 vols (1789)

Fordyce, J., *Sermons to Young Women,* 2 vols (1767)

Fordyce, J., *The Character and Conduct of the Female Sex* (Dublin, 1776)

Gale, Thomas, *The Representative History of Great Britain and Ireland: Being a History of the House of Commons* (1816)

Gardenstone, Lord, *Travelling Memorandums Made in a Tour upon the Continent of Europe in the Years 1786, 1787 & 88* (Edinburgh, 1791)

Grigg, J., *Advice to the Female Sex in General* (Bath, 1789)

Hanger, George, *The Life, Adventures and Opinions of Colonel George Hanger, Written by Himself,* 2 vols (1801)

Hummell, J.L., *Harp Sonata with Violin Accompaniment* (1805)

Hummell, J.L., 'My True Love is on the Sea', words by M.G. Lewis (1803)

Hummell, J.L., *Press the Grape* (1799)

Journals of the House of Commons, from October the 31st 1780 to October the 10th 1782, vol. xxxviii (1802)

Lamb, Roger, *A Memoir of His Own Life* (Dublin, 1811)

Le Roy, Julien David, *The Ruins of the Most Beautiful Monuments of Greece* (1758)

Marat, J., *L'Ami du peuple* (Paris, 1791)

Marshall, Joseph, *Travels through Holland, Flanders, Germany, Denmark, Sweden, Lapland, Russia, the Ukraine and Poland* (1773)

Misson, F.M., *A New Voyage to Italy* (1714)

More, Hannah, *Thoughts on the Importance of the Manners of the Great to General Society* (1788)

More, Hannah, *Strictures on the Modern System of Female Education with a View of Principles and Conduct Prevalent among Women of Rank and Fortune,* 2 vols (1799)

Mussolini, Caesar, *Friendly Advice Comprehending General Heads of Qualifications Requisite for Those Who Wish to Marry Well and Live Happy* (1794)

Norden, Frederick Lewis, *Travels in Egypt and Nubia* (Dublin, 1757)

Nugent, Thomas, *The Grand Tour* (1756)

Oldfield, T.H.B., *The History of Boroughs*, 2 vols (1794)

Oldfield, T.H.B., *The Representative History of Great Britain*, vol. 3 (1816)

Pennington, Lady S., *An Unfortunate Mother's Advice to Her Absent Daughters* (1773)

Pigott, Charles, *The Jockey Club, or a Sketch of the Manners of the Age* (1792)

Pigott, Charles, *The Female Jockey Club* (1794)

Pococke, Richard, *A Description of the East and Some Other Countries* (1745)

Richardson, Jonathan, *The Science of a Connoisseur* (1719)

Savary, Claude Etienne, *Letters on Egypt Containing a Parallel between the Manners of its Ancient and Modern Inhabitants*, 2 vols (1787)

Smith, H., *Letters to Married Women* (1774)

Society for Constitutional Information, *A Meeting of the Society for Constitutional Information Held at Holyland's Coffee House, 24 January 1783* (1783)

Stephens, Alexander, *Public Characters* (1803)

Stuart, James and Revett, Nicholas, *The Antiquities of Athens and Other Monuments of Greece* (1762)

Von Archenholz, Baron J.W., *A Picture of England Containing a Description of the Laws, Customs and Manners of England*, 2 vols (1789)

Von Riedesel, Johann Hermann, *Travels through Sicily and That Part of Italy Formerly Called Magna Grecia and A Tour through Egypt* (1773)

Wilkes, W., *A Letter of Genteel and Moral Advice to A Young Lady* (1753)

Wotton, Thomas, *The Baronetage of England* (1771)

Wyndham, H.P., *A Picture of the Isle of Wight* (1794)

NEWSPAPERS AND JOURNALS

Annual Register
Bon Ton Magazine
Connoisseur
European Magazine
Gazetteer and New Daily Advertiser
Gentleman's Magazine
Hampshire Chronicle
Leeds Intelligencer
Leeds Mercury
Lloyds Evening Post

London Chronicle
London Gazette
Monthly Review
Morning Chronicle
Morning Herald
Morning Post
Public Advertiser
Rambler's Magazine
St James' Chronicle
Salisbury and Winchester Journal
Sussex Weekly Advertiser
The Times
Town and Country Magazine
Whitehall Evening Post
World

PUBLISHED SOURCES

Arnold, Dana (ed.) *Squanderous and Lavish Profusion: George IV, his Image and Patronage of the Arts* (1995)

Atkinson, T., *Regimental History of the Royal Hampshire Regiment*, 3 vols (1950)

Ayling, Stanley, *Fox: The Life of Charles James Fox* (1991)

Bamford, Francis, *A Short History of Newchurch in the Isle of Wight* (Newchurch, 1996)

Barrell, John, 'The Body of the Public', in *The Political Theory of Painting from Reynolds to Hazlett* (New Haven, 1986)

Bartlett, P.R.H. and Worsley, H.M., *A Short Guide to the Church of All Saints Godshill, Isle of Wight* (1898)

Beckett, John, *The Rise and Fall of the Grenvilles* (Manchester, 1994)

Benjamin, Lewis Saul, *The First Gentlemen of Europe* (1906)

Black, Jeremy, *The English Press, 1621–1861* (Stroud, 2001)

Black, Jeremy, *The English Press in the Eighteenth Century* (1991)

Black, Jeremy, *The Grand Tour in the Eighteenth Century* (Stroud, 2003)

Blanc, Olivier, *Last Letters: Prisons and Prisoners of the French Revolution* (1987)

Blanning, Tim, *The Pursuit of Glory: Europe 1648–1815* (2007)

Bibliography

Bleackley, H.W., *Ladies Fair and Frail* (1909)

Bleackley, H.W., *The Story of a Beautiful Duchess: Being an Account of the Life and Times of Elizabeth Gunning* (1927)

Bloch, I., *Sexual Life in England, Past and Present* (1938)

Blyth, Henry, *Old Q. The Rake of Piccadilly* (1970)

Brent, Colin, *Georgian Lewes, 1714–1830* (Lewes, 1993)

Brent, Colin, *Historic Lewes* (Lewes, 1995)

Brent, Colin (ed.) *William Verrall's Cookery Book 1759: Master of the White Hart in Lewes* (Chichester, 1988)

Brewer, John, *The Pleasures of the Imagination* (1997)

Brewer, John and Benmingham, Ann (eds) 'Elegant Females and Gentlemen Connoisseurs', in *The Consumption of Culture, 1600–1800* (1985)

Broadley, A.M. and Melville, Lewis (eds) *The Beautiful Lady Craven* (1914)

Broers, Michael, *Europe under Napoleon 1799–1815* (1996)

Browning, Oscar et al., *The Despatches of Earl Gower, English Ambassador at Paris* (Cambridge, 1885)

Buffenoir, Hippolyte, *La Comtesse d' Houdetot, sa famille, ses amis* (Paris, 1905)

Bullock, John M., *Bisset of Lessendrum: 1757–1821* (1929)

Burford, E.J., *Royal St James* (London, 1988)

Burford, E.J., *Wits, Wenchers and Wantons* (1986)

Burke, J.B., *Burke's Extinct Baronetcies* (1844)

Burke, J.B., *Burke's Landed Gentry* (1937)

Campbell, Susan, *A History of Kitchen Gardening* (2005)

Cannon, John, *Aristocratic Century* (Cambridge, 1984)

Chalus, Elaine, *Elite Women in English Political Life, c. 1754–1790* (2005)

Chancellor, Beresford E., *Memorials of St James' Street Together with the Annals of Almacks* (1922)

Chancellor, Beresford, E., *The Pleasure Haunts of London* (1925)

Chester, J. (ed.) *Westminster Abbey Registers* (1876)

Christie, I.R., *The Benthams in Russia, 1780–91* (1993)

Christie, I.R., *The End of North's Ministry: 1780–1782* (1958)

Clair, Colin (ed.) *Literary Anecdotes of the Eighteenth Century by John Nichols* (1967)

Cockerell, C.R., *Travels in Southern Europe and the Levant: 1810–17* (1903)

Cokayne, G.E. and White, G.H. (eds) *The Complete Peerage of England*, vols 1–12 (London, 1953)

Constable, W.G., *John Flaxman* (1927)

Constantine, David, *Fields of Fire: A Life of Sir William Hamilton* (2001)

Conway, Stephen, *The British Isles and the American War of Independence* (Oxford, 2003)

Cook, B.F., *The Elgin Marbles* (1997)

Crossley, Alan and Elrington, C.R. (eds) *Victoria County History: A History of the County of Oxford*, vol. 12 (1990)

Cruickshanks, Eveline (ed.) *Memoirs of Louis Philippe, comte de Ségur* (1960)

David, Saul, *Prince of Pleasure: The Prince of Wales and the Making of the Regency* (1999)

Davidoff, Leonore and Hall, Catherine, *Family Fortunes: Men and Women of the English Middle Class, 1780–1850* (Chicago, 1987)

Davies, Norman, *God's Playground, A History of Poland*, vol. 1 (Oxford, 2005)

De Beer, G. (ed.) *Tour on the Continent by T. Pennant, 1765* (1948)

De Madariaga, Isabel, *Russia in the Age of Catherine the Great* (2002)

De Zurich, Pierre, *Une Femme heureuse: Madame de la Briche, 1755–1844* (Paris, 1934)

Elrington, C.R. (ed.) *Victoria County History: A History of the County of Middlesex: Hampstead and Paddington*, vol. 9 (1989)

Ensing, R.J., 'Brompton Park Estate', in *Kensington Society Annual Report* (1974–75)

Erskine May, Thomas, *Constitutional History* (1863)

Esdaile, C.J., *The Wars of Napoleon* (1995)

Farr, Evelyn, *Before the Deluge: Parisian Society in the Reign of Louis XVI* (1994)

Fitzgerald, Brian (ed.) *Correspondence of Emily, Duchess of Leinster (1731–1814)* 3 vols (Dublin, 1949–57)

Foreman, Amanda, *Georgiana, Duchess of Devonshire* (1998)

Gascoigne, John, *Joseph Banks and the English Enlightenment* (1994)

Gatrell, Vic, *City of Laughter: Sex and Satire in Eighteenth Century London* (2006)

George, Dorothy M., *Catalogue of Political and Personal Satires in the British Museum, 1771–83* (1935)

George, Dorothy M., *Catalogue of Political and Personal Satires in the British Museum, 1784–92* (1938)

Ginter, Donald E. (ed.) *Voting Records of the British House of Commons, 1761–1820*, vol. 5 (1995)

Girouard, Mark, *Life in the English Country House* (1980)

Gleeson, Janet, *An Aristocratic Affair* (2006)

Gordon, Catherine, *The Coventrys of Croome* (Chichester, 2000)

Greig, James (ed.) *The Diaries of a Duchess: Extracts from the Diaries of the First Duchess of Northumberland* (1927)

Gristwood, Sarah, *Perdita* (2005)

Gronow, Captain R.H., *Last Recollections* (1866)

Gross, Jonathan David, *Byron's Corbeau Blanc: The Life and Letters of Lady Melbourne* (Liverpool, 1998)

Guédé, Alain, *Monsieur de Saint-Georges: Virtuoso, Swordsman, Revolutionary* (2003)

Hamilton, Elizabeth, *The Mordaunts* (1965)

Hampson, Norman, *Prelude to Terror* (Oxford, 1988)

Harewood House Trust, *Harewood, A Guide* (Leeds, 1992)

Hecht, Jean J., *The Domestic Servant Class in Eighteenth Century England* (1956)

Herbert, Lord George (ed.) *Henry, Elizabeth and George, 1734–80: Letters and Diaries of Henry, 10th Earl of Pembroke and his Circle* (1939)

Herbert, Lord George (ed.) *The Pembroke Papers, 1734–1794: Letters and Diaries of Henry, 10th Earl of Pembroke and his Circle* (1942–50)

Heward, Edmund, *Lord Mansfield: A Biography of William Murray, 1st Earl of Mansfield 1705–1793*, 2 vols (1979)

Hibbert, Christopher (ed.) *An American in Regency England, Louis Simond* (1968)

Hibbert, Christopher, *George IV, Prince of Wales* (1972)

Hibbert, Christopher, *The Grand Tour* (1987)

Hickman, Katie, *Courtesans* (2003)

Hill, D., *The Satirical Etchings of James Gillray* (1976)

Hindle, Wilfrid, *The Morning Post: 1772–1937* (1937)

Hitchcock, Tim, *English Sexualities, 1700–1800* (1997)

H.M.S.O. *Private Papers of British Diplomats, 1782–1900* (1985)

Home, James (ed.) *The Letters and Journals of Lady Mary Coke*, vol. 4 (Edinburgh, 1896)

Horn, D.B., 'British Diplomatic Representatives, 1789–1852', in *Royal Historical Society, Camden 3rd Series, vol. 50* (1932)

Houlding, J.A., *Fit for Service: 1715–1795* (1981)

Huish, Robert, *The Memoirs of George the Fourth* (1830)

Ilchester, Countess of and Stavordale, Lord (eds) *The Life and Letters of Lady Sarah Lennox*, 2 vols (1902)

Imbruglia, Girolamo (ed.) *Naples in the Eighteenth Century* (Cambridge, 2000)

Jenkins, Ian and Sloan, Kim, *Vases and Volcanoes: Sir William Hamilton and His Collection* (1996)

Jesse, J.H. (ed.) *George Selwyn and his Contemporaries* (1901)

Jones, Colin, *The Great Nation: France from Louis XV to Napoleon* (2002)

Jones, John, *The History and Antiquities of Harewood in the County of York* (1859)

Kelly, Ian, *Beau Brummell, The Ultimate Dandy* (2005)

Konstan, Angus, *Historical Atlas of the Napoleonic Era* (2003)

Langford, Paul, *A Polite and Commercial People: England 1727–1783* (Oxford, 1989)

Laprade, William Thomas, *England and the French Revolution: 1789–1797* (1909)

Laprade, William Thomas (ed.) *The Parliamentary Papers of John Robinson: 1774–1784* (1922)

Laws, Richard and O'Donohue, William, *Sexual Deviance: Theory, Assessment and Treatment* (1997)

Lever, Sir Tresham, *The House of Pitt* (1947)

Lewis, Judith Schneid, *Sacred to Female Patriotism: Gender, Class and Politics in Late Georgian Britain* (2003)

Lewis, W.S. (ed.) *Horace Walpole's Correspondence*, 48 vols (Oxford, 1983)

Lloyd-Verney, Lieut.-Col. J. Mouat and Hunt, F., *Records of the Infantry Militia Battalion of the County of Southampton from 1754–1894* (1894)

Macken, Arthur (trans.) *The Memoirs of Jacques Casanova de Seingalt*, 8 vols (Edinburgh, 1940)

Manning, Jo, *My Lady Scandalous* (New York, 2005)

Mannings, David, *Sir Joshua Reynolds* (2000)

Mansel, Philip, *Constantinople* (1995)

Matthew, H.C.G. and Harrison, Brian (eds) *Dictionary of National Biography* (Oxford, 2000—)

Mauchline, Mary, *Harewood House* (1974)

Mavor, E. (ed.) *The Grand Tour of William Beckford* (1986)

Michaelis, Adolf, *Ancient Marbles in Great Britain* (Cambridge, 1882)

Minto, Emma Eleanor Elizabeth Elliot, *A Memoir of the Right Honourable Hugh Elliot* (1868)

Mitchell, Leslie, *The Whig World* (2005)

Montefiore, Simon Sebag, *Prince of Princes: The Life of Potemkin* (2001)

Moore, Lucy, *Liberty: The Lives and Times of Six Women in Revolutionary France* (2006)

Morris, Anne C. (ed.) *The Diary and Letters of Gouvenour Morris* (1970)

Muhlstein, A., *Memoirs of the comtesse de Boigne* (2003)

Murray, Venetia, *High Society in the Regency Period, 1788–1830* (1998)

Bibliography

Namier, Sir Lewis and Brooke, John, *The History of Parliament: The House of Commons, 1754–1790*, 3 vols (1985)

Nevill, Ralph, *London Clubs* (1911)

Norton, Rictor, *Mother Clap's Molly House: The Gay Subculture in England, 1700–1830* (1992)

Page, William (ed.) *Victoria County History: A History of the County of Hampshire*, vol. 5 (1912)

Parker, Derek, *The Trampled Wife: The Scandalous Life of Mary Eleanor Bowes* (Stroud, 2006)

Peakman, Julie, *Lascivious Bodies* (2004)

Pevsner, Nikolaus and Bradley, Simon, *The Buildings of England, London 6: Westminster* (2003)

Pevsner, Nikolaus and Cherry, Bridget, *The Buildings of England, London 3: North West* (2002)

Pevsner, Nikolaus and Lloyd, David W., *The Buildings of England, The Isle of Wight* (2006)

Picard, Liza, *Dr Johnson's London* (2000)

Porter, R., *English Society in the Eighteenth Century* (1984)

Postle, Martin (ed.) *Joshua Reynolds: The Creation of Celebrity* (2005)

Read, John Meredith, *Historic Studies in Vaud, Berne and Savoy* (1897)

Reverend, Vicomte A., *Titres, anoblissements et pairies de la restauration*, 6 vols (Paris, 1903)

Ribeiro, Aileen, *A Visual History of Costume: The Eighteenth Century* (1983)

Rice, H.C. Jr, *Thomas Jefferson's Paris* (Princeton, 1976)

Roscoe, E.S. and Clergue, Helen (eds) *George Selwyn, his Letters and his Life* (1899)

Royal Academy of Arts, *Citizens and Kings: Portraits in the Age of Revolution, 1760–1830* (2007)

Royal Commission on Historical Manuscripts, *The First Report of the Royal Commission on Historical Manuscripts* (1870)

Rubenhold, Hallie, *The Covent Garden Ladies* (Stroud, 2005)

Russell, Gillian, 'The Theatres of War: Performance, Politics and Society, 1793–1815', in *Eighteenth Century Women Dramatists*, ed. Melinda C. Fineburg (Oxford, 1995), pp. 33–51

Russell, Gillian, *Women, Sociability and Theatre in Georgian London* (2007)

Russell Barker, G.F. and Stenning, A.H., *Record of Old Westminsters* (1928)

Sagan, Eli, *Citzens & Cannibals* (Lanham, Maryland, 2001)

See, R.M.M., *Masquerier and his Circle* (1922)

Shawe-Taylor, Desmond, *The Georgians: Eighteenth-Century Portraiture and Society* (1990)

Sheppard, F.H.W. (ed.) *Survey of London: The Museums Area of South Kensington and Westminster*, vol. 38 (1978)

Sheridan, Richard Brinsley, *The School for Scandal*, ed. Paul Ranger (1986)

Sheridan, Richard B., *Sugar and Slavery: an Economic History of the British West Indies 1623–1795* (Baltimore, Maryland, 1973)

Shoemaker, Robert, *The London Mob* (2004)

Smith, John Thomas, *A Book for a Rainy Day; or Recollections of the Events of Sixty Years, 1766–1833* (1861)

Smith, W.G. (ed.) *The Amorous Illustrations of Thomas Rowlandson* (1983)

Staves, Susan, *Married Women's Separate Property in England, 1660–1833* (London, 1990)

Steinmetz, Andrew, *The Gaming Table, its Votaries and Victims* (1870)

Stokes, F.G. (ed.) *A Journal of My Journey to Paris in the Year 1765* (1931)

Stokes, Hugh, *The Devonshire House Circle* (1917)

Stone, Lawrence, *Broken Lives: Separation and Divorce in England, 1660–1857*, (Oxford, 1993)

Stone, Lawrence, *The Family, Sex and Marriage in England, 1500–1800* (1979)

Stone, Lawrence, *Road to Divorce: England 1530–1987* (Oxford, 1992)

Summers, Judith, *The Empress of Pleasure* (2003)

Sutherland, D.M.G., *France 1789–1815: Revolution and Counterrevolution* (Oxford, 1986)

Swinburne, Henry, *The Courts of Europe at the Close of the Last Century* (1841)

Thompson, J.M., *The French Revolution* (Oxford, 1985)

Tillyard, Stella, *Aristocrats* (1994)

Tillyard, Stella, *A Royal Affair* (2006)

Timbs, John, *English Eccentrics and Eccentricities* (1969)

Toledano, Ehud R., *Slavery and Abolition in the Ottoman Middle East* (Seattle, 1998)

Vectis, Philo, *The Isle of Wight Tourist and Companion at Cowes* (Cowes, 1830)

Walford, Edward, *Old and New London*, 4 vols (1878)

Wallace, Nesbit Willoughby, *A Regimental Chronicle and List of Officers of the 60th or the King's Royal Rifle Corps* (Oxford, 1879)

Wark, Robert E. (ed.) *Rowlandson's Drawings for a Tour in a Post Chaise* (San Marino, California, 1963)

Werkmeister, Lucyle Thomas, *The London Daily Press, 1772–1792* (1965)

Western, J.R., *The English Militia in the Eighteenth Century* (1965)

Whitehead, John L., *The Undercliff of the Isle of Wight* (1911)

Williams, Eric Eustace, *Capitalism and Slavery* (Chapel Hill, 1994)

Williams, Kate, *England's Mistress: The Infamous Life of Emma Hamilton* (2006)

Wilson, Richard and Mackley, Alan, *Creating Paradise: the Building of the English Country House, 1660–1880* (2000)

Winter, C.W.R., *The Manor Houses of the Isle of Wight* (1984)

Wortley Montagu, Mary, *Life on the Golden Horn* (2007)

JOURNAL ARTICLES

Anon., 'A Georgian Ladies Club', *Times Literary Supplement*, 11 August 1932, pp. 561–2

Anon., 'The Brocklesby Paintings', *The Connoisseur* (June 1957), p. 64

Alger, J., 'The British Colony in Paris, 1792–93', *English Historical Review*, 1898

Andrew, Donna T., 'Adultery à-la-Mode: Privilege, the Law and Attitudes to Adultery, 1770–1809', *History*, vol. 82, no. 265 (1997), pp. 5–23

Barnhart, Russell T., 'Gambling in Revolutionary Paris – The Palais Royal: 1789–1838', *Journal of Gambling Studies*, vol. 8, no. 2 (June 1992)

Barrell, John, 'The Dangerous Goddess: Masculinity, Prestige and the Aesthetic in Early Eighteenth Century Britain', *Cultural Critique*, no. 12 (Spring 1989)

Bermingham, Ann, 'The Aesthetics of Ignorance: The Accomplished Woman in the Culture of Connoisseurship', *Oxford Art Journal*, vol. 16, no. 2 (1993), pp. 3–20

Fulton, Gordon D., 'Why Look at Clarissa?', *Eighteenth-Century Life*, vol. 20, no. 2 (May 1996), pp. 21–32

Gilbert, A.N., 'Law and Honour among Eighteenth Century Army Officers', *History*, J. xix (1976)

Habakkuk, H.J., 'Marriage Settlements in the Eighteenth Century', *Transactions of the Royal Historical Society*, fourth series, 32 (1950)

Herbert, Charles, 'Coxheath Camp, 1778–1779', *Journal of the Society for Army Historical Research*, no. 44 (Fall 1967), pp. 129–48

Rendell, Jane, 'Almacks Assembly Rooms: A Site of Sexual Pleasure', *Journal of Architectural Education*, vol. 55, no. 3 (February 2002), pp. 136–7

Rizzo, Betty, 'Equivocations of Gender and Rank: Eighteenth Century Sporting Women', *Eighteenth Century Life*, vol. 26, no. 1 (Winter 2002), pp 70–93

Russell, Gillian, 'The Peeresses and the Prostitutes: The Founding of the London Pantheon', *Nineteenth Century Contexts*, vol. 27, no. 1 (March 2005), pp. 11–25

Sherbo, Arthur, 'A Suggestion for the Original of Thackeray's Rawdon Crawley', *Nineteenth Century Fiction*, vol. 10, no. 3 (December 1955), pp. 211–16

Straub, Kristina, 'Reconstructing the Gaze: Voyeurism in Richardson's *Pamela*', *Studies in Eighteenth Century Culture*, no. 18 (1988), pp. 419–31

UNPUBLISHED SOURCES

Bray, Peter, *Appuldurcombe House* (Ventor and District Local History Society, undated)

Clark, Gregory, 'The Secret History of the Industrial Revolution' (unpublished paper given at the University of California, Davis, October 2001)

Jessel, Christopher, *A Firm of First Rate Connexion; Farrer & Co.* (unpublished booklet for the firm of Farrer & Co.)

INDEX

Abbott, Captain Charles, 44
Abergavenny, Lady Catherine, 82
Abergavenny, Lord, 82
Abergavenny v. Lyddel, 82
Adam, Robert, 19
Adams, Lady Margaret, 176
Aiguillon, Duchesse d', 244
Ainslie, Sir Robert, 210, 238
Akenside, Mark, 161
Albani, Francesco, 252
Alexandria, 209
Alfieri, Count Vittorio, 79, 177–8
All Saints Church, Godshill, 260
All Saints Church, Harewood, 26
Almack's, 175, 182
Alresford, 40, 99
America, 44, 45, 49, 99–100, 131, 132, 138, 159, 160, 161
Amey, Countess d' (Madame Palmerini), 255
Amherst, Lord, 46
Ami du Peuple, L', 242–3
Andalusia, 205
Andrea del Sarto, 258
Angelo, Henry, 229
Answer of Sir Richard Worsley to the Epistle of Lady Worsley, The, 197–9

Antiquities of Athens (Stuart and Revett), 206
Appuldurcombe: as Worsley family seat, 7–8; Sir Richard Worsley plans renovation of, 23; purchase of lands adjacent to, 25; as backdrop to portrait of Sir Richard, 28; renovation and extension of, 29–30; collection of books, art and antiquities moved to, 31; Sir Richard destroys wife's belongings at, 101; Deerhurst questioned about his visit to, 124–7; Sir Richard's display of his wife at, 166–7; Sir Richard no longer wishes to live at, 254, 259; as repository for Sir Richard's collection, 259; sale of objets d'art at, 260; brief references, 33, 42, 43, 57, 72, 94, 262
Aretino's Postures, 166
Argyll, Duchess of, 129
Armistead, Elizabeth, 135, 179, 181, 199–200
Ashburton, John Dunning, Baron *see* Dunning, John, Baron Ashburton
Astle, Thomas, 236
Aston, Henry Harvey, 138
Athens, 206, 207–8

www.vintage-books.co.uk